Poverty and Human Wellbeing

About the Author

Dr. Sudip Chakraborty is an internationally known researcher in Economics of Child Labour. He is presently working as Associate Professor in Economics at Ananda Chandra College in Jalpaiguri, West Bengal. He has published numerous books and articles on poverty and child deprivation. His participation and presentation on Economics of Child Labour in Belgium in 2004 and in Norway in 2005 was appreciated by scholars across the globe. His participation and presentations on children's issues, in Sion (Switzerland), in Amsterdam (Netherlands), in Oxford University (U.K), in Florida (U.S.A), North Dakota (U.S.A), Minnesota (U.S.A), in Australia, in Kampala of Uganda, in Accra, Ghana (West Africa), in Delhi as well as in Kolkata, on several occasions are manifestations of his keen interest and scholarship on the subject. He was a Fulbright Visiting Scholar in the U.S.A during 2008. UGC nominated him in 2013 as Visiting Research Fellow at the Central European University in Budapest, Hungary.

Poverty and Human Wellbeing

The Indian Context

Sudip Chakraborty
Assistant Professor in Economics,
Ananda Chandra College
Jalpaiguri, West Bengal

CONCEPT PUBLISHING COMPANY PVT. LTD.
NEW DELHI-110059

ISBN-13 : 978-93-5125-062-3

First Published 2014

Published and Printed by

Concept Since 1974

Concept Publishing Company Pvt. Ltd.
A/15-16, Commercial Block, Mohan Garden
New Delhi-110059 (India)
T: 25351460, 25351794, F: 091-11-25357109
E: publishing@conceptpub.com, W: www.conceptpub.com
Editorial Office: H-13, Bali Nagar, New Delhi-110 015, India.

Cataloging in Publication Data—*Courtesy:* D.K. Agencies (P) Ltd. <docinfo@dkagencies.com>

Chakraborty, Sudip.
Poverty and human wellbeing : the Indian context / Sudip Chakraborty.
p. cm.
Includes bibliographical references (p.) and index.
ISBN 9789351250623

1. Poverty—India. 2. Poverty—Government policy—India. 3. Well-being—India. I. Title.

DDC 339.460954 23

Preface

This book delves deep in to the issue having relevance to human survival for all times focusing primarily on India. Poverty is a subject of much debate and disagreement. It implies scarcity of anything including of economic resources. Interestingly economic poverty is described as poverty in popular discourse as well as in scholarly dialogue on the subject. We are used to this expression that drops its prefix. The reason for detaching is obvious. Of all deficiencies in the lives of human beings, that of economic means come first. Physical survival drives away all other needs for life. Poverty has its long past as well as its pervasive present in the contemporary world. It will have a flourishing future if we fail to contain it through local as well as global action. The United Nations' Millennium Development Goals pave the way for global partnership. It sets the goal to eradicate extreme poverty and hunger by 2015. The World Bank, according to its new study, reveals that one in three of the world's poorest people are living in India. But this revelation does not match with India's remarkable feat as second fastest growing economy. The World Bank's figures show that the number of those in extreme poverty around the world, surviving on 82 pence per day or less, has declined significantly. Unfortunately India now shelters a greater share of the world's poorest than it did thirty years ago. During 80s, India was home to one-fifth of the world's poorest people, the magnitude now stands at around 400 million, one-third of the world's poorest.

The study entitled 'The State of the Poor: Where are the Poor and Where are the Poorest' undertaken by the Bank recently, brought to the fore that the number of extremely poor people had dropped from half of the world's population in 1981 to one-fifth in 2010, but it also aired apprehension at its rise in Sub-Saharan Africa and persisting higher magnitude in India. World Bank President, Jim Yong Kim takes pride in drumbeating the global success in the overall decline of poverty. He quickly described it as "remarkable progress". However his euphoria is watered down by the exposure of the very harsh fact that 1.2 billion people were still living in extreme poverty. He rued it as "a stain on our collective conscience." He asserts the World Bank's global effort has resulted in reducing poverty, but he also regrets that nearly one-fifth of the world population is still below the poverty line. Poverty alleviation initiatives will necessitate synchronized endeavour by the Bank, individual nations, and the international development agencies.

The scale of unwavering extreme poverty in India, despite her outstanding economic growth in recent times does not augur well for a nation celebrated as the largest democracy in the world. We have reason to be apprehensive about "ticking time bomb". India's population is projected to touch 1.5 billion figures and she is on her way to become the world's most populous nation surpassing China by 2026. Indian economy is not growing fast enough to create the 20 million new jobs per year to stem the tide of escalating poverty. Her precarious plight is worsened by poor health care services, child malnutrition, child mortality and inadequate education and skill training. School discontinuation of children is still alarming.

Enrolment in schools has gone up significantly but quality of learning is missing as revealed in the research reports. Consumption poverty has declined during the decades after economic reforms measures adopted in 1991. Surprisingly, caloric poverty has not declined and as many as 80 per cent of rural Indians were caloric-poor in 2004-2005. Economists of the neo-liberal camp assert that people at the bottom of the ladder are giving up coarse cereals. They are turning to expensive foods as a result of enhanced purchasing power. They validate this argument by referring to the findings of two research surveys. One is self-reported hunger study that reveals drastic fall in hunger perception during the period from 1983 to 2005. The other is the world Gallup Poll survey conducted in 2006 which reports that half of the respondents in India were getting better now in economic standing. But inter-State and intra-State disparity in the level of poverty in India is certainly worrying. One feature of India's contemporary growth scenario is that urban prosperity has been contributing to reduction in poverty in the rural areas encircling the urban centres. Expansion of urban economy has been helping the rural non-farm economy to grow where agriculture is languishing, rural workers are moving toward non-farm jobs. But the quality of non-farm employment is on the wane. Steady reduction of consumption poverty in India does not match with her deplorable score card in human development indicators. While the score for the nation as a whole is upsetting, some States have already touched the level of the developed countries in this regard. Scores of some other States resemble those of poor African nations. We are helplessly witnessing the emergence of India sharply divided in two parts: the prosperous pockets and the poor regions. India as a nation should emulate her own 'best achieving' constituting State. Indicators of child well-being, as estimated by the government agencies, are causes of concern for all. While decline in consumption poverty is a cause for rejoicing, the increase in income inequality in the growing India is enough cause for worry. We are now on the way to join the league of high unequal counties of the world along with Brazil and South Africa.

The widening inequality in India is driven by differential return to education of the participants in economically productive activities. The caste division, still powerful in globalizing India, have a say in the distribution of the fruits of development. Poverty and low caste are habitual bedfellows. Social exclusion and economic exclusion have been reinforcing each other. The lesson we learn from India's growth trajectory since her birth as a free nation is rich to learn and disseminate. Economic growth, on its own does not take care of disempowered people. Appropriate public policies can only drive the growth juggernaut in such a way that it lifts the underdogs incapable of getting into it by themselves. Those powerless Indians have to be empowered through appropriate public action, through creating opportunities for the underdogs, the major part of which must be meaningful education and quality health care for all.

Sudip Chakraborty
Ananda Chandra College
Jalpaiguri

Acknowledgements

At the very outset I would like to convey my heartfelt gratitude to my former teacher Dr. Prafulla Chandra Sarkar who, couple of decades ago, supervised my Ph.D. work on the issue of poverty. The seed inside me was sown by him. All my research outputs that followed are fruits of the tree that had emerged out of the seed. Extensive field work under his supervision enriched my understanding about the lives of the underprivileged people plagued by extreme economic adversities. Hundreds of household members in the rural area of Jalpaiguri district in West Bengal deserve my appreciation for copious cooperation in course of my household survey. The University Grants Commission provided me with generous grants to carry out my research project on food security and child labour. I must acknowledge this assistance wholeheartedly. My recent visit to Africa, twice by turn, gave me the opportunity to interact with people in those African nations engaged in improving the lives of the people over there. I had learned much from them about the issue of global poverty and the need for global cooperation in fighting poverty. I must acknowledge the continuous support and inspiration from my dearly loved colleagues at Ananda Chandra College. However, the assistance I received from my beloved student Sri Suman Basu Roy as my research assistant is immeasurable. It would be unjust if one name is missed out and that is of my beloved student Sri Debojit Jha. He takes time out of his hectic schedule in his present capacity as DREO Jalpaiguri for evaluating my papers and articles. Last but not the least is the immense contribution made by my wife Soma and my daughter Saroni. They always tried to keep my spirit up during the preparation of this manuscript.

Contents

Introduction

Poverty as a particular feature of human distress afflicts millions of our fellow human beings on this planet. Destitution persists globally but its enormity widely varies across the global regions. Sub-Saharan African region stands in stark contrast to Scandinavian region. The former is the desert of destitution while the latter is the oasis of opulence. These two regions share the same planet, the sweet home of mankind in the universe. It may appear that poverty is a modern day peril. But scarcity of material goods had visited mankind well before the beginning of human civilization. The great exodus of our earliest ancestors from the 'cradle of humanity' was crisis-driven. Our distant forefathers abandoned their place of origination in Africa thousands of years ago in search of food and shelter somewhere else. Scarcity of material goods had befallen on them. Poverty had compelled our earliest ancestors to take on a hazardous journey to unspecified destination. Poverty persists now overwhelmingly over one-third of the world. The beginning chapters of the book look for the foundation of poverty. They take us to the long past of the onset and diffusion of it. Poverty or the state of material insufficiency for a section or whole of population had inconvenienced our ancestors. But human beings did not bother and did not act collectively to mitigate the menace. In short, this was not a pressing problem to them as human minds did not think over it nor did they chew over it as a problem.

Mankind began to realize it much later, during seventeenth and eighteenth century in the light of enlightenment philosophy.

The idea gained ground that people's well being is not determined by any unseen forces or external agency beyond the comprehension of human minds. The hold of church in explaining the human existence loosened gradually by series of discoveries one after another. Physical world was no longer a mystery and incomprehensible to men. The upshot of enlightenment wave was humanitarianism. Man was placed at the centre of the social world. Poverty or any sort of human distress was thus anathema to humanitarianism. The physical world is subject to fixed rules of nature which enlightened human minds began to understand. Man freed themselves from the darkness of ignorance. Like physical world, social world was also understood by human minds drawing on new insights from enlightenment philosophy. The new lights of knowledge revealed that poverty in particular and human distress in general was unacceptable. Reason of poverty is not beyond the comprehension of human minds. Solution to poverty is achievable by human action. Reduction in poverty in the aftermath of the evolution of state is attributed to two processes; economic growth and political process. The former create opportunities for better living overcoming poverty and the latter develops and perpetuates institutional arrangements that tend to work for safety nets and redistributive provisions. Welfare states must engage themselves with these functions. State formation has two obverses: economics and politics. One is growth focused and the other is welfare focused.

Democratic state and totalitarian state stand apart in dealing with the destitution of the people. Democratic state, by the nature of its formation, is committed to the people. Poverty reduction is thus an obligatory task and priority agenda in governance. Totalitarian states are not obligated to take up the task of eliminating poverty through anti-poverty initiatives. But Democratic states may not be always developmental states. The efficacy of the democratic states in reducing poverty depends on the institutions, the functioning of which depends on the internal dynamics and politics. Chapter two of this book 'poverty and society' brings to the fore the issue of cultural connection of poverty. While nature of state and institution arrangement therein influence the occurrence of poverty, culture also counts. Cultural theorists emphasize the role of culture in explaining the generation and perpetuation of poverty. Samuel Huntington is the leading proponent in this 'culture school'. He invokes the examples of Ghana and Korea to establish his argument that culture matters. Amartya Sen, the leading light in the contemporary development discourse, however, does not endorse Huntington's cultural explanation. Sen situates public policy and geo-political location of the states far above culture as determinant of poverty. Poverty in the present-day India has to be understood in the light of her long colonial past, imperial exploitation, and crisis of nation-state, politics of independent India, partition, communalism and inward looking economic policies. Independent India had opted for planned economic development to remove poverty in the long run. But for short run amelioration, anti-poverty programmes in India, in line with many other developing countries, are being implemented. They comprise of two types. One is through creation of self-employment opportunities for the poor and the other is through the provision of wage work. Both of them are means to achieve the ends of removing poverty. Both of them have advantages and disadvantages and should not be placed in the race for getting the tag of the 'best instrument' in the fight against poverty. They are to be coupled in a mutually complementary way for the best result. Wage work programme during the lean season in agriculture in rural India could be coupled with self employment programmes for the unemployed poor. They are to be coupled in a mutually complementary way for the best result. Nationalized banks were asked by the government during early eighties to hand out low interest loan to the small entrepreneurs in villages. Government on its part gave generous subsidies to the recipients of low cost credit. Assistance from both sides helped them in acquiring micro productive assets. IRDP was a trendsetter in this genre. Its results were mixed. Success somewhere was belittled by failure in other places. Self-help groups comprising mostly of adult women are current strategy to fight poverty. National Rural Employment Guarantee programme confers entitlement to the unemployed poor in the rural India for wage work of 100 days in a year.

Wage work programme during the lean season of agriculture is the suitable project for rural India where agriculture is the mainstay of livelihoods for the majority of Indians. Agriculture and its allied activities cannot provide employment round the year for all working adults. The root of poverty lies in the pathetic state of agriculture for its inability to sustain life and livelihoods of people. Wage work for the idle workers in the lean season of agriculture protects them from virtual starvation and semi-starvation. India's long stint with both of them since the initiation of First Five Year Plan has met with mixed results. The results fell short of target. The magnitude of poverty instead of coming down seems to be on the rise despite huge budgetary expenditure.

Anti-poverty government programmes are meant for the poor. Therefore, poor has to be identified for targeting beneficiaries of anti-poverty programmes. Democratic state is duty bound to free the people out of the shackles of penury. Success or failure in the battle against poverty is a test of government's affirmative action. Credit goes to the government if the number of poor could be brought down. Wrath is in store in case of failure. Thus counting of poor is the crucial task of the government. In case of India, this task is more problematic as the heads to be counted are too numerous.

The level of development substantially varies across countries. The rich nations of today's world had undergone same economic situations being experienced by the poor sub-Saharan African nations or South Asian nations at present time. Affluent nations of the Western world two centuries ago were poor by today's standard or outlook on poverty. Human misery there in the long past was quite pervasive. People would die of preventable morbidity. Bubonic plague, for example, took away lives relentlessly centuries ago in those rich countries. Life was very short compared to present day's average life span of around 80 years in these rich countries. Scandinavian nations are on their way to achieve average longevity of hundred years. Four hundred years back, they could hardly cross forty years. The average longevity in Sudan, Liberia and in war- ravaged Afghanistan at present are near the figures achieved by the rich nations in the western world three centuries ago. Average life span of the citizens is an indicator of country's economic progress.

Citizens of the poor nations live on earth for much shorter period than their fellow beings in the richer nations. Economic advancement and consequent rise in living standard over the years have made it possible. Average height of the citizens like longevity is also an indicator of economic standing of the country. Citizens of the rich industrial nations in the western world are much taller, healthier and stronger now than they were two to three centuries ago. The difference in heights as well as in other health indicators between the people of the North and of the South of this planet is noticeably sharp. Economic prosperity of the today's rich nation over last many centuries has made it possible. Economic development over the last many centuries in these nations has freed the people from the shackle of poverty. The improvement over the years has been manifest not only in the achievement in health condition and much higher income but also in many other dimensions of human progress. The horrific destitution in vast swath of the sub-Saharan Africa appears too stark alongside vast opulence of the people of rich nations. No one needs a measuring scale to testify the enormous difference in life attainments in both the contrasting world. Without undertaking the task of measuring poverty in these two contrasting settings, one can easily infer after a casual observation that poverty is pervasive in one part of the world while the other part of the world has almost removed it once and for all. The governments in all states undertake poverty measurements from time to time. Developed nations despite having least incidence of poverty occasionally count the poor according to poverty characterization of their own. The rich nations have to provide for social security net for the underprivileged. Thus counting of the poor is essential for fixing the budgetary provision for them to be made by the state. The provisions include wage employment, shelter and health care for the poor segments of the society. The extent of provision and the reach of coverage however, depend on respective states commitment to welfare. Rich nations are less bothered about the magnitude of their poor citizen as they constitute a negligible segment of population in their respective societies. Poverty eradication measures, unlike in the developing world, do not receive the governmental priorities in the rich nation. Legislation for same sex marriage in the U.S would receive political priority much more than free housing schemes for the Latino immigrants. Developing nations prioritizes the anti-poverty programmes in the governmental actions as their poor citizens constitute a huge segment of the citizens. The totalitarian poor states are less concerned about the magnitude, counting and reduction of poverty. They are neither answerable nor obligated to reduce poverty. The huge horde of poor is not going to pose a challenge to their authority.

Democratic poor states on the other hand, cannot escape that responsibility. They are accountable to the people. Victory in the fight against poverty brings electoral dividend as the party in power has to face the electoral battle armed with achievements in mitigating poverty during their tenure in office. The number of poor in case of India is counted by the state machinery from time to time. This is an important task of the government. The number is the test of efficacy of the government's anti-poverty programme. Rapid reduction during a particular time interval place the government in good stead while sluggish diminution and rise of the number in any case, show the government in poor light. Electoral defeat looms large. In India, the National Sample Survey Organization undertakes the task of recording Monthly Per Capita Consumption Expenditure from sample households selected across the country. This Organization, as an organ of the Planning Commission, counts the poor in India.

Chapter 3 titled 'Issues in Poverty Measurement' describes India's initiatives to measure poverty. Poverty line was adopted by our planners as dividing line between poor and non-poor citizens. Nutritionists in India, in the early years of poverty estimation had prescribed 2400 kcal and 2100 kcal for rural and urban areas respectively. These calories requirements have been coming under scathing attack in recent times. The chapter unfolds the reigning debate and concludes that calorimetric poverty line needs to be re-examined in the light of the emerging consensus on the broadening the definition of poverty. Chapter 4 brings to the fore the current debate on poverty in India. Poverty line is dubbed as reductionism which according to Amartya Sen, is rooted in commodity space. Poverty line ignores and discounts wide variety of development deficits that cripple the underprivileged in the society. It does not take into account intra-household disparity in the endowment of productive and non-productive assets. The chapter lays bare that there could be divergence between gross caloric intake and net caloric absorption. Poverty line approach is further weakened by the recent revelation about pervasive malnutrition among children and women in India. This sounds funny that the numbers of poor in India is on the wane while the numbers of malnourished Indians are on the rise.

Calorie anchored poverty line fails to explain this mismatch. Chapter 5 brings to the light the government's belated realization of the meanness of calorimetric measure of poverty. Professor Suresh Tendulkar was invited by the government to lead the committee constituted to relook and redefine poverty line in India. This chapter offers a balanced treatment of Tendulkar report. Recommendations are a mixed bag that contains positive ideas as well as manifest inadequacies. Chapter 6 comes next. It deals with a crucial issue that has political ramifications in the context of electoral politics. Identification of poor for targeting is a tricky task in a situation where too many heads vie for grabbing the tag. Once a family is identified by the local elected authority as poor, it almost gets a gate pass to enter heaven of facilities. Identified families are allotted BPL card of entitlement to various facilities. But the methodology for such identification since the beginning of this exercise has been coming under stern criticism. Chapter 6 presents a critical analysis of the methodologies so far adopted one after another, since the beginning. The current one has been crafted by professor Saxena. There is veritable shift in the outlook on poverty in the Saxena methodology. Multi dimensional approach to poverty is replacing one dimensional poverty.

Chapter 7 begins with an in-depth analysis of the connection between poverty and democracy. Does democracy as a form of government compels the state to undertake poverty alleviation programmes and actions? How India, since her birth as a free nation, has been doing in this regard? Children and women, as vulnerable member in the society face, double disadvantages. Child poverty and feminization of poverty are issues of concern, voiced vociferously in the current dialogue on poverty in India. Globalization process currently underway has been dubbed by anti-globalizers as villain. They argue that faster economic interconnectedness has been accentuating the poverty. Advocates of globalization, on the other hand, finds immense possibilities in global connection for reducing poverty. This chapter tries to reconcile these conflicting strands for arguments. Poverty stands as a barrier to enjoy freedom to lead a life with full enjoyment. The freedom pertains particularly to lead a decent life, free from hunger, ill health, illiteracy and many other disadvantages. Amartya Sen's capability approach to the understanding of poverty has added new insights on poverty as capability deprivation. From the prospective of universal human rights, onslaught of poverty is the violation of human rights.

Chapter 8 presents the current debate on poverty reduction in contemporary India. Government of India takes pride in its remarkable accomplishment in reducing the head count poverty which has declined as per the estimate provided by the National Sample Survey in 2004-2005. Government's euphoria got further boost from the findings of two research surveys. One is self reported hunger study that reveals drastic fall in hunger perception during the period from 1983-2005. The other is world Gallup Poll survey that reports that half of the respondents in India were getting better now. But the steady reduction of consumption poverty in India does not match with her deplorable score card in human development indicators. Inter-state variation in human development performance is quite large. School enrolment has gone up in recent years but quality education is lagging far behind quantitative expansion. Increasing inequality in growing India is an issue of concern. We are now on way to the league of most unequal Nations of the world. Differential returns to the education of the participants in economically productive activities have been contributing to the generation and perpetuation of the inequality. But the structural inequality as an offshot of India's hierarchical social order is more harmful. Economic inequality is further reinforced by social exclusion. Inclusive growth must be the ultimate goal of poverty eradication projects.

CHAPTER 1

Poverty and Human Civilization

1.1 Poverty and the Beginning of Humanity

Is poverty a present day human misery and did never occur in the humanity's past? Did it come in the wake of the advent of modernity that radically changed the course of human history? This historic turning point had changed our world view. We began to see ourselves in different ways, a sweeping departure from our long established outlook. The beginning of poverty is as important as its magnitude at present in the contemporary world. The genesis of poverty is as important as its proliferation now. The birth of poverty and its association with human progress is an issue that invites intelligent scrutiny. Development economists, sociologists, anthropologists and historians are engaged in their respective fields of enquiry to trace the beginning of poverty. These separate endeavours must not be construed as race among the disciplines to dominate the discourse on poverty. These individual pursuits of disciplines of social sciences are not exclusionary. They are mutually interactive and beneficial. These individual efforts make up a comprehensive whole through which origin and trajectory of poverty could be studied and understood. Informed policies can be taken up to have a leash on it with a view to remove it altogether. Each discipline contributes to 'enlightened' understanding of the genesis of poverty as a social problem. The study of mankind is incomplete without the study of material wants that affects mankind and its course of civilization progress over thousands of years. The living conditions of man as a social being form the foundation of the discipline of sociology. The birth of society as collection of individuals and the beginning of social living in place of individualized living marked the recognition and acceptance of society as an entity over them. The social living demanded some compliances and obedience. This compliance to social norm came to be known at a later stage as social contract. This was a primordial understanding among the human persons to live in unison to share with the fellow beings the benefits of nature and to face with them the wraths of nature. The sharing of feelings and communication among members gave rise to ideas for the better living as social beings.

Social living of man is contingent on material endowment. Living in this world is dependent on resources provided by the nature and it includes the earth, air, water, vegetation, light and everything that produces material goods indispensable for living. Man would cease to exist if nature stops providing these basic ingredients for living. Some of the material needed for human living are product of nature and, therefore, unlimited in supply. Air, water, rainfall, vegetation, light, the changes of season are natural endowments beyond human creation. Man cannot create and distribute air, the vital ingredient for living. The same is true for all natural endowments that make life possible on earth. But human beings who make use these products of nature are least bothered about how these products are created and made available in plenty to all living organisms on earth. They are not haunted by the ill thought of any eventuality of stoppage of benevolence of nature. The early man did not produce anything needed for his living. His shelter was a cave or a branch of trees or a ground under the sun in the open sky. His shelter was nature's benevolence and his clothes are also the same. The early man had used bark or animal hide at later stages when humanity had left behind the primitive stage when covering of body was out of fashion. Food was available in the lap of nature. Hunting and collection of foods were dominant activities of the early men. Fruits, honey and edible leaves were available in his natural surroundings. Animals were hunted for meat using tools provided by nature. The tools for hunting include wooden sticks, flints, stones, and sharp bones of dead animals. Man's platter had contained raw meat for thousands of year until the discovery of fire.

Poverty did not exist during this primitive stage of mankind when this material supply and bounties of nature did not tapper off. All resources were in plenty. Scarcity never befell on our early ancestors. Poverty defined universally as a state of human living marked by material want was not even thought of. Poverty was non-entity during this phase of material abundance. This was primarily due to the conception of the accessibility of minimum goods for such living. Poverty is a social construct and was identified much later in the course of human history as a social ill. Early men fewer in head count lived in opulence in the lap of nature that bore everything for them. But that opulence or lack of scarcity did not last for long for our early ancestors. The great migration that took place more than a million years ago was caused primarily by the shortage of foods. Anthropologists have established with strong evidence that man first appeared in some corner of the east African region. They lived there for long, had negotiated with natural adversities. They had faced all odds, had fought the wild animals, had overcome the fear of death and destruction but had never moved else where in search of safer places to live. The large scale migration of our ancestors to the safer pastures leaving behind the place of their birth was crises-driven. They would surely die of starvation in those places where they were born and grew. Why did they migrate? There are two reasons known to the world. The first one is the swelling in the number of feeding mouths over the years. Thus poverty caused by the population explosion is traceable to our early history. Poverty in a sense induced our forefathers to abandon their familiar land of habitation. It forced them to take on an unchartered journey for the unknown destination, beleaguered by uncertainties and threatened by dooms and decay. The availability of food per head in the habitation and around them began to plummet over a period of time. Population swelled and the demand for food went up concurrently, but the production of food by nature fell short of the heightened demand. Nature takes its own time to produce and reproduce food for human consumption. Trees would take time to bear fruits; the animals would take time to replenish the missing supply chain of animals for hunting. It would take time to refill the depleted food stock. The depletion was faster with the growth of population. Men have to look for new areas for hunting and to the great migration by our early ancestors in search of food and water. Sociology as a distinct discipline in social sciences deals with formation of society. Origination of poverty is, therefore, an important area of sociological discourse. Does poverty accompanies the social process? Dose it exists and perpetuates in particular social structure? Sociology deals with the question of generation and perpetuation of poverty in a particular society. Poverty and inequality are traditional bedfellows. One reinforces the other to grow and persists simultaneously. Development Economics focuses on the issue of distribution of opportunities among members of society. What are the basic rules that regulate distribution of resources among members of the society? In the absence of any rule to regulate the actual behaviour of people, the society would be turned into one man show of the tyrants where most powerful of the world rules the roost and the rest of the people in the human society would be pushed to sub-human state of life.

The powerful would usurp power to rule the society without popular mandate. This type of society still exists in many locations in Africa, the cradle of human civilization where tribal lord rules ruthlessly with the help of military might. They remain in power by incarcerating the opponents, by muffling the voices of dissenters and by spreading terror among the powerless citizens. Poverty in the sense of economic destitution would go up manifold in such dictatorial regime that is not backed by popular mandate. The dictators are ruthless in exploiting their subjects to generate income as much as possible. They spend not for enhancement for social welfare but for further strengthening his military might to terrorize the people in a bid to rule out any possibility of his removal from the throne. Many poor African states are glaring examples of dictatorial regime when poverty, starvation deaths and ethnic cleansing had haunted several times in the past. The cradle of humanity had also witnessed terrible genocides, the root cause of which embedded in the persisting poverty and concomitant powerlessness of the people. Thus social rules and institution largely determine the distribution of opportunities and resources among people. If the distribution is extremely skewed in favour of a few, poverty would befall on the majority. Thus the social rules are important. The social rules would govern the institutions that ultimately govern the society. The dictatorial African nations did not frame its rule and establish its institution for delivery of governance in the spirit of fairness as justice.

1.2 Individual Well-Being and Social Living

How and why did individuals come together to give birth to society? This question regarding the genesis of human society had preoccupied the social thinkers for a long time. For a long period individual living without caring for fellow people was the dominant mode at the beginning phase of human civilization. Instinctively, this atomized living gave way to communal living or living in groups. Group living was advantageous than the individual living, which men had learnt themselves through living actual lives in the earliest phase of human civilization. Before the emergence of human society and the adoption of social order, man had to negotiate with the natural world alone for his survival or had at best a loose affiliation to a group without having legal, moral or any obligatory commitment for each of the member of the group. In the state of nature where social rules for conduct did not come up to regulate individual behaviour, man could do anything as he liked. He did not ponder over the consequences of his action. He did not bother whether his action could jeopardize the lives of other. A man could hunt as many animals and collect as much food without bothering about his fellow beings who were forced to starve because of his non-altruistic behaviour.

The state of nature was the theatre of anarchy. Lives of children, women and aged people were in constant peril. They gave in to the masculine power of the powerful. The demarcation or the dividing line between right and wrong was altogether absent. Instincts rather than intellect had regulated human behaviour. Freedom to do anything was unbounded in the stateless living. Early human beings used to live in close contact with their fellow beings. They moved and stayed together. But this togetherness of human living was driven by instincts not by any intellectual impulses. Early men learnt from life experiences that hunting together is more beneficial than moving out alone for a kill. An individual venture was always fraught with danger of backlash from the preys. It was almost difficult for a single man to chase and kill a speeding deer or running boar but the collective hunting can easily accomplish the task. A man alone could not carry the heavy load of the carcass of dead animal to the place, safe for savouring the meals. Men used to collect fruit, herbs, and berries together not out of fellow feeling or emotional bonding but for fear of attack by the big cats which hunted on human beings. They used to live in caves or on an isolated highland not as an extended family unit tied by kinship relation. The group living and sharing food gathered collectively is impelled by the need for putting some deterrence against attack by wild animals. Man learnt that security of life in the kingdom of nature was greatly enhanced by living together. Man was more exposed to beastly attack in the solitary living mode. However, this collective living as compulsion was instinct-driven rather than the result of informed collective decision. This was, of course, a remote precursor to human society and emergence of family as a smallest unit of human living mode. Society as collection of family units had emerged much later in course of human civilization. The first difference between this collective living of "human tribes" and society relates to freedom. In the state of nature characterized by anarchy and chaos freedom to do any thing was unbounded. No one was answerable to any one for any deeds or misdeeds.

1.3 The Genesis of Society and State

Social living demands some compliance with the social rules. This compliance manifestly takes away some freedom. Society by the nature of its formation develops certain unwritten rules, custom and behavioural mode which binds human beings as social animals. Historically, it is very difficult to ascertain the exact period from which the journey of human society began. But the birth of society, state, government and institution in course of the progression of humanity is the outcome of long-drawn social process. The genesis of such institution and the circumstances in which the human society and social institution came into being are to be found in the social contract theory. The fundamental idea developed by a group of philosophers and social thinkers during seventeenth and eighteenth century is that society and state were born as a result of informal contract or covenant by the people who would "be governed". The transition from the state of nature to the system of social order was deliberate decisions by the people themselves. The English philosopher Thomas Hobbes wrote Leviathan in 1651. He said mankind abandoned nature as the life of man was 'solitary, poor, nasty, brutish and short' in the state of nature. Every man was enemy to other. John Locke and Rousseau the French philosopher had also joined Hobbes in support of the exposition of such a contract or agreement as foundation for the formation of state and evolution of social order. The society cannot run and flourish without the framing and adherence to social order mutually agreed upon.

Hobbes the earliest proponent of the trio of ***'contractarian'*** philosophers found nothing good in the state of nature. He pointed out that mutual enmity among people and the resultant violence had created an atmosphere from which men had aspired for emancipation. The social contract was the culmination of a long drawn process of human intercourse and realization of pent up demand for an ordered living. Unrestrained freedom in the state of nature was associated with brutality, violence, death and destruction. Hobbes in his book had mentioned that the state of nature was not social and man could not tolerate the happiness of others. The inner urge of man to get rid of the unhappy, ever-haunting and violent mode of living turned into a collective aspiration for society to be formed where peace would be guaranteed. Freedom to do anything could not co-exist with unfreedom of violence and brutality. The state of nature was not marked by any behavioural restriction. A man was free to kill a bird or animal to satisfy his need for food and this was unrestrained freedom in the state of nature. But his catch as a product of his hard labour could be snatched by other man by his sheer strength and physical power. The actual hunter could resist this action by other but that would surely result in bloody violence and death. The actions of both of them were driven by instincts. The question of legality or morality of this action did not arise. The man who snatched the kill by brute force did not consider his action as sinful. He did not think of any legal consequence of this action. In the state of nature, the dividing line between moral and immoral, legal and illegal was absent. When society came in to being, men by default became members of the society. The key to the survival and flourishing of society is the social order established by men through mutual agreements. The social order evolved by men, was not only the manifestation of collective desire of man to get rid of the disorderly and brutish living, it was also the reflection of human aspiration for prosperity and peace.

Thomas Hobbes was joined by John Locke, another English political philosopher in the espousal of the social contract theory as the genesis of society and state. They agree as well as disagree on some points on the preceding contingencies. Locke unlike Hobbes was admirer of the state of nature. In his classic book, *Two Treaties on Civil Government*, he had extolled the natural world as congenial habitat of mankind. He said that man lived in peace in the lap of nature and had enjoyed boundless freedom. This was a state of 'peace, goodwill, mutual assistance and preservation'. But this peace and prosperity in haven of perpetual freedom was exposed to severe disturbance that generated gloom and adversities. But this disturbing demon was not the nature itself but some men who were vicious and corrupted. The degenerated miscreants used to create fissure to destabilize and break peace in the state of nature. The state of nature was ruled by laws of nature not by rules framed by men. The offenders neither had any moral inhibition nor any legal prohibition to stop them from these misdeeds. It was natural for a few people to break the peace and unleashed disturbance in the state of nature.

1.4 Poverty: Past and Present in Sub-Saharan Africa as World's 'Poverty Zone'

Poverty is not uniformly distributed over the entire globe. It overwhelmingly plagues some regions of the world and not sighted at all in some regions. The regions of its dominant presence are well-known. Sub-Saharan Africa as a world region of pervasive poverty tops the list of the poverty regions in the world. South Asia comes after that and is still witnessing poverty on a massive scale despite India's remarkable economic growth performances in recent years. Pakistan and Afghanistan are breeding grounds for Islamic terrorism. The governments in both the countries are engaged more in fighting home grown terrorists instead of fighting the poverty. India occupies almost three-fourths of the geographical landmass of the south Asian region. India's growth performances have received mixed feedbacks, neither pure applause nor unmixed denunciation. In some circle India's remarkable economic success has been hailed as example for the other developing countries struggling to reign in poverty to emulate. There are some pockets in the Caribbean as well as Latin America where poverty still persists among certain communities. Most of them are out of bounds in the development mainstream. The development process currently underway there manifestly bypasses them. We were used to the news of recurrent famine visiting Ethiopia. The news did not stir us at least in our childhoods. We do not hear such catastrophe nowadays. Situations over there have improved significantly. Sporadic adversities may come to pass for a short period in a particular region in the country, but that can never take the shape of a famine now. The country has come a long way during the last few decades leaving behind the dark days of extreme economic destitution. The underlying causes of frequent famine in that country has been addressed by undertaking development programmes. Productive base of the economy is primarily agrarian and still exporting primary products to the world. Policy paralysis has almost gripped many nations in Sub-Saharan region, the dark poverty zone in the world. The World Bank in its recent estimate has shown that almost half of the people populating this region that comprises of 48 countries in the African continent live on $1 per day. The bank describes this precarious living as extreme poverty.

Chronic Poverty Research Centre, a global body under the auspices of the UN has recently identified 16 countries belonging to Sub-Saharan region as "desperately deprived". From 1990 to the present time, income poverty has fallen in all world regions excepting this dark African region where the same is either unchanged or has gone up for some countries. Why does it happen in this region? Economists offered the answer, Breton Wood institutions; the World Bank and the IMF accepted it. The reason for the sticky poverty in that region is entrenched in the particular context of the region. The ground situation varies, therefore, poverty reduction has not been uniform throughout the world regions. Few would invoke the example of South Korea and Ghana to bear out the contention that culture matters. During 1950 Korea and Ghana had same level of per capita income. Both of them were poor on equal footings. But now, Korean economy ranks

15th in the ranking of the economies of the world in terms of size. Some factors are present in this region that perpetuates poverty. Firstly, the tropical ecology of this region gives rise to risk and vulnerability in its only source of living, i.e., agriculture. The fear of crop failure likely to be brought about by severe drought always haunts. Untimely rainfall in abundance can cause harvest failure also. Strike of natural calamities runs havoc in the absence of institutional arrangement. Institutional structure for agricultural credit, insurance, and farmers' cooperatives are still many miles away here. Crop failure as a result of natural calamity does not hit the crop producing farmers alone. It severely affects non-farm income and employment. The economy is adversely hit because agriculture is the dominant sector of production activity in this region. In fact, it is estimated that in late 2002 as a result of crop failure the lives and livelihoods of as many as 16 million people in Lesotho, Malawi, Mozambique, Swaziland, Zambia and Zimbabwe were threatened.

The state fails to appear as rescuer, as the size of the sufferers and the amount of crop loss are too high to compensate by budgetary support. The states have to look forward for donor agencies to tide over the crisis. Market failure like crop failure also heralds doomsday for the farmers. Markets where the farmers bring the crop for sale are not well-organized. Information asymmetry is quite large for the farmers in the absence of information network. Prior information about the prevailing market price of crop can help the farmers in organizing production so that loss could be minimized. Isolated communities do not have the idea about the price of their produce. They run the risk of market failure. For example sudden drop in the export price for coffee brought about disaster among the coffee producing small farmers of Uganda and Ethiopia few years ago. Sporadic ethnic conflicts were regular features in many countries of this region. Conflict within the state caused by fights among tribes for supremacy not only perpetuates but also deepens poverty. There is positive association between low income of countries and occurrences of ethnic conflicts. The recent revelation is amazing. Countries exhibiting lowest HDI score are the same countries that are witnessing internal strife, race riot, ethnic cleansing and terrorism. Sudden or prolonged ill health often results in a downward spiral of asset loss and impoverishment as people are forced to abandon productive activities. The relationship between ill health and poverty is complex and works in both directions: illness can cause poverty and poverty can contribute to poor health. Untreated sickness contributes significantly to low life expectancy. For example, seasonal conditions such as diarrhoea, water- and mosquito-borne diseases result in poor health outcomes, and given that they commonly coincide with the rainy season and, therefore, the most highly labour-demanding agricultural season, such illnesses can have broader poverty implications.

Health Shocks

Ill health diminishes working capacity. Health statistics in this region are alarming. The under-five mortality rate in 2005 was 166/1000—a figure that has hardly improved in two decades and is twice the developing world's average. Poor maternal health is just shame. Probability that woman will die from complications during pregnancy and childbirth at 1 in 16. This is too much high compared with a developed world rate of 1 in 3800. Life expectancy in SSA is today lower than it was three decades ago, with an average life expectancy of about 50 years in 2000-05 according to a report published by United Nations Development programme released in 2007. The HIV/AIDS pandemic has reduced life expectancy and contributed to high levels of mortality. The number of people dying from AIDS in SSA continues to increase, reaching 2 million in 2006, as does the number of new cases and the number of people requiring treatment for advanced infection (United Nations Department of Public Information, 2007: 2). HIV/AIDS has an impact on households' livelihoods and labour productivity and on the ability of households and communities to cope (Van de Waal and Whiteside, 2003). Households affected by HIV/AIDS commonly have less income, reduced food security and are more vulnerable to other shocks, such as drought (Harvey, 2004). Dependency ratios (dependents as a proportion of the working population) in SSA are the highest in the world, with the dependency ratio 0.8 (young) and 0.1 (old) in 2004 (World Bank, 2006a). This is partly driven by the HIV/AIDS epidemic in SSA. HIV/AIDS is also putting considerable strain on public resources.

Low Capability

Income poverty is now a narrow measure of wellbeing of people. Capability approach has far greater acceptance among policy makers and development economists. Low capability formation among the people of the Sub-Saharan Africa is the cause of the persisting penury among the people. Capability is the opportunity or freedom to live a life without hunger, ill health, preventable death, illiteracy and many handicaps that deters the full enjoyment of life. Public policy can substantially enhance capability. Bad governance and anarchy can lead to diminution of capability. Take the example of Uganda where a large number of people were victims of internal displacement caused by political strife. The UN sponsored relief centres managed by the fragile state over there were almost a *ghetto*, reminiscent of the fascist torture on the Jews people. The refugees live miserable life in those camps which did not have sanitation, potable water and other facilities for decent living. Food was inadequate and medical care was absent. Mortality went up manifold in the camp life. Poverty added by inequality in the distribution of current income generates extreme hardship. Inequality persists also in the distribution of asset ownership by the people. Non-income economic inequality gives rise to income inequality. The world dreadful poverty region that geographically overlaps with Sub-Saharan African territory is also plagued by extreme economic inequality. Economist's favourite tool for measurement of economic inequality is statistical formula called Ginni Co-efficient and this 47.4 per cent in the region. This level is quite alarming. Poorest 20 per cent of population earn only 5 per cent of total income. Kenya as a big country in this region can be cited as an example for individual nation where inequality has reached its nadir. Here 10 per cent of households receive 42 per cent of total income and bottom 10 per cent less than 1 per cent.

Exclusion from political, social and economic institutions is part of vicious cycle that leads to low capability. Majority of people do not participate in the political process, leaving this field to the hands of privileged tribal leaders. Democracy is deeply undermined. Horizontal inequality becomes pervasive. Inequality that arises because of association with a group characterized by ethnicity, gender, region, religion and so on is damaging. Discrimination on the basis of personal traits like gender, age and impairment are equally worrisome. Adverse incorporation instead of promoting social equality reinforces inequality by engaging people from the lowest rung in terrible work environment. This employment situation is not only marked by low wage but also by uncertain and exploitative terms.

Ethnicity instead of national citizenship decides everything in Africa. It generates discrimination, conflict, bad governance, chaos and anarchy. State formation is hindered and the process of nation building is derailed. Choices and opportunities shrink. Ethno-territory plays central role in determining poverty and wealth. Poverty has deepened here in recent time because livelihood opportunities have been shrinking over last many years. Employment does not drive away poverty among the working people. They constitute the rank of working poor. The phenomena of working poor persist when real wages of the workers fall behind the escalating cost of living. Livelihood opportunities do not come by for number of reasons. Firstly, market as an institution is precariously imperfect. Markets are few and far between. Geographical distances in the absences of transport and communications deter the primary producers to engage them in the market and exchange. Non-market productive activities keep them entrapped in perpetual penury. Agro-ecological conditions and vagaries of nature brings irreparable blow to the suffering farmers. Public investment for infrastructure is very low. The added fuel to the fire is sporadic ethnic conflict. Capital formation is hindered not only by low savings but also by lack of financial institutions to mobilize the savings. Rural-urban divide in the incidence of poverty is conspicuously present. People living in the rural areas are more likely to be poor than their urban counterparts.

The nature of politics prevailing in the region is fundamentally non-developmental. Neo-patrimonial power relation gives rise to hybrid state where demarcation between private sphere and public sphere is blurred. Private appropriation of public resources is quite rampant. Nepotism and patron-clienteles relation guides the framing of public policies. Issue-based politics has given way to clan interest of the ruling elite. Political parties without any exceptions are born and reared to serve the parochial interest instead of broad national interest. Poverty as an issue never comes on the eve of election. The colonial legacy of this vast region has left behind a human settlement without any means to build their own destiny. The imperial power fostered the culture of ethnic conflict. Therefore the nation-states formed by the common citizenship, fairness, equality and participation were born here as crippled child. Here the state exists to serve and swell the interest of the few who bends the law at will in their favour. The majority suffers at the hands of the powerful few. International aid is a short term measure that can heal the wound for some time but long term solution lies in the good governance, rule of law and building of institutions. The Donors responses are not always prompt and positive. Aid is never the good option. The African aid-dependent states should now move forward for self-reliance to live and flourish with dignity.

1.5 Poverty in South Asia : The Other 'Poverty Zone' on this Planet

Sub-Saharan Africa is closely followed by South Asia in sheltering the staggering magnitude of poor people. Governments of the South Asian region have been publishing poverty statistics on almost regular basis overcoming many deficiencies that come in the way in this type of massive exercise. However, Government data on poverty is not well received by everyone. Many ventilate their reservations. NGOs allege that government tries to hide its own incapacity of fighting poverty. The World Bank goes by the official data furnished by the respective government. Development economists are posed by a very crucial question on historical backwardness of this region. Its South East Asian neighbours close by geographically have been posing as contrast as if dark and luminous locations stay side by side. Japan first showed the light in Asia's eastern region and her followers took up the journey later as shown by their leaders. The road to development in Japan was paved during Meiji Restoration in Japan when she first abandoned her isolationist stand she had been clinging for thousands of years. Poverty did not come in the way of universalizing elementary education and public health care in this country two hundred years ago. The idea, quite radical in those days in an isolated land in the Far East, laid the foundation on which today's Japan stands imposingly. The demonstration effect of wonderful ideas of Japan was immense in her neighbourhood. Japan had demonstrated, by offering her own example that a nation can economically prosper despite having nothing underground what we term as 'natural resources'. The deprivation by nature is added by distress caused by frequent earthquake that rocks harshly the 'land of rising sun'. The key to prosperity in case of Japan and her followers is the human capital formation. The process of which set off hundred of years ago. Japan is reaping the benefits. South Korea, Singapore, Taiwan had followed Japan to give shape to what is now known as ***'East Asian Miracle'***.

South Asia, in which India holds a majority of geographic as well as demographic shares did not go the East Asian way. Her destiny was different as her present day neighbours surrounding her. British imperialism for two hundred years over the Indian subcontinent is held responsible by many for the contemporary India's poverty and underdevelopment. The dominant political discourse puts the blame at the door of imperial exploitation of the colonies. There was political India before the onset of colonization whose boundaries were always changing according to monarchy. War among kings to gain control over territories to expand the contour of empire was regular feature but the fascinating aspect of India's village society as a self-sufficient little 'state' has been invoked by many times as an unique case of political life. These self-contained village communities, independent of each other, are referred by many as village republic having separate system of internal arrangement of administration. Democratic ambience had prevailed in this self-sufficient village where agriculture was the mainstay of occupation. Farming was followed far behind by small manufacturers of farm implement and rudimentary service undertakings along with crafts. The idyllic village society during India's pre-colonial stage has captured the imagination of number of thinkers and writers. Karl Marx had analysed the structure of Indian village communities as independent units in his discourse on 'Asiatic Mode of Production'. These villages units dotting the landscape of India remained undisturbed for centuries even though the kings were fighting among themselves to conquer each other territory somewhere away. The peasant societies for long remained intact unaffected by the storms hitting the political sky. Colonial administration had completely destroyed these self-sufficient village structure in Indian subcontinent.

The British administration was concerned only with collection of land revenue. They put in place number of intermediaries to ensure smooth flow of land revenues in the colonial coffers. Peasant distress went up manifold in the wake of installing layers of intermediaries between them and the state. Peasant's precarious plight caused by the exploitation by landlord, neither reached nor stirred the British administration. Public investment in agriculture was very little or almost nil. Agriculture did not flourish for lack of productive investment. Productivity remained stagnant during the colonial period. Destitution of the masses dependent on the agrarian economy during colonial regime was occasionally deepened by the affliction of natural calamities. Flood and drought brought about disaster for the peasants in the absence of state protection. The British laid the railway lines to facilitate transport of military and merchandises. The upcoming textile mills in the Great Britain needed raw cotton as well as market for clothes produced in the mills. The railways did not lay the foundation for economic development in the British India. Independent India inherited from the colonial master the baggage of poverty and underdevelopment. The subcontinent was partitioned on communal line that sowed the seed for religious fundamentalism. Pakistan and Bangladesh, India's eastern and western neighbours, have been grappling with home-grown religious fundamentalism that weakens the democracy and formation of nation-state. Afghanistan is now gasping for breath on getting suffocated by long-drawn war waged by fundamentalist forces. At times, it seems that state has virtually disappeared from the scene leaving the site to terrorists to do whatever they like. Poverty of the Afghan people is reinforced by absence of good governance. The World Bank goes by the official data furnished by the respective government. The pace of poverty reduction is manifestly varied across the region. From 1990 to 2005, during the period spanning 15 years, head count poverty has come down in India, in Nepal as well as in Bangladesh. Inharmoniously, poverty has increased in Pakistan and it has been almost unchanged in Sri Lanka during the same period (Fig. 1.1).

This is in contrast to what has happened to economic growth in recent years for countries of this region. Pakistan and Sri Lanka have posted much higher growth rate than India and Bangladesh. Thus GDP growth and poverty reduction does not move side by side at least for the period from 2001 to 2004 as evident from the

World Bank's report. There is no one to one correspondence between economic growth and poverty reduction. Economic growth can reduce poverty fast if the trickle down of growth is

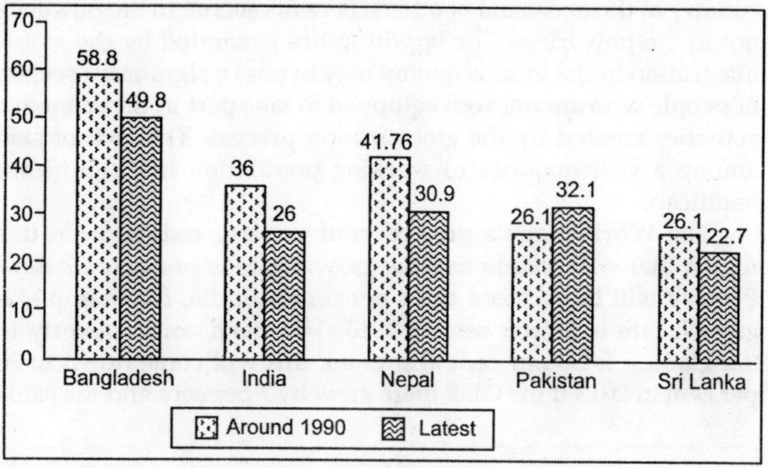

Source: The World Bank Poverty Report 2012.

Fig. 1.1: Poverty (Head Count Index) in South Asia is Declining in Recent Years

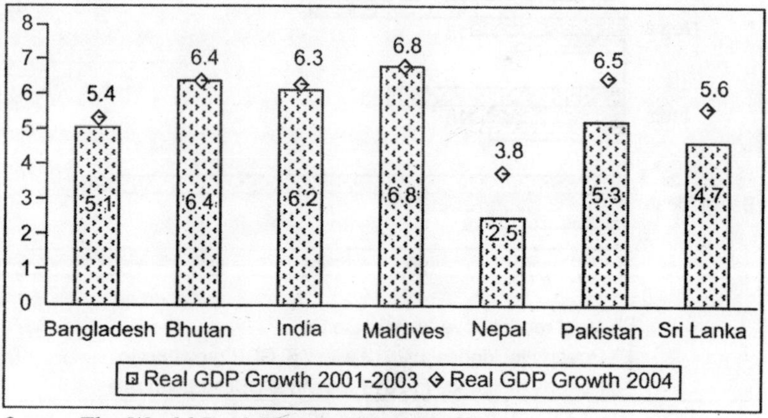

Source: The World Bank Poverty Report 2012.

Fig. 1.2: Real GDP Growth in South Asia has been Impressive in the Recent Past

spontaneous. This has been an issue of debate in contemporary discourse on development whether growth can lift the people who are perpetually trapped in poverty. Growth may not be inclusive in all the situations. It may benefit a section of population in the country at the exclusion of others. Benefits accrue to the powerful not to the powerless. The opportunities generated by the global integration in the local economy may bypass a significant section of people who are not well equipped to take part in the economic activities created by the globalization process. The lack of skill among a vast majority of working population is a significant handicap.

The World Bank's projection of poverty reduction in this region that will accompany the growth rate is presented below. Poverty will be reduced to 13 per cent in India, for example, if growth rate is 10 per cent in 2013. The Head count poverty in Bangladesh is 50 per cent at present; this will come down to 20 per cent in 2013 if the GDP there grow by 7 per cent and the same

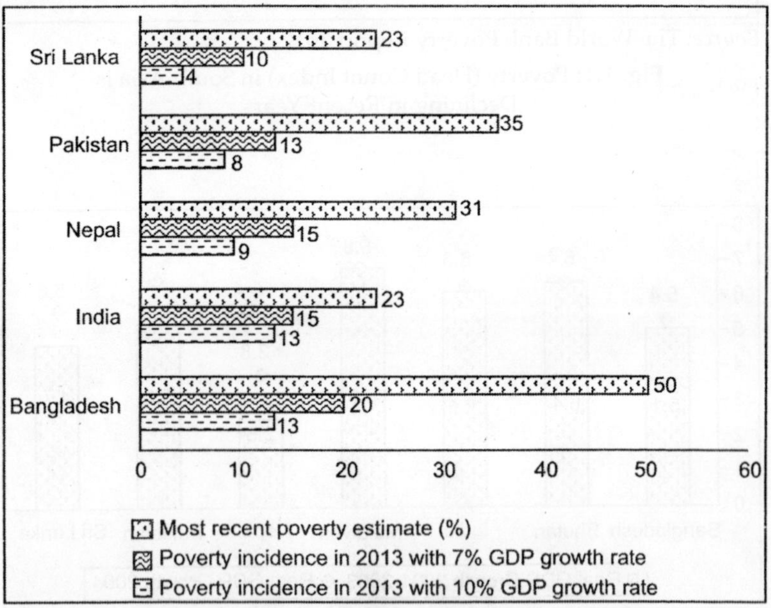

Source: The World Bank Poverty Report 2012

Fig. 1.3: Poverty Reduction in South Asia associated with Economic Growth

will further come down to 13 per cent if the GDP grows by 10 per cent (Fig. 1.3).

Though economic growth has brought down the incidence of poverty in South Asia, its total number of poor has escalated. The number of poor people living on less than $1.25 a day increased from 549 million in 1981 to 595 million in 2005. In India, where almost three-quarters of these poor live, the number increased from 420 million in 1981 to 455 million in 2005 (Ravaliion *et al.*, 2009). Moreover, human development has been lagging far behind the pace of income growth. Children and women are suffering more than the others. More than 250 million children are malnourished and more than 30 million children do not go to school in South Asia. More than one-third of adult women are anaemic. The share of female employment in total employment is among the lowest in the world. South Asia is a land of sharp contrasts and astonishing inequality (Devarajan, 2006). It has more pronounced regional disparities than the rest of the world and is in fact divided into two 'Asias'. A lot of attention has been given

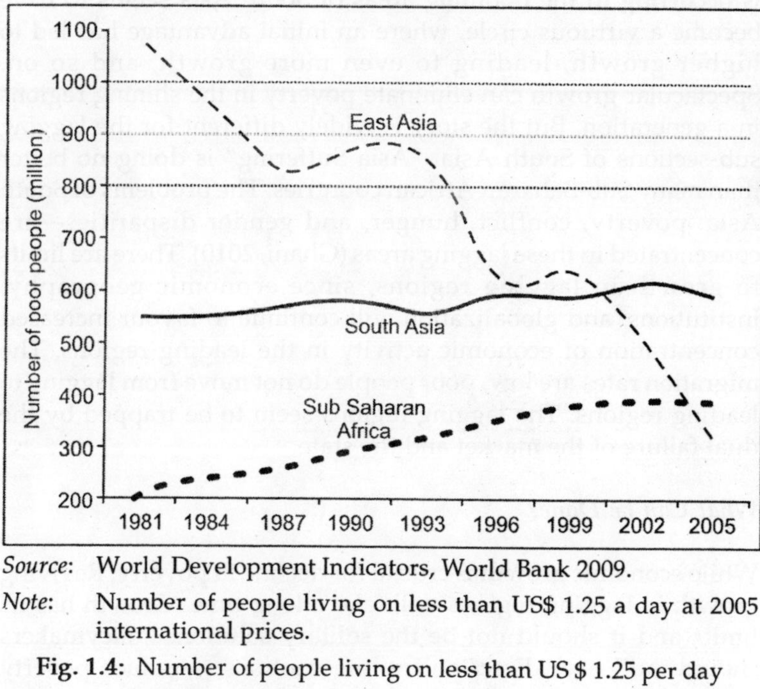

Source: World Development Indicators, World Bank 2009.

Note: Number of people living on less than US$ 1.25 a day at 2005 international prices.

Fig. 1.4: Number of people living on less than US $ 1.25 per day

to "Asia Shining". But there is another Asia that exists in parallel, "Asia Suffering". The distinction between the two is so pointed that they seem to be set in two different centuries. And the gap is mounting (Fig. 1.4).

Spatial Disparities

The selected flourishing locations in the South Asia can appear as an enigma to the rest of the world. These sparkling lights are the gateways connecting South Asia with the developed economies. The city of Bangalore in India is an example of this, and it is flying on the back of globalization in services. Technological externalities that entail self discovery, demonstration effects, learning by doing, pecuniary externalities that includes surplus labour markets that promotes better matching and agglomeration (Krugman, 1999) has generated growth in that sector. Bangalore has come up like a nucleus of schools and universities that promote professional learning and entrepreneurship (Glaeser, 2010). The makeover that is occurring in the booming areas of South Asia seems to have become a virtuous circle, where an initial advantage has led to higher growth, leading to even more growth, and so on. Spectacular growth can eliminate poverty in the shining regions in a generation. But the story is widely different for the lagging sub-sections of South Asia. "Asia Suffering" is doing no better than many Sub-Saharan African countries. The problems of South Asia: poverty, conflict, hunger, and gender disparities—are concentrated in these lagging areas (Ghani, 2010). There are limits to growth in lagging regions, since economic geography, institutions, and globalization will continue to favour increased concentration of economic activity in the leading regions. The migration rates are low, poor people do not move from lagging to leading regions. The lagging regions seem to be trapped by the dual failure of the market and the state.

What Can be Done?

While economic growth is crucial for decline in poverty. Reviving growth in lagging regions will take a long time. Growth has its limits and it should not be the solitary solution. Policymakers should mull over direct policy interventions to reduce poverty

(Banerjee and Duflo, 2007). Direct interventions can have a double benefit. They will lessen human misery, which could set off growth. A high priority should be given to increasing the pro-poor fiscal transfers. Poor regions have a low base of economic activity to tax, and characteristically these regions have lower revenues. This revenue constriction prevents governments from extending safety nets, investing in human and physical capital, and adequately providing government services. Achieving equity through fiscal transfers can ensure a level playing field. This equity is particularly important if the government provides important inputs into future growth potential, such as in developing a healthy and educated workforce. Simply directing financial resources to lagging regions, however, may not be adequate. It must be complemented with an improvement in capacity, accountability, and participation at the local level. Frictions and imperfections in the labour market seem to be hampering less skilled workers more than skilled workers. This is reflected in lower migration rates for uneducated than educated migrants (Caglar, 2010). In India, the mobility rate increases with the education level. The mobility of university graduates is much higher than the mobility of unskilled workers. Removing barriers to human mobility—such as labour laws, state-specific social welfare programmes, and housing market distortions—should be an integral part of development. Human mobility allows poor people to move to geographic areas and economic sectors where the demand and the returns are higher. By pulling up wages in lagging regions, migration benefits non-migrants in these regions. Migration also empowers the traditionally disadvantaged groups, particularly, women.

CHAPTER **2**

Poverty and Society

2.1 Social Contract Theory

The desire of many people to get rid of occasional disturbance committed by few wrongdoers found its expression in the formation of civil society. Locke called it Social Contract and this formation put an end to the state of nature. Rousseau, the French writer of the eighteenth century in his famous book "The Social Contract" published in 1762 wrote that the "man in the state of nature was a novel savage who lived a life of primitive simplicity and idyllic happiness'. Like Locke, Rousseau had heaped praise eloquently on the world of nature. He described that man in the state of nature was independent, healthy, self-sufficient, fearless and good. In this the French philosopher visualized the state of nature as the wonderful habitat of mankind without having sense of any sin in the activities of men. The demarcation or the dividing line between right and wrong did not come up in the minds of men. Men in the natural world were innocent like other creatures of nature. They did not bother about the consequence of these actions on themselves, on fellow human beings and on the surroundings they live. They neither could judge nor was impelled to reflect on the righteousness of his action. Society bereft of any value system or ethical judgment would be anarchic in nature where weaker members are decimated by the strong. Rousseau's description of the antecedent circumstances giving birth to society based on rules had emerged in many ways. It reflected the evolutionary process of the building of society, espoused by his predecessors hundred years ago. They agreed that state emerged out of social contract but the need and circumstances of the meeting of human minds differed in a significant way. According to Rousseau, society and the state come into being to prevent dispute over disparate claims on property.

Population was skimpy in the state of nature. It grew manifold over thousands of years. Thus sustaining the lives of this huge number was the daunting task of mankind. Food had to be provided to all feeding mouths. The human living in the hunting and gathering stage was unsustainable for natural reason. The growth of population far exceeded the capacity of earth to produce food for them. Human dispersal in search of better pastures had already began. Men abandoned pastoralist living and settled in places close to large waterbodies to undertake agriculture and livestock for flesh and farming. While agriculture and livestock were dominant occupation in the settled agricultural society, they did not altogether give up hunting. Historians cannot make any comment on the pattern of food available for our early ancestors in this pre-historic period. It was plausible that food available per head had certainly gone up in the 'agriculture phase' than the earlier phase of roaming for hunting and gathering. Discovery of agriculture was a turning point in the history of civilization. It heralded a settled living for mankind and ended the practices of looking upon only on nature for supply of food. After the advent of agriculture, men could produce food in plenty not only for present consumption but for future also. Surplus production of food crops was traded for other necessities of life. It helped in the beginning of trade and exchange not only within the same settlement but also with other distant areas of human settlements.

Hobbes contended that limited material prosperity of mankind in the wake of discovery of agriculture was fraught with degeneration. The prosperity threw challenges to mankind to make provision for sustaining the prosperity. The enactment of property law or enunciation of property rights through discussion and dialogue among people was the only measure that could stop the property going haywire. Agricultural technique, in its earliest form, could enhance production of certain crops to a significant extent. In the absence of state and institution, the issue of employing one's own labour and resources and the exclusive command over the produce remained tricky and problematic. Pilferage or stealing of crops planted by others was widespread. The stealing or forcibly taking away the crops from the field was neither morally unacceptable nor legally prohibited. Man in this phase of civilization did not give any thought on moral judgment on any action. Man could not differentiate between what is right and what is wrong. So grabbing the product of other labour was an instinctive action and was an acceptable activity. But this attitude could singularly turn the wheel of human progress in reverse course instead of moving forward. If everyone steals the crops raised in the field by others, then at certain point of time no one would put any labour in cultivation crops in the field. Cultivator would be demoralized if he would find to his dismay that his crop was being harvested by others. The man who produced was kept out of his enjoyment of the product. These disincentives would stop production and material prosperity would wither.

Hobbes explained that articulation of property rights stemmed this degeneration and slipping into destitution and death. Men began to think that the fruits of their labour should be protected from stealing by others. Social contract had emerged out of felt-need for such protection. The social rules came into place through mutual agreements and consensus. The society conferred entitlements or rights for the piece of land, from which crop produced by his labour, to the individual. This right of, ownership was legally enforceable. The rule conferred individuals exclusive rights over his land. This made her exclusive owners of its produce from land. No one can encroach or trespass into other's land and take the produce. Such action would invite punishment for the offenders. The rules of punishment were laid down by the state through the judicial system. Material prosperity of mankind through heightened agricultural production and increase of livestock owes much to the emergence of property law. Conferment of rights through stipulation of some rules and codes had a boosting effect on the morale of the persons who cultivates and raise live stock. He devotes much energy and time when he came to know that his produce of labour would be his exclusive command. The snatchers and thieves would be brought to book for the offence of stealing. Social contract was thus a historic turn in the progress of human civilization that had provided protection of property rights. The proponents and architects of the social contract theory had made immeasurable advancement of social thinking. The contemporary social analysis owes a great deal to these founders of the social contract theory.

The philosophical thinking about man and society that made the fundamental premise of enlightenment thinking of the seventeenth and eighteenth century was largely influenced by the shining lights of the ***contractarian*** philosophers. They had started their expositions on different notes but ended with a converging tone. Society and state were born out of collective wishes of men to lead a happy life, secured and prosperous life for all members of the human family. Firstly, the social living had given men the security and protection which were absent in the state of nature. When the human society came up men began to accept it as an entity that demanded allegiance and respect from each member of society. Society made certain rules for social behaviour the compliance of which was mandatory for all. Those who defied were offenders to be brought to book according to rules articulated through collective dialogues and free discussion among themselves. The human journey from world of nature to the world of social living was associated with gain as well as loss. The loss relates to the sacrifice of some amount of freedom to the regulatory system of the society. In the state of nature men were absolutely free as no rules regulated their behaviour. But the social world is not without rules or code of conduct which men had to adhere. Men had parted with some amount of freedom and got in exchange the security and rule of law in which his life and properties would be protected.

The state came into being as an institution or governance with the consent of the 'governed'. The state draws its legitimacy for governance from the people. The state was born out of collective will of the people to get rid of anarchy in the state of nature. The power of the state to rule was the collective power of the people vested with the state. The people who would be governed had themselves consented to be governed by a set of rule or behaviour code collectively articulated and agreed upon. The state is empowered to frame rules for the best interest of the people. Rules making is the important function of the state. But the making of rules involves two fundamental issues to be addressed in the light of the functions of the state as a ***'super body'***. The first one relates to "how and what rules would be conceived and articulated ?" Secondly, what would be the basic premise or value on which this rules would be formed? ***Contractarians*** aptly provided the answer to the first question. The state or its legitimate organ would frame the rule that reflects the will of the 'governed'. As to the nature of the rules, they emphasized that rules reflected the social priorities. Law makers must be formed in the spirit of freedom and fairness, security of life and properties of the governed, creation of opportunities for development, raising taxes from the subject in a fair manner and making provisions for some of the essentials for survival.

Some distinctions between law and rule in the functioning of the state were brought to the fore. Some rules for conduct of individual in a society were not enacted through acceptance by people over successive generations. Behaving rudely with fellow citizens is not unlawful as per the letters of the law. But the social rule and conduct disallow this rudeness. Some rules are conventional and respected over time by people without incorporating them in the law book. Let us take an example of such a rule based behaviour or good behaviour appreciated in the society. A man comes across another man lying down on the street, bleeding profusely as he was hit on his head by a speeding truck. There is no law to compel the 'passer by' to stop on the spot of accident instead of reaching his office in time. The law cannot direct him to lift the suffering old man in his arms, take a taxi and rush for the hospital. The man undertaking this human work is never haunted by the fear of breaking law in case he just ignores and leaves the spot. But he takes all these trouble driven by inner urge or the call of the consciences or the social rule or convention that glorifies this empathy. This is an act of benevolence, a concern and feeling for the fellow citizens and the proclivity to abide by the social rules and codes of good behaviour. Thus the basic difference between the law and social rules relate to enforceability. The law is enforceable and the social rules are not. But it is no way it renders social rules a useless instrument in the functioning and life of society.

2.2 The Enlightenment and People's Wellbeing

The enlightenment period is the defining historical phase in the progression of human civilization. It was a turning point that had tremendous impact on how the people used to see and understand the world around them. The enlightenment period is referred as age of reason. It was a confluence of ideas sprouted throughout the Western Europe, England and America during seventeenth and eighteenth century. The enlightenment age closely follows the European Renaissance signifying an indelible influence of the former on the latter. Renaissance followed the end of the Dark Age in the human history. The sequences of these historical occurrences are important in interpreting our past. The link among them is manifest and provides us with food for thought in enriching our understanding of human civilization. But the naming of this epoch making period spanning almost two centuries has to be explained before any attempt to bring the period and its significance to the fore. Some people in that era were more enlightened than their peers in the society. Light of knowledge fell on selected few and they were ahead of others in critical thinking and questioning the foundation of humanity. They were pioneers and front runners during their period to give priority to reason instead of accusing to every dictates of the authority. They were enlightenment thinkers as they started questioning everything around them instead of lessons and wisdom imparted by the church.

Ill-being in general and poverty in particular was not questioned by the governing authority. No one did explore the possibility that material wellbeing could be enhanced through appropriate actions and policies. The enlightenment thinkers had reflected on the living conditions of the people and had thought on the way out to remedy the economic adversities that had engulfed the multitude of the people. The prevalent belief that the state of being in the material world is unalterable was propagated by the church and the ruling elites. The Orthodox Church in the western world had passed on the heavenly sermon of allegiance to the authority by the subjects without questioning. The unquestioned loyalty of the subjects to the dual authority of church and kings was expected and realized by invoking divine wish. The church and the monarchs worked in tandem to rule the people for ages and this mandate was showered on them by the divine authority. The advent of enlightenment thinking among the leading lights heralded a virtual end of the hegemony of the ruling duo. Enlightenment thinkers were few and they were far ahead of others in thinking about physical and social world around them. Some of them were enlightened while the rest of fellow citizens remained in darkness. They did not ask themselves about their worldly living. They took everything as wish of the super power which is far beyond the human understanding. The belief was deep rooted among the people that nature obliges the dictates of God. The king rules by the dictates of God. The church and the priest are worldly representative of God. They are the ultimate custodians of men. The teachings they impart is infallible. Their lessons could not be questioned.

Thus church stymied the growth of intellectual exercise of the people. People were neither allowed nor encouraged to reflect on anything. The age of enlightenment was the age of reason that gradually replaced the acquiescent mindset. People began to argue and reason on everything around them. The authorities of the church in controlling human lives were challenged by the leading thinkers of the enlightenment age. Most stirring challenge was posted by the discovery of the solar system pioneered by Galileo and followed by leading scientists of the seventeenth and eighteenth century. The dominant wisdom fervently spearheaded by the church before this discovery was that earth is a fixed object and the sun rotates around it. Night and days occurs because of solar rotation. This was proved wrong by astronomical discovery that earth on which we live also rotates on its own axis causing night and day. This was the first blow to the authority of church. The study of the universe began with pioneering enquiry by Copernicus and was followed by Keplar. This earliest study on the nature of universe had placed sun at the centre of the universe refuting older beliefs. Galileo was immensely encouraged by this revelation and had engaged himself in deeper probing to unravel the mystery. He had developed telescope to observe the position of the celestial objects and planetary motions. He personally took scientific enquiry and experimentations based on facts. He confirmed through these experimentations the observations about the universe made by his distinguished predecessors. With the help of the instrument he had made himself, he found that moon's surface was uneven. His epoch making discovery paved the way for scientific discoveries in different fields of physical world but it spelt disaster for him. He was summoned by the Pope in Rome and was accused of disobeying the church. He was put to house arrest until his death in captivity. He was forced to sign a declaration scripted by the Pope that what he and his predecessors had discovered was wrong.

Roman Catholic churches were scared by the scientific revelation regarding the natural world. But this punishment meted out to the pioneers of enlightenment thinking did fail to stop further discoveries that followed. A great number of leading lights appeared to follow the footsteps of Galileo who had lost his life so early for committing the sin of unravelling the truth. The search for truth was fraught with danger posed by the church which is used to wield the exclusive power of teaching the truth of existence. After Galileo three names are prominent in the realm of science. They collectively contributed to laying the foundation for establishing science as the tool for unravelling the truth and revealing the mysteries of nature. Francis Bacon and Rene Descartes were perfect inheritors of the tradition of scientific enquiry set in motion by Galileo. Bacon wrote philosophical treaties that had placed logical analysis at the central place. He is credited with giving birth to the method of scientific enquiry, the hallmark of enlightenment thinking. The advances in human civilization owed much to the human attitude instilled by the enlightenment thinking.

Bacon was the earliest proponent of state funding for scientific enquiry. Rene Descartes, the leading follower of the enlightenment period, had delved in geometry to understand the laws of physical world. Geometry, as a distinct discipline based on mathematics and logic was born out of his tireless engagement throughout his life. Sir Isaac Newton almost gave birth to the science of Physics during the period when scientific discoveries had already set in motion and the urge to know more about the nature of universe. He was born during the advent of the age of reason but was not altogether free of the influence of church in shaping his world view. Newton was perfect follower of Galileo who relied on observations and testing to determine the veracity of a statement about the laws of nature. Galileo was less fortunate despite his remarkable feat as a trendsetter. He had invited the wrath of the Orthodox Church by his discovery that had falsified the age-old belief system held by them. Sir Isaac Newton at least did not meet the same fate. Galileo was born and made the stirring discovery at a time when the age of reason had just begun. Unquestioned loyalty to the church and the state was still intact. Sir Newton was born quite later at a time when enlightenment thinking was catching up to the dismay of the Orthodox Church. Laws of Gravity were his discovery. His ***Principia*** the epoch making book came out in 1687. As the title of the book makes hints about the content, he had shown the world for the first time that the physical world is guided by a set of principles. He laid bare the fact that the universe is governed by a set of unchanging laws. Only scientific study, based on observation and data, could understand the law. The universe exists; the physical world run and all the nature's phenomenon are not divine dictates beyond the comprehension of human mind. The laws of nature are unchanging and guided by logic. Human mind could successfully grasp these laws. Reason and empiricism marked the period of enlightenment which gradually unsettles the hold of church fathers on the citizens. Teachings of the churches began to loosen its impact on the people's mind. The enlightenment thinking began to be received by a scientific section of the people. The schism between two strands of teaching of minds persisted. The beginning of the enlightenment age did not instantly herald the end of church teaching. It took at least a century to enfeeble the hold of church and enlightenment ideas to spread across length and breadth of the world. It took considerable time to reach all segment of human society and all areas of thinking of human minds but it swayed and lasted. Thus enlightenment was in a sense the celebration of ideas originated and propagated during this defining period of human history. One fundamental idea that was unequivocally established was the immense potentiality of man. Unbounded possibilities of human intellect were established. Man is the reservoir of potentialities and it is not the passive recipients of the fruits of nature and benevolence of state and the church. Man could make his own fate by intellect and positive action. Unravelling the mysteries of nature could lead the way to material advancement of the humanity.

The worship of reason, precisely expressed in a set of philosophic ideas was undertaken by the scientists in the first go closely followed by philosophers and theologists. The literary community took up the new ideas and began to spread the new ideas through writings. It touched the upper middle class at first as literacy was yet to be universal in the western world. The focal point in the massage of enlightenment thinkers was faith in nature as well as in human potentiality. Nature appeared as a complex system of interacting laws governing the universe. Individual human being, as part of system was designed to act rationally. Man can enhance the happiness of others and improved his surroundings if they are allowed to undertake reasoned judgment free of influence of any commanding authority. The restraints imposed on man by the state and the church had to be removed to allow free thinking. Thus enlightenment teaching bears the seed for antipathy towards organized religion and hegemony of state. Many of the ideas were political in nature. A section of people began to contemplate a society where freedom and democracy would overwhelmingly prevail. Citizens would be conferred fundamental rights by the state. Egalitarianism would be the hallmark of the state policy for the citizens. Argumentations as the style of decision making grew of the new scientific method that invited multitude of hypotheses to be put of test. Empiricism was elevated to the level of public discourse.

The Western Europe, comprising of England, Holland and France, was the epicentre for the generation and spread of enlightenment ideas. Philosophers as pioneers in the enlightenment thinking, hailing from France, began to be known as philosophers. This breed of scholars in France gave rise to new philosophical thinking. Montesquieu was leading figure in this assembly. He was the earliest challenger of absolute monarchy. His world view was shaped by his foreign travel he made during the early part of the eighteenth century. He was highly impressed by English liberty. The spirit of law, his maiden book on political philosophy, came out in 1748, where he expressed his concern about the government failings. His suggestion for instituting checks and balances in governance was adopted later in different European nations. He forcefully recommended the uncompromising defence of liberty against tyranny. Voltaire was no less vocal against traditional religion and unjust old regimes. He did not ventilate his displeasure in plain language. He was a prolific writer and had used caustic language to air his grievance against the existing social order. He began to preach Newtonian science in France, campaigned for freedom of the people and began to harp scathing attack on churches. Through his writings he preached human freedom, fairness and egalitarian attitude for the people. The best known among the Philosophers was Rousseau. His social contract theory had vehemently indicated absolute monarchy. He said "Man is born free but today he is everywhere in chain".

Immanuel Kant, the German philosopher was deeply influenced by the enlightenment thinking. His ideas contained primarily in 'the critique of pure Reason' (1781) ushered in a new age of philosophic idealism. Kant agreed with Lock on the role of senses in acquiring knowledge but insisted that sensory experiences had to be interpreted by the mind's internal pattern. He taught us that certain ideas were a "priori". They existed before the sensory experience occurred. The innate ideas were width, depth, beauty, cause and God. All were understood but these are not learned through senses. Kant concluded that some truths were not derived from material objects through scientific study. He said that realism beyond the material world was unapproachable by science. Reason according to Kant went beyond the mere interpretation of Physical realities. He said that pure reason is close to intuition as well. The idea of God came from mind's penchant for harmony

2.3 Humanitarianism

Enlightenment movement had trickled down to the bottom of the society over a period spanning almost two hundred years. This movement gave birth to humanitarianism as an outlook. The attitude towards human beings by the religious authority had undergone change as a manifestation of impact of the movement. Demand for reform in Christian principles had gathered momentum. Christianity was redefined and its earlier garb was removed to bring it close to common men. Concern for man got the priority than any other concern.

The grip of the Roman Catholicism was weakened by the advent of the new humanism. The new wave sought to relive human sufferings of children and women. Anglicans, Evangelicals, Methodists and Quakers came together to strengthen the humanitarian movement unleashed by enlightenment wave. A court case in 1774 ended slavery in England and abolition of slave trade followed. The wave of humanitarianism also hit the legal institution, the offshoot of which was legal reform accepting the basic premise that human beings were basically good by nature. Criminality is not basic instincts but the creation of circumstances. Legal reform was closely followed by jail reform which began to insist on humane treatment of prisoners. The religious groups were strongly demanding such reforms. The rationalist thinkers advocated education for children for building a better society. Enlightenment wave gave rise to multifaceted impacts in almost all realms of thought and actions. The age of the reason heralded by scientific discoveries reached all strands of thought. Rational thinking and application of logic in understanding the world took firm ground. Newtonian discovery of unchanging law that govern the universe also had deeply impressed the social thinkers who were engaged in finding out any such law that governs our social world. Social contract theory was the fruit of such collective engagement of leading social thinkers of the enlightenment era. The fundamental premise of the social contract theory is human being's collective desire to lead a social life to be governed by law to be formulated by people themselves. Human beings are rational, therefore, their collective action and thoughts would be rational. Collective action would lead to maximum social welfare.

Society came into being out of collective desire to lead a secured life instead of constant uncertainties, hazards, insecurity and threat to survival. The state came into being as super entity holding power to govern. Men vested some power on the state sacrificing some freedom to be governed by the state. The state in return would protect the men. Thus the state was born out of social contract, an unwritten covenant, among individuals craving for a social order marked by law and governance. The state will not only protect some inalienable right of its citizens but would also promote the welfare of its subjects to the highest extent possible. The enlightened ***contractarians*** believed that the man held rights, enjoyed freedom and liberty in the natural world. Man must enjoy the freedom in every circumstance irrespective of whether he is in the natural world or in social world. This freedom oriented feature of human nature was revealed by the enlightenment thinkers. This thinking and its propagation set in motion the popular displeasure with absolute monarchy that characterizes the nature of state in the pre-enlightenment era. Absolute monarchy and freedom of people are anathema to each other. The

Divine mandate to rule began to face challenges of reasoned agreement and questionings by the citizens. The Enlightenment movement gave rise to basic principles about human affairs. Reason was the key to truth, not the lesson imparted by the established churches. The progress was possible if people would be set free of domination by church and the state. Socialist thinkers, not as mainstream enlightenment ideas, began to advocate abolition of private property in a bid to build an egalitarian society.

Mary Wollstonecraft, the leading feminist thinker, argued that political rights and freedom should be extended to women. She had aired her displeasure about male centred views of the most of the enlightenment thinkers. Mary's insistence on women's rights as equal citizens was not accepted universally in the beginning but she was successful in setting the ball rolling for reflection on the most crucial aspect of freedom of mankind. But she must be credited for launching the movement that culminated in popular demand, at much later stage, for enacting right to equality irrespective gender, age and any other considerations. The triumph of feminist movement during twentieth century owes much to Mary and her co-fighters. Equal treatment for women is still a far cry in many territories of the world. The seed of enlightenment movement is yet to blossom in many parts of the world of the twenty-first century. But we have enough reason to be optimistic. Our cherished destination for gender equality in all aspects of life, at all places in the world is still away but within reach. Some of the developments relating to status of women even in traditional sexist society are encouraging. Conferring voting rights to women in the democratic countries is one such positive step toward equality of political rights. The United States, despite being the oldest democracy did not provide for voting right for women from the very beginning of their electoral process. They later realized that democracy is heading towards wrong direction if half of its citizens comprising of women could not take part in election process.

The US action of conferring voting right to women was emulated by other democracies in different parts of the world at later stage. The enlightenment thinking and Mary's crusade against denial of equal right to women had laid the ground for movement and action for fair treatment of women in this world. The other remarkable achievement begotten by the enlightenment movement that have received comparatively less attention is related to the plight of children. Well before the onset of enlightenment wave that had hit at the Western Europe, children in the parental homes were treated as good as livestock. During the medieval period, children were considered as evil incarnation. They were put to hard work in family farming as well as in the raising livestock. The dominant social outlook towards children was characterized by neglect and maltreatment. The enlightenment movement could successfully change the social attitude towards children. Older method of discipline through harsh treatment was gradually replaced by restrained behaviour moulded by empathy. It was accepted that children were naturally innocent and good creatures. They are as human beings as adults are. They deserve human treatment, care and protection. The enlightenment, movement had instilled the notion that good treatment and proper education can make them good adults. They have self-esteem and self worth and bears immense possibility for flourishing. Only education can bring out these potential. Duty of the state and responsibility of the parents toward children was charted out.

2.4 Poverty and Enlightenment: Some Observations

Poverty as a manifestation of human distress may appear to be unrelated to the revolutionary episode in human history later came to be known as enlightenment. One significant contribution of the new ideas embodied in the enlightenment philosophy is bringing man in the centre stage of world view. The dominant social outlook framed by the Orthodox Church sponsored by the ruling state predating the enlightenment kept man outside the core idea preached by them. For thousands of years, men were not regarded as human beings blessed with immense possibilities to flourish. They were considered by the authority as passive beneficiaries of benevolences, recipients or cruel treatment and filled with animal instincts devoid of intellect and capacity to judge. Enlightenment thinkers, the assemblage of great souls of visionary intellectuals, knocked at very premise of the prevalent notion about man. Man was free in the natural world and man would be free in the social order that came into being out of collective desire to lead an ordered social life with freedom and security of life. The enlightenment thinkers reflected on poverty in its comprehensive obverse not particularly as a state of living characterized by inadequate nutrition. They did not even go beyond nutrition to include inadequate shelter, clothing or ill health as a mark of poverty. But they pointed out that human distress or disadvantage including the economic adversities could be remedied through corrective actions. The plight of man, as they had propagated, is not wish of the divine power. This predicament is not the creation of any invisible super power beyond the comprehension and reach of man. Surrender to fate as the determinant of human predicament propagated by the church was challenged by the enlightenment thinkers.

The era preceding the age of reason spanning thousands of years did not focus on human living conditions. Therefore, poverty as a disadvantageous living condition did not come to mind of anyone to reflect on. The age of reason as brighter phase in human history stood apart from medieval traditions of nonchalant attitude to human affairs. The leading thinkers began to apply reason to understand the plight of man as they had delved into unchanged law of the natural world. They had focused on the law of the social world with reasoned judgment. The enlightened revelation of the thinking had the far reaching effect on the future course of humanity. The humanitarianism underlying ideology of social policies and actions in the aftermath of enlightenment era insisted on development of man. This focus of social policies implicitly indicates a shift and a radical departure. The reasoned understanding of man and his surroundings would result in creating an environment in which man can enjoy his life with freedom instead of subjugation under an authority without any obligation to man. Humanitarian worldview does not accept subhuman conditions of man that characterizes state of poverty. The enlightenment thinkers set in motion the resound understanding of poverty as ill-being. Humanitarianism had asserted that poverty is an inhuman condition of living of a segment of people. It could be remedied with appropriate social action. Poverty as a state of living came to be known as the outcome of unjust social order.

The social order which men had been cherishing for long before the social contract is supposed to be built on the edifice of humanitarianism. This world view places humanity as the target for social actions and policies. The humanitarian social order must pursue freedom from want for all the citizens. Man in the social order would apply reason to understand the material standing around him. The collective mind would reflect on the circumstances that causes distress in daily lives of men. The enlightenment thinkers had showed the way to eschew the long held belief that human predicament is created outside the reach and actions of human beings. They have taught us to forsake the belief that the past deeds during the past lives determine the present predicament. The causes of poverty are to be diagnosed in the present world where we live and these are not hidden in an unknown realm beyond human understanding. The causes for human distress including economic adversities are not only comprehensible but also alterable through suitable actions within framework of the social order. Poverty as a state of economic ill-being began to be understood in the era of enlightenment as the outcome of dysfunction of social order. Scarcity of material goods and services that cause poverty can be corrected by appropriate social actions based on reasoned understanding of the problem. The perpetuation of poverty and its cruellest manifestation in the shape of persistent hunger goes against the ethos of humanitarian worldview in the post enlightenment world.

2.5 Poverty in Ancient India

Before the beginning of the social living of mankind, the law of nature ruled the human lives. This was a universal phenomenon so India was no exception to the natural world. Social structure based on rules framed by collective minds evolved over thousands of years. Men wilfully got rid of the plenty of nature unbounded by any rules that interfere with daily lives. Men agreed to be bound by rule for the sake of security and to gain the benefit of collective social living. The rule of nature did not restrict human liberty in seeking their livelihoods in the lap of nature. Man could collect as much food as he could from his natural surroundings. He could kill as many animals as he could in the jungles. The property or resources including food and shelters were common for all; no one could claim exclusive right on nature's bounties. The free ride for men came to an end when society emerged as collection of human persons mutually agreed to abide by the rules. Property rights came much later when conferment of rights over productive resources was felt necessary for social progress. If man could not harvest the fruits of his labour, he would be discouraged to invest his labour in the next round. The bounties of nature allowed for the free ride when human effort did not go into production of food. It was benevolence of nature. Nature went on showering its bounties by providing food for men so long as it could sustain.

Poverty could befall when nature would stop bearing food for men. In the normal circumstance without any calamities, nature kept on producing food. So the problem was not posed from the side of earth, but from the side of the men. As men could not interfere with the production process of nature, evidently until the advent of agriculture, total food supply could not be expanded to meet the incremental demand from men. The demand for food would rise as a consequence of population growth or immigration. Our early ancestors, living in groups for the sake of safety and security would depend on their physical surrounding for food, water and shelter. The physical surroundings were not boundless. Thus the capacity of the earth to produce every necessity for men living in the area was also limited. Even a miniscule increase in the number of feeding mouths would cause scarcity. This scarcity could be overcome by migration to new places, never visited by men before. Our early ancestors had to compete with wild animals in the race of hunting. Neither the historians nor the anthropologists did paint a rosy picture of life, our ancestors led. Life was uncertain, threatened, and crisis-ridden and was always haunted by hazards. Human distress was omnipresent at this stage of human civilization. Discovery of agriculture had ended the days of distress caused by uncertainties with regard to food collection. The settled agriculture had changed the course of civilization. Food began to be produced in plenty and it freed the man from the hazards of roaming in the forest to gather food. Domestication of wild animals began in the aftermath of agriculture. Agricultural civilizations in different parts of the world had flourished during this period.

The sources for knowledge about prehistoric India are epics, religious texts and archaeological findings. However, the latter relates to the specific period beyond which it cannot reveal about the period preceding it. For example, the artefacts, the pots, and the seals, discovered by the archaeologist from the sites of Indus valley civilization speaks a lot about the lives of the Indus people who lived in the great walled and planned cities around more than five thousand years ago. Their discoveries give an idea about lives and livelihoods of the people. The available evidences do not shed any light on the living conditions and adversities for any segment of population. Presence or absence of poverty among the Indus people would just be guesswork for economic historians engaged in researching the living conditions of people. Evidences in support or against the prevalence of economic destitution among them are yet to come by to initiate such probing. But relative affluence of the Indus cities came to the fore after the excavation. These were agricultural civilizations and, therefore, had ensued and flourished on the bank of rivers. Availability of water in plenty not only had helped agriculture but also had facilitated the rearing of livestock. The remnants of the huge granaries discovered during excavations bears testimony to the fact that crops, particularly foodgrains used to be produced in abundance. The surplus food was stored in the granaries skilfully built by the Indus people. While agriculture was dominant economic activity, small scale manufacturing and trade were also undertaken.

The surplus foodgrains were traded in exchange for other essentials. Trade was an important activity during Indus period and trade was extended to far off places within India. The end of the Indus valley civilization saw the beginning of the Aryan settlement in India. They had migrated from Central Asia according to the dominant theory of the origin of the Aryans in Indian subcontinent. They were superior race well conversant with improved technique of agriculture and could skilfully used horses as mode of transport. Civilizations moved ahead faster on the back of the Aryan race. They had first settled in the North-West and then advanced to northern Gangetic plains populating vast fertile plains which are known at present as ***'Aryabartya'***. The region prospered quite rapidly by dint of the hardworking and intelligent race. Abundance of food as a consequence of improved agricultural technique bestowed affluence on them. Surplus food and cattle might had freed the Aryan people of anxiety of impending scarcity of food and the threat of natural calamities like flood, drought and storms. This affluence could bestow enough leisure to take up other activities not related to production. Feelings of the material security in life led the Aryans to reflect on the world and the problems of existence. *Veda*, the greatest literary treasure of the humanity, came out during this period. The great epic of India, *Ramayana* and *Mahabharata* were written in the post-*Vedic* period. We can gain some idea about the society and the people of the period over which these great epics were scripted.

The period from Indus valley civilization down to the epic age did not witness any incidences of hunger, persistence poverty and pervasive distress. We don't have the evidence of the occurrence of such calamities in the period. Our rich literary texts that came into being from the dawn of our civilization do not mention anywhere about this unwelcome occurrence. We don't come across any character or a community in our ancient literature living under severe distress caused by crop failure or giving rise to famine. There are no references to massive poverty in the religious texts during the *Vedic* period. In place of the depiction of distress among the subjects of kingdoms, the post-*Vedic* literatures enlightens us with the celebrations of ***yagna*** (sacrifice) as recurrent social rituals organized by the kings. Kings were advised by their religious mentors comprising of priest and saints to undertake charity (***dan***) on the day of sacrifice not only as means of pleasure but also to pave the way to heaven after death. It was believed that cycle of birth and death are perpetual. Good deeds such as charity would ensure better life after death. Subjects of the kingdom who were materially less endowed were assisted by this benevolent gesture of the kings. Kings could earn laurels and their fame would reach far and wide if they could keep their subject in happiness, maintain peace and provide enough food and clothing. This royal gesture seems to succeed in preventing abysmal poverty in the post-Vedic period particularly in epic period.

The period between the end of the epic age and the beginning of the Maurya Empire during the third century B.C. remains a missing link in historical evolution. During Maurya Empire, India had emerged as strong, huge, and unified kingdom, the fame of which had rapidly reached far and wide. A prosperous empire had emerged under the able leadership of Maurya kings. There is no reference of large scale economic distress among the people in any literary or other types of historical sources. In the absence of the recorded sources for the period pertaining to the beginning of the first millennium, it is hard to say that the economic poverty did persist. One particular reason for the absence of references to poverty might be the value judgment of the people in that period about mode of living. Poverty as particular feature of distressed living of a section of population was not defined by the society for thousands of year. Poverty didn't emerge as an issue of concern until the advent of enlightenment thinking during eighteenth and nineteenth century, that for the first time in human history, accepted humanism as the end objective of collective human actions and thoughts. Poverty began to be conceived as human deprivation. Man should not suffer from economic destitution. Poverty is, therefore, unethical and unacceptable living conditions of the persons or groups of persons. Humanism demands that each human being should live happily without going through any harrowing experience of acute scarcity of food, shelter and clothing. The state can't abdicate the fundamental duty of protecting her citizen from the pangs of poverty and hunger.

2.6 Nature of State and Poverty

State had emerged out of the social contract as an institution to rule the people who had empowered it through sacrificing some freedom. Human freedom not to be ruled by anybody or any institutional arrangement was boundless in the state of nature. The natural world did not impose any restriction on the movement of the people. Men could undertake any activity not bothering about its impact on his neighbours. For example, a man could pick up all fruits from trees oblivious of the hunger of his neighbours. In case of fights among men for the survival, the powerful would survive and weak would be banished. The powerful would finish off his weak rivals for the sake of survival in the environment of fierce competition for food. When nature provides more than what all the living beings in the particular area need to keep their body and soul together chaos would be less visible. Anarchy would prevail in the situation of crisis when available food would fall short of demand for all living beings inhabiting in the area. In that case, man had to fight not only with the wild animal to grab foods but he had to do the same with his fellow creature. There was freedom to do anything in the natural order but the nature did not provide security of life from all inhabitants in the world of nature. Men had aspired to get rid of this short, brutish and hazardous life.

State was born out of the collective wish to live in social order. The state as an entity or super-guardian was vested with power to rule the subjects. The state was entrusted to enforce the social order and to live peacefully with safety and security of life. The social order demands obedience to rule of the state. The acceptance of obedience is the mark of departure from the anarchic natural order to the rule-based social order. The journey was long drawn but the state and the society evolved everywhere. State as super guardian of the human society bears the following marks. It has power to rule the citizens of the state. The rules are formed by the states. The basic principles underlying the rules for governance is set by the state as the governing authority. The state should have mandate to rule the people. On the ethical or moral grounds that mandates are most essential. The legitimacy of the state as a supreme entity to govern has to be acquired first to have the moral authorities. The nature of the rules for the governance is contingent on the nature of the state. As per functioning features a state can be either totalitarian or democratic. The former is characterized by the absence of people participation in governance. The ruler may be emperor of the empire constituting the state. The king rules the kingdom. The Lord rules over his fiefdom. Monarchy as a feature of the state was in vogue everywhere until the advent of democracy as a form of governance that made inroads gradually. Nobody questioned the moral authority of the enlightenment thinking that paved the way for popular resistance against totalitarian state.

Monarchs and kings got the mandate to rule from the catholic churches which were sole representative divine power. People were led to believe that the state was the arm of the church. They were vested with divine power. So obedience to state was tantamount to allegiance to God. The king was free to rule as mandate by the established church. The strong nexus between the church and kings had helped in perpetuating the monarchy for prolonged period. All social practices, we condemn now, like slavery, torture, incarceration, bonded labour system, and exploitation were in vogue during the period of absolute monarchy mandated by the church. King as a supreme authority could do anything that suited his purposes. The churches did not object or resist any royal misdeeds, so far their material interests are satisfactorily served through the generous gift and grants from the states coffers. Kings could collect as much land revenue and taxes as they wished from his subjects. Pauperization of peasants did not bother the king who was hell-bent on swelling his coffer to enhance his military might. People who silently suffer the inhuman treatment from the rulers had nowhere to go to seek justice. The royal court meted out punishment to those who dared to disobey the order. The church imparted the lesson that dissidence was immoral act that goes against the will of God. Monarchy as a particular form of totalitarian state could survive and flourish so long as people did not air their collective anger.

The number of the totalitarian states is on the wane but still they exist at many places in the world in the form of military dictatorships. They assume power by the force through military coup. The religious fundamentalist groups are trying to capture the power by spreading terror and jeopardizing the existing democratic polity. The situations of Pakistan and Afghanistan point out to that condition where democracy as an institution is under constant threat requiring life saving support from the overseas power. Middle Eastern countries are boiling now after prolonged years of dictatorial regime. The resistance movement taking place in Middle Eastern nation popularly known as 'Arab Spring' is collective aspiration to get rid of this totalitarian regime. The world attention is focused on the happening of the trouble torn region where conflict has gone to an extreme extent between the government forces and rebels. The former wants to remain in power and the latter is determined to overthrow. Observers and analysts around the world are divided on the political outcome of this organized rebellion. One strand of observation predicts arrival of democracy in these theocratic or totalitarian lands. The other groups are less optimistic about the ushering of democracy and secularism in the event of the overthrowing of the present dictatorial regime. They smell religious fanaticism in the organization of resistance movement. Despite all these unwelcome traits in the movement for regime change, the advance of democracy is remarkable. Many African nations have embraced democracy and on their ways to build a modern nation based on democracy and secularism. The victory of democracy seems to be inevitable despite the fact that the path to democracy is paved with thorns. The barriers are erected by the enemies of democracy and forces of totalitarianism.

2.7 Why Totalitarian Regime is less bothered about Poverty?

Poverty affects the underdogs of the society who lack the means to overcome it. Income as primary means is inadequate for those hopeless people to keep the body and soul together. Poverty as a state of being was not defined in earlier times despite manifest presence of penury among the underprivileged in the highly stratified society. Poverty was omnipresent among artisans, among peasants and among social underdogs during early regimes under absolute monarchy. The state ruled by monarch is totalitarian regime, concerned only with the continuity of his tenure in the throne. He is haunted by the fear of losing the throne to the invaders more powerful than he is. This fear of impending attack and apprehension of defeat impels him to strengthen his military might through swelling the ranks of soldiers and expanding the stock of arsenals. Attainment of military power could not only provide defence to invaders but also helped in responding the empire by defeating the neighbouring kingdoms. Thus, the rules were interested only to fill the coffer as much as possible to spend for manpower and logistics. Land revenue, as the only source of income, increased manifold. The exorbitant land tax virtually squeezed the peasants. Poor peasants were pushed to the brink of survival. On getting no way out, they turn on village moneylenders who ultimately pushed them further to the depth of extreme penury.

Economic hardship was added by the invasion of epidemic sporadically that increased the sufferings manifold. Crop loss caused by natural calamities like flood or drought used to hit peasants most. So many perils waited for them to engulf. One danger that constantly haunted was running out of foodstock for their families. In the absence of food distribution programme of the government, the variant of which we come across today, the peasants were to undergo starvation. Over and above, the peasants had to pay the land revenue to the state. They cannot appeal for exemption the particular year under the dire eventuality of calamity-led crop failure. The revenue officials of the state would not pay heed to the saga of the distraught peasants who has almost turned into mendicants. The revenue officials would be unfazed at the sight of the starving members of the family. He would insist for the land tax which is already so high. The peasants had no option. He has to cough up. The village money lenders always looked for such prey beleaguered by penury. The peasant had to borrow at an exorbitant rate of interest to pay the land tax. Non payment could land him in prison or could lead to eviction from land. Turning to village money lenders at that moment of crisis was thought to be the last option for face saving. Poverty of the peasant, caused by occurrence of flood or drought or by the onset of epidemics and coercive land tax system hardly reaches the palace from where the king or emperor rules. Even if the terrible news reaches the seat of royal administration, it hardly jars the ruler as his throne will not be stirred by the sufferings of his subjects.

The enlightenment thinking that swayed the western world during eighteenth and nineteenth century has established humanism as the fundamental premise of public policy. The totalitarian regime by very nature of its formation skirts humanism. They are concerned with holding on to power by force. They are not accountable to people, and people cannot dethrone them in normal circumstances. The totalitarian rules whatever public policies they frame lacks humanism. A democratic state on the opposite end of the spectrum has to worry about the poverty primarily because it draws its essence from the humanist approach committed to the pursuit of greatest benefit of the largest number of people. Democracy as a form of government runs on people's participation in all stages and spheres of governance. Policies are formed by the legislators elected by the people through open, free and fair electoral process. Policies are implemented by the executives who are accountable to the legislatures. The latter is accountable to the people. This accountability in governance makes the democratic system work for the best interest of the people. The poor constitute a significant section of electorate particularly in a developing nation. The democratic state is obligated to craft antipoverty programmes to alleviate poverty. The state is under compulsion to implement those policies at the ground level so that positive outcome is visible. The ruling government can take a pride in reducing the number of poor during its tenure. The ruling party face election on the back of the success on the fight against poverty. Failure in the fight can spell disaster by way of electoral outcome.

The relationship between the state and the poverty is an engaging area of research for social scientist. The latter group of must be interested to know about the impact of the state action on alleviating poverty. Does the departure from the rule of nature to the rule of social world made of any differences to the lives of many people facing survival adversities in the form of scarcity of the material goods. There remains hardly any doubt that any reduction of poverty is possible only in the state system. Reduction in poverty in the aftermath of the evolution of state system is attributed to two processes: economic growth process and political process. The former create opportunists for better living overcoming poverty and the latter develops and perpetuates institutional arrangement that tends to work for safety nets and redistributive provision. Thus the state formation has two obverses: economics and politics. One is growth focussed and the other is welfare focussed. But both of these are possible if the state is not only effective but also developmental. Generally we speak of two types of state; police state and welfare state and this sharp division is based on the nature of state intervention. The police state is concerned and occupied with the task of maintaining law and orders. Welfare state in addition to policing is committed to welfare of the people. The latter strives to be effective state. State may be ineffective and examples of such positions are plenty in contemporary world. Our western neighbour is the glaring example where non-state actors are more visible and powerful than the state in controlling and managing the state institutions.

Rapid poverty reduction is possible in effective as well as developmental state through direct intervention. Market driven economic growth tends to be exclusive leaving behind a significant section of population or some regions within the 'geographical' state. Market driven economic growth in Brazil or in post-apartheid South Africa contributes very little to reduction of poverty and economic inequality. The trickle down seems to be very trifle. Economic growth and redistributive policies must stay together to ensure poverty reduction and social justice. Stateless society used to exist during 'hunting gathering' stage of human civilization well before the discovery of agriculture. Pre-modern states were made up of feudal state, princely state, imperial state, absolute monarchy, kingdoms and so on to rule the agricultural society. But modern state came into being after the great transformation from agricultural society to industrial society. The fundamental difference between modern and pre-modern states relates to the provision of social and economic institutions. Modern states are characterized by establishing institution for provisioning of public goods that includes peace, stability, safety and security for the citizens. The state must create economic institutions to provide livelihood security, creation of economic opportunity and employment generation. Political arrangement of a modern state categorically can take three shapes: Socialist, Capitalist and Mixed. Development state may take any of the form but the efficacy of the state in the reduction of poverty depends on political process. The latter is the primary condition for institutions in the modern states to work for poverty reduction.

2.8 Poverty and Developmental State

Developmental states are those states whose successful economic and social development performance illustrates how their political purpose and institutions are developmentally driven. But the objectives and targets of the development drive of the state are linked to the political process. There are various forms of these developmental states. Some are autocratic like Korea and Taiwan. Botswana and Singapore are democratic states but the latter is characterized by single party dominance. Some democratic states are run by coalitions of political parties agreed upon a common programme and rules for governance. But the efficacy of the democratic states in reducing poverty depends on the institutions whose functioning, in turn, depends on the internal dynamics and politics. Developmental state may be democratic or authoritarian depending on the particular context and the history of the formation of the state. Totalitarian state may be developmental if the development drive keeps in continuity of authoritarian regions. The authoritarian regime can facilitate economic growth by forging synergies with private entrepreneurs to develop in a bid to gain the benefit mutually. The exclusive growth can enrich the authority as well as private business ignoring the vast mass of people. Economic growth thus empowers the ruling regime militarily.

Swelling military might emboldens the authoritarian regime as they are more equipped to resist and overcome any possible internal movement by the people for restoration of democracy. Resourceful regime can also go for military build-up to resist external aggression.

Thus effective state that must be developmental one and which should create and strengthen institutions that not only fosters but also works for distributive public policies and actions. The formation and consolidations of institutions however depends upon politics and political process. In the absence of soldier and legitimate institutions the development drive can flounder. "Thinking of the states in terms of the way in which political processes function to produce such outcomes helps deepen our understanding of strong states, weak states and failed states and their respective capacities to promote growth and social justice, at least in the form of poverty reduction" (Leftwich, 2011). Ultimately, poverty reduction is contingent on the state formation and state capacity; State capacity falls on *'institutional domain'* which means the effective institutions must come in place to work for reduction and inequality. Efficacy of institutions, not this number does matter. But the crucial issue is how the institutions are run. The design and quality of their functions are directly linked to political process and that play an important role. Thus politics and state actions towards promotion of growth, reduction of poverty and delivery of social justice widely varies among states despite having institutional arrangement. Anti-poverty policies and action take direct route in conformity with the domestic political process. For example, E1 Salvador, aimed at breaking the inter-generational poverty trap by conditional cash transfer system. Botswana adopted job creating strategies.

Wage employment programmes currently underway in poor nations as a tool for poverty alleviation may be either welfare-based or rights-based. India's ongoing wage employment programme known as National Rural Employment Guarantee Scheme (NREGS) adopts right based approach instead of 'welfarism'. This job creating programme of India is the largest in the world now considering its coverage and financial expenditure involved in the project. This mammoth programme began in India in the wake of the passage of a bill in parliament that proposed to provide state guarantee of job in the rural areas for 100 days in a year. The government conferred rights to employment for 100 days to the unemployed job seekers by enacting the employment legislation for the first time in India. The birth of such employment guarantee programme after six decades of India's independence was possible by intense political pressure. Civil society organizations, citizen groups, trade unions and farmers' bodies have been clamouring for rights based employment programme for the poor in the rural India. Independent India's antipoverty initiatives are not only quite diverse but also quite old. Women not only constitute the half of India's population but they can play a wonderful role in alleviating household poverty through participation in productive activities. Women were encouraged to form groups among themselves to take up economically gainful activities. These women groups are self-help groups formed mostly by women desirous of changing their lots by undertaking group activities. Micro finance institutions came up in village to assist these groups through provision of microcredit to run business activities. Political pressure from women's groups and a movement for women's empowerment and women's rights are largely responsible for initiating these self-help group programmes.

Strategies, policies and programmes whether aimed at job creation or social provision would depend on the circumstances, level of economic development, endowments and the politics of the possible (Leftwich, 2011). But the effective state and particularly developmental state would not set in development momentum but would strive to forge synergy with private sector for the sake of building infrastructure and institution to foster economic growth. It has been observed that effective modern state works to enhance the growth process. It means that an effective state can only be driven by economic growth. Modern states in Europe came up in the era of competitive nationalism. The prevailing motto was that the nation must grow stronger militarily. Military strength could be realized through rapid economic growth. The fear of invasion by the more powerful nations and the urge to expand territory of control drove the nation to pursue economic growth mainly through rapid industrialization. All modern states that come up in course of 'Great transformation' from agriculture society to industrial society confronted four main challenges: internal security, external aggression, building and strengthening the national economy and the provision of social welfare benefits for the underprivileged. Characteristically, four types of modern nation State had emerged in the world depending on the geographic location, irrespective of legacies, context and circumstances. The first was the Anglo-American model that had produced liberal states in the western world.

This state would promote market driven growth, secure property rights, fair and efficient judicial systems and set rules for market based economic activities. The second category of state follows social democratic model. The social democratic state would actively undertake social transformation from pre-modern feudal structure to democratic institution. This state would strive to contain the excess of capitalism by adopting redistributive policies. Social democratic state cannot tolerate inequalities of opportunities among the citizens and would be proactive in removing the inequalities. The third in the categories is the soviet model state where the economy is characterized by state control and ownership, centralized decision through state planning board about the allocation of resources and top down industrialization. Private enterprise and private profit are anathema to the system. The fourth model is 'developmental states' typified by East Asian nations prominently. These are many examples scattered in the contemporary world that also stands for rapid development as the ultimate objective and enlargement of the state. Japan was the pioneer in this genre of states which had initiated development drive during eighteenth century in the wake of Meiji restoration. Japan embarked on the strategy of human resource development through provision of universal education and health care. Japan reaped the fruit of her bold steps undertaken one and half century ago. She stands for an example of a nation that can grow economically so fast without having natural resources beneath her earth. Japan sets herself as an illustration for human capital-led growth. She has succeeded in developing such a technology purely indigenous that could leave the western nations many miles behind.

The exclusive credit for the remarkable economic prosperity of Japan during last century goes to the Japanese state. Japan's spectacular prosperity brought about by technological innovation and entrepreneurial ability was not confined to her own sovereign geographic boundary. Its spill-over effect is manifest. Her neighbours, mainly South Korea followed and emulated Japan in the pursuit of technology led growth. It was almost a trend set by Japan and Korea to move ahead on the strength of skill and innovations on micro chips, microprocessor, automobiles, robotics and micro electronics. Japan is the first Asian country to pose the challenge to the western domination in science and technology. This was possible by active state intervention and state leadership in promoting entrepreneurial and encouragement of industrial enterprises. She did not look forward to western aids in all aspects of her development drive. Japan and later Korea are examples of human resources-led development. State, not only created skilled manpower to take up the challenges of technological breakthrough, it consistently provided an enabling environment. Japan's public investment in universal education and healthcare, at a time when she was a poor country by today's standard, had paid rich dividend. Japan's march to prosperity by her exclusive focus on human capital was emulated by her neighbours in the South East Asian region. The developmental states gave birth to the Asian tigers. The spectacular economic performances of these developmental states are referred as 'East Asian Miracle'.

But the prospect of developmental states that gave birth to Asian tigers is severely constrained now. The overwhelming presence of state in all spheres of economic activities is looked upon as retrograde steps. It harms rather than helps the people. This negative attitude towards developmental states has been created and nurtured by the protagonists of neo-liberal states. The developmental states seems to be on the verge of extinction in the face of the challenges thrown by the neo-liberal global regime currently underway leaving behind way back the state-led development regime. Neo-liberal policies embodied in the economic reform measures calls for downsizing the governmental role, dismantling the public sector, promotion of private sectors, delicensing and deregulation. Economic ills in the form of high unemployment, inflation and slow growth were diagnosed as a problem associated with excessive state intervention by way of doling out enormous amount of subsidies. Burgeoning fiscal deficits caused by escalating subsidies on unproductive heads of expenditure stood as a villain to be decimated forthwith. Development states all over the world could emerge and flourish in the period following the end of colonial period.

'Developmentalism' through intense state intervention and participation as a reigning principle of governance came under severe pressure during many times. But its virtual roll back was triggered by the advent of neo-liberal global order. The Breton Wood institutions have taken U-turn. They prescribed our panacea for all, invoking the contextual realities of the present world. Size of the state has to be curtailed. This is widely held that poverty has gone up manifold in the post-liberalization era.

While development states, the overwhelming presence of which we find in East Asia are threatened by the onslaught of external factors, the non-effective states are in more jeopardy. The least developed countries of the world as identified and ranked by the World Bank are characterized by many deficiencies and fall short of what is known as effective states. The locations of the majority of the least developed countries of the world in African continent alone speak volumes of the skewed development that has taken place in the post-colonial world.

2.9 Poverty and Culture

Economists tend to explain the casual process of poverty in terms of economic endowments. Poverty, according to them, is a state of material adversity that stands in the way of attaining a minimum level of living as standard minimum set in a given society. Economists hardly include culture as correlate of poverty. Ever since investigation in the nature and causes of poverty began, mainly after the end of the Second World War, economists viewed culture as residual or at least intermediary factor. It affects, indirectly. Culture defined grossly as a set of behavioural norm for the individuals in the society making the world view of the people, did not find its place in the casual forces. This is primarily because of emergence of poverty as global issue affecting the humanity in the post-colonial world. More than half of the world region was colonized by the imperial powers of Europe for centuries. The 'other world' comprising of three continents of Latin America, Africa and Asia had a long tryst with colonial domination. The race for imperial expansion among the imperial power in the other world was caused by finding market for their industrial products and for sourcing of raw materials to run the factories. The race among the new industrial power was triggered by what is now known as competitive nationalism in Europe. Colonial exploitation in different form, from remittance to plunder, is held responsible for stifling the growth potential of the colonies. Poverty in the periphery was deliberately planted by the centres for the sake of primitive accumulation by the capitalist world as per Marxian explanation. The imperial powers of the centre located in Europe were least bothered about the poverty in the peripheries. They occupied and ruled for the sake of their own nations striving to overtake rival neighbours in the race for grabbing overseas market for their industrial products. When the beginning of the capitalist development was underway in the centres, the colonies were deliberately kept backward. The purpose of the imperial inaction was to pave the way for unhindered exploitation of the colonies to benefit the imperial power. The colonial power kept the subjects in darkness denying them access to modern education and technology. They ruthlessly ruled caring very little for the future of the subjugated people. The world views of the subjects that fostered aversion to enterprise and hard work for material wellbeing was never questioned by the imperial government. The colonial master had introduced English education in India during eighteenth century for the chosen few among the urban middle class to serve the interest the British *raj*. The British administration had needed massive manpower to rule this vast country while the key post would be held by the British officers. Educational institution under the auspices of the British *raj* began to groom a section from elite class to assign the graduates from their schools the task of assisting the British officials particularly in matters of revenue administration. The education system taught them sycophancy, allegiance and unquestioned loyalty to the colonial masters. The colonial education system was geared to produce docile native workmen to assist the imperial administration. The retrograde values and obsolete belief system that bound the colony subject for centuries was never questioned and challenged in the education system. Education delivery system can effectively alter the deep rooted mindsets of the people that sometimes inculcate aversion to changes for the better world and the higher level of material prosperity. The culture of unquestioned loyalty to the rulers was nurtured and promoted during the colonial era in India. The attitude to take up challenges and brave the adversities in life could be instilled through education that can shape the mindset of the nation. Inertia or fatalism can be defining feature of a race, or of a community, even of a nation. Inertia of mind can be best described as proclivity to continue with and live within the usual setting of life. This is a tendency to avoid any course that leads to any change. This is a mindset of aversion to adapt any alternative life course. Poverty stays fixed in such a situation where people love to accept and take pleasure in the present predicament. Inertia can overwhelmingly define the culture of a race or group of people within the nation-state. Economist tends to ignore inertia of mindset as possible candidates for explaining poverty. Economists in early years of their desperate attempts to identify the causal factors for endemic poverty did not consider culture for influencing factor. The axiomatic promise that drives economist's overlook of the culture is the notion of rationality in the behaviour of human beings. The fundamental principle is the assumption that human beings are guided by self interest.

Therefore, nothing can hold back man's inherent craving for material prosperity. A poor any where in the world would not accept his predicament, presently constrained by wants of resources. She would desire in the depth of her mind a better life. But this idea of economist did not come true in many instances. Despite massive development programme undertaken in the past in the poverty-stricken zones of the world, the outcome are not encouraging. The culture of the apathy also count in determining the impact of development efforts.

Economists and international development agencies are now accepting the crucial role of culture. People for whom new development initiatives were taken up were themselves unwilling to take risk. It was a form of irrationality a preference for living in the past. This is called affliction by cultural inertia. Does this inertia afflict universally? It was found that West Indians who left Caribbean for better living in Europe had showed remarkable zeal for prosperity. They were apathetic at home but quickly accepted the challenges of life abroad. Thus culture cannot be responsible for reluctance to take challenges to get out of poverty. However, this argument was opposed by cultural theorist on the ground that emigration is selective process. Decisions to immigrate to lands of prosperity are made by individuals. They were better human material. They could overcome the pervasive apathy prevalent among their fellow beings. Culture cannot trap the entire community in perpetual poverty. Some of them can easily defy culture. Thus, theory of culture now turns into theory of individual psychology as explanation for differential poverty. Those who are poor, love to embrace the culture of apathy. Economist, as a dominant group in poverty analysis is uncomfortable with this assertion of the influence of cultural traits in determination of poverty.

Culture is the moral and intellectual spirit of a particular form of organization. Culture is a dynamically interactive and developing socio-psychic system. Therefore, the culture of apathy is a weak position. Development theorists do not accept the idea that antipoverty development drive can be derailed by the culture of apathy among the poor. However, they admit that mismanaged development drive can also cause harm rather than help. One such instance was put forward by eminent historian Stephan Gudeman. He mentioned that Panama, a tiny country in the Middle America, adopted commercial farming in sugarcane in expectation of huge export earnings. Government swayed by the prospect of export led growth, taking place in many other locations of the world, undermined the traditional rice farming. Fall in export demand for its commercial crop pauperized the farming community in Panama. The outsiders and landlords reaped the profit but the poor peasant was left in the lurch. The former took the decision about the economy which forced them to struggle for survival. Such development adventurism may harm the community rather than benefiting them. Mismanaged development can deepen poverty.

Of late economist tend to view culture, variously referred as ideology, in formal institutions, informal rules, lifestyle as collective product of rational persons trying to coordinate their lives. Christopher Bliss an eminent economist observed "People are not simply individuals. They live socially and their views, their values and even their beliefs, as well as their abilities are formed and sustained with social groupings, families, and communities. Perhaps the consideration of lifestyle offers an alternative to the methodological individualism" Cultural theorist asserts that each cultural tendency provides its own view of poverty, its causes and remedies. Thus poverty cannot be understood without any references to culture. Poverty thus is not culture-free concept. Culture of a particular community can hold back development initiative as a measure to fight poverty. Culture of inertia as explained above, has resemblances with fatalism as established worldview among certain community. Belief in fatalism destroys innovation and craving for higher material wellbeing. For fatalist, life chances and opportunities are given. One would not attain better life without the ordain of fate. Thus poverty among people is ordained by fate which ordinary mortal cannot remove.

Under the spell of fatalism, people accept their precarious predicament as will of God that cannot be altered by human initiative. Reluctance to take up challenges thus stems from a belief system that a powerful force beyond the reach and comprehension of ordinary human beings decides the destiny. This attitude adversely affect the development drive of the state in which the poor are stakeholders, the fatalist poor take part in economic transformation with a mind convinced of futility of the exercise. Thus, the culture of the suffering poor believing in invincible fate keeps away development outcome from reaching them. Samuel Huntington the leading exponent of cultural determinism forcefully argues that culture determines development course of nation. The widespread variation in the level of development among nations in the contemporary world is caused largely by cultural differences. Lawrence Harrison and Samuel Huntington jointly edited a book entitled *Culture Matters*. Huntington in one of his essays called 'Culture Counts' observed

> *"In the early 1990s, I happened to come across economic data on Ghana and South Korea in the early 1960s and I was astonished to see how similar their economies were then... Thirty years later South Korea had become an industrial giant with the fourteenth largest economy in the world, multinational corporations, major exports of automobiles, electronic equipment and other sophisticated manufactures, and per capita income approximately that of Greece. Moreover, it was on its way to consolidation of democratic institution. No such changes had occurred in Ghana whose per capita income was now about one-fifteenth that of South Koreans. How could this extraordinary difference in development be explained? Undoubtedly many factors played a role, but it seemed to me that culture had to be a large part of the explanation. South Koreans valued thrift, investment, hard work, education,*

> *organization and discipline. Ghanaians had different values. In short, culture counts.*

Amartya Sen, however, does not accept this one to one causal relation between culture and economic development. He cites four influencing reasons behind South Koreas growth performance compared to Ghana. Firstly, the business class was bigger and proactive in the South Korea. Ghana did not have such entrepreneurial class in their society. Secondly, domestic political priority between them differed. South Korean government promoted pro-business economic environment which was absent in the Ghana. Thirdly, geographical location, being close to Japan, played a positive role. The demonstration effect of Japan's spectacular economic rise witnessed very closely had a stimulating impact on South Korean society. Ghana did not get that light in her surroundings. South Korea came in touch with the USA much earlier. Fourthly, South Korea by 1960 had attained much higher level of literacy and much more expanded school education system. Sen concludes that public policy matters more than cultural determinism.

CHAPTER 3

Issues in Poverty Measurement

3.1 MPCE and Poverty Line

Poverty has to be defined and the number of poor has to be counted. The primary task of the welfare state is to identify the poor citizens for the sake of targeting. The state must bring all underprivileged citizens within social security net. But how Indian authority measures poverty? The consumption expenditure data for each sample household is the unit level data of construction of Monthly Per Capita Expenditure (MPCE). The MPCE class with respective frequencies are constructed to see the distribution of population according to MPCE class for rural areas as well as for urban areas. Poverty line is constructed as market value expressed in prevailing price of food as Recommended Dietary Allowances (RDA) that contains 2400 kcal for rural areas and 2100 kcal for urban areas plus minimum consumption of non-food items. The minimum level of living requires the minimum expenditure one has to incur. Poverty line is thus the minimum level of consumption expenditure as set by the Planning Commission to enable a person to fulfil the basic minimum needs to lead an active and dignified life in the society. The persons whose income or expenditure falls below the basic minimum are poor. In India poverty lines is revised upwards every five years to take into account inflation. Without this exercise, the estimate of poor is sure to be underestimated.

Thus the person who is MPCE does not allow to access the basic level of living is poor. MPCE class distribution result provides us the magnitude of such people whose MPCE falls below this basic minimum or poverty threshold. The estimate of poverty at a certain point is measured by this procedure. The MPCE must contain food expenditure that allows a *'reference'* person to access the normative caloric intake of 2400 kcal and 2100 for rural and urban areas respectively. But this minimum requirement was not arbitrarily fixed. This had been derived from age-sex-occupation-specific nutrition norms by using the all-India demographic data from the 1971 Census. Requirement for minimum nutrition varies widely across sex, age, living conditions and nature of job. Thus there is no common minimum caloric need in a highly diverse country like India. Females require fewer calories than males in the same social environment. Likewise a child of ten years would need less calories than an adult agricultural labourers in the rural setting. Thus *'adult equivalence scale'* was introduced to rule out any possibility of underestimation during calculating per capita expenditure in a household. Average consumption of child and females were converted into average adult consumption by taking child consumption or female consumption as a fraction of adult consumption.

3.2 Caloric Controversy

Caloric is the source of energy that keeps the body-engine on work. The engine stops to work when energy supply comes to a stop. Human body receives the needed calories from the food intake. Body metabolism does come in the way to convert the food absorption into 'energy making' in the body. Why a human body does require energy? The rudimentary knowledge in the biological science. is sufficient to answer to this question that seems, in its outer face, to be the exclusive subject of physical science. It should not have anything to do with Economics that does not at least deal with functioning of human body. But interestingly this is not the case and Economics is not being accused of trespassing in the areas earmarked for other disciplines. But the central focus of

Economics is man; therefore wellbeing of man is the natural concern of Economics. This wellbeing obviously entails physical wellbeing as well as emotional wellbeing where both are interdependent. Health is the physical state of being of any individual. Malnutrition is one of the unwelcome manifestations of ill health. There are two possibilities that trigger malnutrition in a human body. One is the inadequacy of nutritious diet of the afflicted person obviously caused by inability to afford such balanced and nutritious food. The person lacks the purchasing power because of low income. He cannot travel through other route bypassing the *'market'*, the other route is subsidized food distribution for the poor and distressed. Therefore, malnutrition and debility can be caused by poverty in general.

There is other ground for malnutrition not directly linked to poverty. Even a rich person can suffer from malnutrition whose plates of meals would be wholesome, nutritious, balanced and adequate. Opulence and adequate food intake do not automatically convert into energy. The body metabolic system is the converting agent. That system might be dysfunctional temporarily for some affliction or may be permanently impaired for genetic causes. The system may be corrected by medical intervention. Where health care system is free for the poor, the medical intervention is not *'poverty deepening'*. But the medical treatment might be too expensive for the poor where free health care delivery system by the state is absent and market cost is too prohibitive for the poor. Therefore, inability to correct the malfunctioning of the system is poverty driven. Health and hygiene are, therefore, emphasised alongside nutritious food for better physical health. Gastroenteric diseases afflict a vast segment of population in India during and after the monsoon season. The disease takes its toll in urban slums and in impoverished localities in villages bereft of any sanitation and provision of safe water distribution system. Child mortality goes up in the wake of such outbreak. Thus safe water, drainage system, cleanliness that prevents vector borne diseases is equally important alongside nutritious and balanced food. Thus food intake does not singularly prevent malnutrition.

While malnutrition is the result of poverty, the latter may also be the result of the former, because, malnutrition and general debility would reduce work capacity. Manual work, particularly wage labour in agriculture as well as in non-agriculture sector requires exhaustive physical labour. Reduced work capacity thus prohibits participation and earning opportunities in the labour market. The majority of the poor in the developing countries depend on wage income for survival. Thus the subsistence wage formation as formulated in the early writings of Adam Smith and David Ricardo incorporated the need for basic minimum living that allows the wage earners to purchase wage goods to keep them physically fit. In India, the differential calories requirement for two types of working environment: one in agriculture sector and the other in urban informal sector was accepted in the seventies without opposition in the beginning. No one then debated the prevailing understanding that work in agriculture and rural occupations was more strenuous than work in urban areas. The agriculture workers have to take a long walk on all working days to find work. The rural areas mostly are bereft of transport facilities that could otherwise lessen the burning of energy for rural workers.

But the minimum biological norm of caloric intake is increasingly opposed in recent years. One, as already been said, is that food intake and caloric absorption in a human body is not automatic. The other opposition to the current norm of calories is its inadequacy. The World Health Organization (WHO) in one of its report published in 1985 said that a representative male subsistence farmer engaged in moderate activity (involving seven hours of farm work) is estimated to require 2,780 kcal per day. Daily energy requirements for a male engaged in manual work in the tropics are in the order of 3,550 kcal (Dasgupta's, Partha, 1993). Thus minimum caloric requirement recommended by India's nutritionist in the early phase of planning exercise is opposed now as inadequate. Therefore poverty estimate in India based on the accepted minimum is sure to be dubbed as underestimate. The other argument is also gaining ground that is also opposing the lower caloric norm for urban work. Some of the scholars and invoking the onset of Structural Adjustment Programme (SAP) currently underway that makes working life of urban poor much harder. Informal sector and casual job opportunities have gone up, uncertainties and fear of jobless also looms large among workers in urban areas. Drive for job search has intensified. This new development mainly in the wake of informalization of urban sector business activities has brought change in the lifestyle of these people. They now need more calories to participate in economic activities. This calls for heightening the prescribed caloric norm for urban poor. Contrastingly, there is just opposite strand of argument in favour of lower requirement of calories. This was put across by Mr. P.V. Sukhatme *"A healthy woman there (in Kerala) has a level of intake of only 1300 to 1400 calories a day, which is much less than the prescribed allowance and yet she has a level of health and activity on par with a northern woman eating much more". Kerala thus provides an illustration of how food is used with greater efficiency at the lower end of homeostatic range"*. However, the illustration of Kerala or a case to bring down the minimum calories requirement has very few takers. The opponents say that what is true for Kerala will not hold good in India's other provinces. This is because general health conditions of all workers, hygiene, sanitation, safe drinking water along with quality public health care system in Kerala are unique. The others States are far off this ideal condition.

There is a startling revelation also that shows the wide discrepancy between number of poor people as measured by head count ratio in India and number of people below the prescribed calories norm. The book entitled *Social and Economic Security in India* published by Institute of Human Development in 2001 brings to light this divergence. The book notes that while head count ratio of poverty has declined from 44.5 per cent in 1983 to 36 per cent in 1993-1994. The percentage of malnourished people was 66 per cent in 1983-84. It remains 66 per cent in 1993-94. Thus during the reference decade, while poverty has lessened, caloric deprivation seems to be unusual and disturbing. It means that a significant section of non-poor population in India is malnourished. The fall in the head count ratio of income poverty did not accompany similar fall in nutritional poverty in India. Prof. Ranjan Roy and Geoffrey Lancaster using household specific estimated nutrient prices have again confirmed that these discrepancies are very wide and show how far the official poverty line have fallen out of line with their true measure.

3.3 Settling the Calorie Controversy

Roy and Lancaster have convincingly put across in their remarkable paper that the discrepancy between the magnitude of caloric deprivation and head count poverty is sharper in socially disadvantaged categories of people. This chapter emphasizes on the urgency of strengthening of public distribution system to stem the alarming rise in the number of malnourished people in the lower rungs of the social category. The poverty line expenditure entails a minimum diet below which healthy living is impossible. The minimum diet must provide the minimum calorie norm prescribed by nutritionists in India. Unexpectedly, in prescribing the minimum diet, local, cultural factors and food habits were ignored. It was taken for granted that the diet would be uniform across the country. Professor Ashwani Saith in his illustrious paper "Poverty Lines *versus* The Poor", appeared in Economic and Political Weekly (*E.P.W.*) has raised some ethical issues in constructing and setting poverty line diet for the poor in India. He raises the question whether that minimum diet that contains minimum required calories is the balanced one. Does it contain five portions of vegetable and fruits widely recommended for maintaining good health? The representative poor for whom minimum diet is recommended may indulge in some kinds of vices like tobacco, opium, alcohol. Children in the mining and quarrying communities are given opium. Children even in poorer households sometimes taste junk food, may be on rare occasions or by chance. The result visible in the data will then be that such households; even though they were supposed to be able to procure the minimum stipulated calories will be consuming fewer calories.

3.4 Non-food Basic Needs

Poverty line expenditure consists of food as well as non-food expenditure. One has to take nutritious diet to lead a healthy physical living in the society. The diet must contain a minimum calorie that transform into body energy for leading working life. The basic need approach speaks about the minimum for food expenditure and consumption as well. But basic need does not apply to non-food items. There is minimum caloric norm for food items but no such 'minimum' is stipulated for non-food items. The latter goes with MPCE that contains minimum caloric norm for food. People do not and cannot survive on food only in human society. One has to wear clothes in a civilized society. But kind of clothes, sizes of them, quality and the amount needed for a person are undefined. There is no defined decent level of clothing. This decency varies across culture and regions. The person residing in the Darjeeling hills or in the upper ridge of Kashmir mountain would need a different kind of clothing than what a person would need in the desert of Rajasthan or in the plains of North India. Cost of dresses would differ widely. It would be unreasonable to set any common minimum clothing expenditure for both these ecologically diverse region. For example, the decent dress for women in culturally conservative communities in India may be just trash for women in other communities not bound by restriction of dress code

There are many other items which go into non-food category of the consumption expenditure. These items are bought and used in certain climatic regions in India, umbrella, for example. A person living in North Eastern States of India would need rain clothes and umbrella as essential commodities as rainy season is much extended and intense in those parts of India. Life is miserable without rain clothes or umbrella in those showery regions. There are many such items demanded as essentials in specific geographical regions for daily lives. Those same items are non-essential or just luxuries in other regions. It would be unjust to specify such clothing requirement for all people that conform to the poverty line MPCE for entire country despite wide dissimilarity in tastes, preferences, culture, customs and climate. Thus while woollen clothes or jacket must be included in the basic need of the hills people, rain clothes for wet regions' people, head turban for desert people and similar such items would not constitute basic needs for people for other regions. There is specification for food items but no specification for non-food items. It appears that poverty has to be gauged by food items only. If a person takes minimum diet as prescribed by nutritionist, she is not poor even if she wears a dress not accepted by the society as decent, not protective enough in harsh climate in high mountains or in sun soaked desert and which is culturally minimum in her social surroundings. This pertains to quality, quantity and outer looks of the clothes not the deliberate wearing of short clothes influenced by latest fashion in the cities. The former is the result of inability to afford and the latter is the matter of choice.

Those who are uncomfortable with the vagueness of requirement for non-food component advocates a fixed proportion for it. They sometimes refer to I.L.O's earlier suggestion of making non-food expenditure as 50 per cent of food expenditure. This specification could clear the haze around the quantum of non-food expenditure. There is other line of argument that stress that like food expenditure, non-food expenditure, should also conform the 'basic minimum' uniformly specified for the country as a whole. But this specification is also beset with problems of misjudgement. There is biologically determined minimum for food but not such stipulation for threshold in the case of non-food. "*Thus the food component is need based whereas non-food component reflects the poverty of the poor with no guarantee that all basic non-food needs are in fact could be satisfactorily met. This is a very serious shortcoming and could have the effect of supposing the visibility of such crucial basic needs as health, education, housing, transport, communication, fuel, information, social and political participation*" (Ashwani Saith, 2005). After spending on food items, poor people are left with very little amount for spending on health and education. It may so happen that a non-poor family may be stuck in a situation where children may not be attending school for this inability to afford too much private cost on education. This vulnerable situation can breed child labour.

When poverty line was mooted by the planners to assess the magnitude of poor in India, it was thought out by them that health and education expenditure would not come within the purview of non-food item. The exclusion was deliberate as no private expenditure is involved to access those provisions. The state will provide for health and education for the people, particularly for the underdogs of society who cannot buy them in the market. The welfare state is bound by her constitutional commitment to provide free education for children. State health care system is supposed to take care of health of the underprivileged. Thus education and health care are public goods to be provided by the state and, therefore, need not be obtained from the market.

3.5 Cost of Education

Universal Education for all children up to fourteen years of age, free of cost, was the solemn commitment incorporated in the Directive Principles of State Policy. The latter is a set of principles that constitute the basic tenets of our Constitution. These are broad directives, a philosophical lights and foundational spirits that underlie the articles in our sacred Constitution. The fundamental difference between the directive principles and fundamental rights pertains to their legal implications. While the principles are guiding spirit in nature not legally enforceable the latter is not. The constitutional provisions for fundamental rights of our citizens are unique, remarkable, and a bold initiative for the young nation just freed from colonial subjugation for nearly two centuries. The incorporation of fundamental rights in our Constitution made the citizens of India holders of rights. The state is made accountable to her citizens for provisioning of rights. In case of failure, the state will be held responsible and will be bound by the constitutional provision to realize the rights of the people. Thus the directives are moral call but the fundamental rights are compelling and make the state duty-bound. The insertion of the pledge to provide free and compulsory education to all children within ten years from the date of commencement of our Constitution is undoubtedly a noble gesture. But there is a yawning gap between expression of lofty intention of the Indian state and its time bound implementation. Such gap is prominent in the case of universal education for children. Even after five decades of our existence as a free nation and despite the constitutional directives, millions of children in India could not access school. They could not access school not because they were unwilling to attend but schools did not come up in and around their habitations. The Kothari Commission constituted by the Government of India in the early years of educational planning recommended the concept of neighbourhood school for India as a condition for promoting elementary education in India. Children must find a primary school within a radius of one kilometre from their residences. It would be unjust to thrust upon them an exhaustive journey to reach school.

Majority of Indians reside in villages where connectivity, particularly, all-weather rural roads are yet to come up. Children are most likely to miss school during rainy season that lingers three to four months in a year depending on the geographical location. Floods also afflict many regions during rainy season adding fuel to the fire of distress for the villagers. The government is expected to bridge the physical distance between the school and the children. It can be accomplished by two ways. Either schools can come up within the neighbourhoods or the government can provide transport facility free of cost for the village children. For the latter, there must be all-weather road connectivity for the villages. Huge public investment is involved to create those facilities. Establishment of school comes within the purview of education budgets of State governments as well as of Central Government. Education in India is included in the Concurrent List. Earlier it was in the State list that made education an exclusive prerogative of the Constituent States in the Union of India. Later the same was brought in the Concurrent List through Constitutional amendment. The implication of such shifting of such an important task of nation building was sharing of responsibility between the Central and the State. The State on its own cannot deliver goods in the realm of expanding and promoting elementary education in India without Centre's intervention. The other objective that prompted the action was to evolve a national initiative on this most vital agenda.

Left to States to take care of education within its control, the progress will surely be differentiated. Some States will move forward because of higher public investment and focused public policy and many of their peers may pathetically lag behind. This uneven development in the realm of elementary education will not augur well for a country looking forward to emerge as a developed nation in not so distant future. We are trying to emulate China in this regard. Universal elementary education is the cherished goal but its accomplishment is a daunting task. It requires dogged determination, firm political will and unflinching consensus among political actors and decision makers to prioritise this task. The State must look for financial resources for creating infrastructure to facilitate physical access to schools by all children, schools have to be built in locations where there is none. Existing school buildings have to be renovated and to be enlarged to accommodate more children. Deficiency of teachers is immense bottleneck on the way to promotion of elementary education. Their numbers always fall short of what is required to take care of all children in a school. Overcrowded classroom in public and government aided schools cannot evade one's sight. Each class or grade under a teacher should optimally have not more than forty pupils. This is standard teacher pupil ratio through which a teacher given his or her ability can properly impart education. Each student can be taken care of individually. The teacher can attend personally the students who may not be catching up or may fail to cope up with the learning process that takes place in school. So many problems crop up when too many pupil scramble in the classroom. Each and every one will vie for the space to sit on the limited space available for the classroom. The over gathering will generate noise and chaos that distract attention of the teacher as well as of the taught, students sitting in the furthest corner are at the receiving end. They can hardly listen to what teacher says from one corner. The teachers' voice is muted by the noise of too many pupils. Class room transaction can be derailed in the overcrowded class rooms. Children in the rural areas are mostly born to parents who had never been to school. These students are, therefore, first generation learners. They stand apart from their counterparts in the cities who are mostly third even fourth generation learners. A student in the latter category can make up at home what he misses in the class room because of the family background of better educational exposure of the adult members. Thus a poor child living in rural areas misses a lot if she fails to follow the classroom transaction. Thus adequacy of teachers is as important as the sufficiency of sitting space for children. Students must fill comfortable within the classroom.

Thus investment in elementary education is an important aspect of public policy decision. This investment of resources is not an action driven by only welfare commitment of the state towards her citizens. A welfare state, as opposed to police state, must take care of health and education of its citizens. The Constitution of our nation obliges the state to go beyond pecuniary return from investment of scarce resources. The poor nations are constrained by inadequacy of resources. But public policies also matter in prioritizing the public expenditure. Examples are a plenty to demonstrate that many poor nations among our Southeast Asian neighbours could prioritize universal elementary education more than a century ago disregarding their resource constraints. They are reaping the benefits of earlier actions by their visionary statesmen of yester years. They did it when they were in the embryonic stage of economic development with least financial support from others. Thus public policy is equally important as resource availability to initiate universal education for children. Japan or South Korea a century ago was not richer than many of the African nations of today. But what these East

Asian nations could accomplish years ago seems to be many years away for the sub-Saharan African nations. The latter countries are receiving foreign aids in bigger amount to supplement their efforts to universalize primary education and health care. They are also beneficiaries of the World Bank's priority spending for human development in poor nations of the world. Donor nations are also coming forward with generous financial aid for these distressing nations.

Despite all these financial flows from outside their continent, these nations are still steeped in endemic poverty. Very little is left for spending in creating infrastructure for promotion of primary education. Millions of children do not go to school in this vast region. This is because the authorities have miserably failed to deliver goods. The nations are afflicted by civil war, ethnic conflicts, popular unrest and a complete absence of the rule of law. Where democracy is derailed, anarchy lurks everywhere, organs of government are not in sync, and public investment is likely to go down the drain. This has happened to many African nations yet to join the development mainstream of the outside world and perishing in perpetual poverty and destitution. Building of schools, having all facilities to retain children in its portals is not only a project that requires budgetary resources, but it also requires strong political will and national consensus. The teachers are to be trained properly to take up the challenge of imparting education to these first generation learners. The teachers themselves have to be motivated first before they can motivate the children from the struggling families. Training of teachers is, therefore, another important task to be undertaken by the governments of African Nations. Framing of course curriculum for the African children to encourage them for participation in the education process is also a challenging task for these laggard nations. Until and unless, a committed government takes up the project with dogged determination, education for millions of African children can be elusive even in the new millennium.

CHAPTER 4

Poverty Discourses in India

4.1 Reductionism in Poverty Line Approach

A very serious question is raised regarding the notion of poverty embodied in poverty line approach and whether that poverty can really reflect the extent, nature and duration of deprivation for a large section of population in a society. Thus poverty line approach is evidently reductionist and embedded in what Professor Amartya Sen has called as commodity space. It ignores and discounts a wide variety of development deficits that cripple the underdogs in various ways. Low income is just one of such diversified deficits. The maldefinition of poverty seems to be further intensified by recent attempts by the government to focus on chronically poor, a subcategory, who are trapped in poverty continuously for last many years. Focusing on this subset seems to have some political implications particularly for pre-poll sloganeering for the incumbent government of its achievement in bringing down the number of poor during its reign. It happens that though the number below a miserly and poorly conceptualised poverty was dropping, the larger section of the population are increasingly being exposed to new forms of insecurities, risk and development deficits of various nature. The poor are always exposed to ups and downs of their meagre income as consequences of their fragile livelihoods. The composition of poor, thus, gets changed frequently even when poverty line and the 'poverty' figure remain unchanged for quite considerable time.

One example would suffice to expose the loopholes in the annual poverty data. Say, head count poverty is 40 per cent during last three years. This annual poverty statistics does not capture some dimension of poverty that is important for policy designing. For example, it does not provide us with the information about the number of poor who remained below poverty line for last three consecutive years. Because some 'old' poor may get out of poverty and vacuum left by them could be filled by new 'entrant' to poverty. Thus the head count figure remains unchanged. Policy framing could be slightly different for the aforesaid two categories: sticky poverty and volatile poverty. The annual average consumption data can hide an extended period of hunger.

Chronic Poverty

The poor are not homogeneous and the poverty is not undifferentiated. Poverty may be transitory or may be extended for a considerable period of time. The latter is generally coined as chronic poverty. There is an organization by the name of Chronic Poverty Research Centre. It publishes in its annual report and provides us with rich information about country-wise number of chronically poor. They define chronic poverty as "still being poor after five years". This centre brought out its report in 2004-05 and noted that while 536 million persons were below the $1 per day poverty line. Those in chronic poverty were between 134 and 188 million. This turns out to be one-fourth of the annual rate.

Another attempt to segregate poor in different categories is worthy of mention for its brilliant insights (Saith, 2005). The survey was undertaken in a group of countries during the period from late 1970s to early 1980s. All the surveyed households were classified in three mutually exclusive categories of 'always poor' (AP), 'sometimes poor' (SP) and 'never poor' (NP). Data available for India during 70s showed that, for every household that was 'always poor', there were another three households that were 'sometimes poor' (SP). The study found that only 12.4 per cent were reported as 'never poor' (NP). For Zimbabwe, the ratio of

AP to SP in the first half of the 1990s was 1 : 6. The same ratio came out to be 1 : 8 in China during the second half of 1980s. This categorization is excellent in its own right. But focussing on 'chronically poor' as well as on 'Always poor' as categorized in the last two studies as mentioned would be a sort of escapism by the governments which tend to take refuge and smug in lower figure. Chronically poor or always poor evidently forms a small segment of population for whom deprivations, deficits and insecurities are no less intolerable. Thus whatever be the poverty line $1 per day global poverty line or national poverty line, these lines are restrictive and exclusionary. Going further down the poverty line is exclusionary in nature. One study (Raghav Gaiha, 1989) has pointed out that chronically poor may not be the poorest of the poor and the opposite is also true. He finds that the households that were poor during successive three years form a small fraction of the poorest of the poor. Then why the governments in the developing world tend to focus on chronic poverty or severest form of poverty. It seems that adopting such a criterion for identifying the target section among the poor would ensure minimum misuse of funds meant for anti-poverty programmes. There will be reduced possibility of benefits reaching the hands of the non-poor. The other reason might be that the foreign donors would be interested in this kind of targeting. But the identification of such chronically poor in a country like India is not only problematic and huge but also runs the risk of committing error in doing so.

4.2 Weaknesses in Income Poverty Line Approach

It has already come to light through the foregoing discussion that poverty line approach is one-dimensional and, therefore, falls short of what should be a comprehensive approach. One weakness of poverty line approach is its singular focus on income criterion as a measure of economic strength of a family. Data on income of a household cannot indicate the amount of assets, both productive as well as unproductive it owns. The relation between household assets and household income is not something having fixed capital output ratio. The economic predicament of two comparable households, one having assets particularly unproductive assets and the other without them must be different in spite of their incomes being equal in amount. Let us consider that both of these households are placed below poverty line. The household endowed with little assets base can endure any sudden economic shock through sale of those assets.

The same economic shock can devastate the other household that do not own any assets to fall back upon. Likewise, income or expenditure data of households do not provide the information about the level of indebtedness of them. An indebted family is evidently poorer than its counterpart which is not in debt despite income being the same. The per capita consumption expenditure that makes the poverty line does not go into the sources of financing the consumption outlay. It makes no distinction between expenditure out of current income or out of past savings or taking consumption loans from the wealthy neighbours.

Demographic structure and profile largely varies among households that render household poverty substantially differentiated despite having same income. Families characterized by higher dependency ratio are more exposed to misery and economic shock than the families having a higher number of working adults. Families, particularly in North India having marriageable daughters, are always in financially frail state of insecurity as the pain of imminent coughing up for dowry imperils them. This precarious living of such families is not reflected in the expenditure or income poverty line. In the same vein, families cursed with one or two severely ailing members are susceptible to misery, the nature and extent of which goes beyond the bounds of poverty line. Adult equivalent scale is introduced to bring in parity in the per capita consumption estimate for all consuming units in a family. This is undertaken on the presumption that the children, female and older member would not consume the same amount as adult would do. But this scale designed to bring in parity in per capita consumption evidently do not take into account the cases of lactating and pregnant mothers in the family. These mothers would need even more than adult equivalent consumption for a considerable period of time. But the scale does not incorporate there additional needs. Interestingly, families incurring medical expenses for ailing members through selling off a part or whole of family assets would exhibit higher per capita consumption expenditure. It may so happen that such distressed families may rise above poverty line for this inescapable expenditure. World wide escalating health cost is pushing the poor families further below poverty line.

Intra household disparities in consumption is not exceptional occurrence, this is widespread in Indian societies where unequal distribution of opportunities within families on gender lines has come to light in many sociological investigations. Thus average consumption in the families does not adequately reflect the welfare of women, children and of elderly members. This gender based discrimination is reflected in the alarming magnitude of malnourished pregnant mothers. Low Birth Weight children are born to these malnourished mothers and chances of survival of these ill-fated children are obviously on lower sides. Children born to unlettered mothers are more likely to miss development opportunities thereby, causing reproduction of deprivations in successive generations. The other demerits of poverty line approach is its independent treatment as consuming units without situating the household in its social context. The poor households suffers not only from want or inadequacy of consumption but they are victims of identity based social exclusion and marginalisation. The poverty line is constructed without taking into account the unequal power relation in the community where the poor households live. Thus the income approach is unidirectional and ignores the socio-political dynamic that generates and perpetuates poverty. Differences in the access to households to social network relations and connection also makes a difference in the intensity of poverty which is overlooked by poverty line approach.

The income or expenditure poverty line approach presumes that consumption of public goods like health, education and other government services that constitute basic needs does not entail private expenditure. These come free of cost. But in reality, these public goods like universal health care and universal basic education is yet to become altogether free and actually universal. Many studies have shown that poor families have to make private expenditure on children's education and the amount is quite substantial. But even we take it for granted that these goods are free the cost of availing such 'free' public goods may be too prohibitive for the poor. Say for example that a rural hospital is situated miles away from the house of the rural poor. The poor not only forgoes the opportunity cost in the form of a day's wage income. She also incurs direct cost on transportation. The poverty line constructed mechanically does not pay attention to the opinion of the poor regarding their own perception of the state of affairs, their own diagnosis of the causes and their own thinking on solutions. The analysts armed with their tools for identification of poor do not value any other judgment of the subjects about their own predicament. But the perceptions of the subjects about their own situations can enrich the analysts' understanding of the extent and depth of poverty they are trapped in. Development studies increasingly recognize the importance of the perception of poor in not only identification but also framing appropriate policies to eradicate poverty. Participatory rural appraisal is now widely accepted as improved methodology for identifying poor and evolving proper policies. Although the methodology of incorporating such self-perception is beset with problem in practical application but its significance cannot be disparaged.

The other most serious weakness of the money metric measure of poverty line is its failure to differentiate between the extent of misery and vulnerability although both of these households show up same level of income. But this is intrinsically erroneous. Let us expose the condition by citing and an example of two families of the same neighbourhood. These two families have same family size and identical demographic structure by way of age and gender composition. Both of these households have same level of income. Now suppose that one of these two families suddenly confront an unforeseen worst situation: one or two of its elder members are afflicted with serious diseases. The other household did not face this situation. The entrenched household would sell the little land it had possessed to spend on medical treatment. Doctors may also advise for supplementing better diet with medication. As a result, this family's per capita consumption expenditure will jump upward. Because of the sudden and relatively big expenditure, the family moves forward economically, an upward move from B.P.L. status to A.P.L. status. But the actual cost of this upward movement is jeopardising its long term viability. This family loses the little asset it could fall back upon in time of crisis. Now the family has no option left other than entering into debt bondage. It appears that the reference family's income poverty has lessened, they are now richer but they are now stripped of their assets.

This income or expenditure poverty does not reflect severe vulnerability of the families. The destitute families are supposed to have productive assets to fall back upon. In this circumstance, they would enter into debt bondage with village money lenders or in the worst case; they can withdraw their children from school and send them to labour market. Now this family's income is supplemented by child labour income and this added income helps the family to rise above poverty line. Paradoxically, this family, in our example, is having one or two child labour but still not poor as per income poverty methodology. Therefore, the expenditure data should not be used as indicator for the fulfilment of the basic needs of a household, because the extent of these needs varies among households. The nature of such variation is illustrated above through depicting the situation of two households residing in same neighbourhood. "Despite its narrow focus, the income-poverty line approach does yield some pertinent information on its choice of scale but it is essentially one-dimensional and overlooks the multifaceted nature of human deprivation. This can easily lead to a superficially and misleading understanding of the nature and causes as well as cures of human poverty" (Saith, 2005).

Calorie-centric and money-metric poverty line is being increasingly dissented on two grounds diagnosed by the opponents of this approach. The first ground for rejection as they point out, is the inadequacy of the rupee values of poverty line basket for meeting normative caloric requirements. The second line of argument speaks against the dependence on caloric intake as only measure of nutritional adequacy. This is a very serious weakness of the poverty line approach if it is found that poverty line expenditure fails to permit the poverty line class, or MPCE class, to consume normative caloric norms. If this happens, then poverty figures published by the government during last many years are manifestly underestimation. Thus there has been forceful demand from many corners to revise the poverty line upward. The charge could not be disregarded. The consumption expenditure survey conducted during 1999-2000 by National Sample Survey was invoked as solid testimony to the allegation of the inability of poverty line income to ensure the recommended calorie intake. It was found that actual calorie intake was lesser in rural as well as in urban areas. In rural areas the shortfall was 25 per cent and in urban areas the same was to the tune of 15 per cent. Therefore, existing poverty line should be raised by 15 per cent for rural area and 10 per cent for urban areas to meet the requirements of normative calorie norm. Those who find nothing unusual in this lower calorie consumption in the poverty line class argue that calorie requirement has come down for the working population in India as a result of change in nature of job and hardship of labour involved in the work.

They argue that the normative calorie requirement 2400 kcal and 2100 for rural and urban areas respectively was prescribed by the nutritionists in India during 1972-73 on the basis of gender, age and work profile of Indian population as was revealed in the 1971 Census. During last forty years, India has made remarkable economic progress that has caused changed in occupational character from hard working job to less laborious job in the expanding service sector. This occupational shift has lessened the requirement of calories in the diet of the working population. However, this observation despite having sufficient empirical validity is opposed by a section of economists who point out there is no evidence to show that this has happened to people around poverty line class. The job diversification that has caused lower calories needs during last forty years is confined to people above poverty line (Sen, 2005). The nature of work and the pattern of livelihood have remained unchanged for people around and below the poverty line. The other argument advanced in favour of condoning the lower calorie intake is about change in dietary preference and taste among the poor during this period. Consumption basket has changed from food to non-food items (Mehta and Venkataraman, 2000). But this observation is also opposed on empirical ground (Sen, 2001). It is agreed that share of food expenditure in total expenditure of the poverty line class in 1973-74 was 81 per cent for rural areas and 72 per cent for urban areas. After, say thirty years, in 1999-2000, the shares are respectively 65 per cent and 59 per cent.

Thus the reduction in the share of food is 16 per cent and 13 per cent as compared to the shortfalls in caloric intake of 25 per cent and 15 per cent respectively. It shows that even if poverty line class spends the entirely on food they would fall short of the caloric norms, most prominently in rural area. Theoretical justification is also missing in the assertion that poors are substituting food expenditure by non-food expenditure. This consumption behaviour is natural in affluent classes but impossible in the poverty line classes who are placed in the subsistence level of living. There is also a possibility that cost for non-food consumption has gone up abnormally, so the poor are forgoing food consumption to cope up with rising cost of non-food items. One line of argument in favour of existing poverty line has come forward and it seems to have some essence. The original poverty lines were developed on the basis of calorie norms, but were specified as currency metrics, which were to be subsequently updated by appropriate price indices. Thus the objective was to protect the capability for consuming caloric norms, not the caloric themselves. Changes in various factors over time, particularly change in taste and preferences, would certainly lead to modification in the actual consumption basket. There is still feasible basket to allow for required caloric consumption by the existing poverty line. Therefore, it is quite clear that the observed shortfall in calorie is not so much the result of a lack of income or purchasing power, but of the choice of a food basket which yields lower calorie per rupee spent than is actually feasible. Thus revision of existing poverty line in India is uncalled for. The National Sample Survey data on consumption for two points of time in recent history, for 1972-73 and 1999-2000 respectively explicitly shows reduced per capita calorie consumption. We need to look for other reasons of this reduction without indulging in accusing per capita as the only causal agent. It may well be the case that with the passage of time, consumption behaviour and economic environment have changed sufficiently to alter the axiomatic basis of not only the poverty measurement methodology but also intervention strategy.

4.3 Relevance of Calorie and its Appropriateness

The poverty line constructed on the basic normative caloric intake is coming under attack from nutritionists in India during recent time. They point out that too much obsession with caloric is meaningless. A balanced diet should contain protein, fat and micro nutrients in addition to calories to ensure better health outcome. It the shortfall in calories intake is satisfactorily compensated by extra intake of proteins and fats and it shows better health outcome, then it is just folly to cry for caloric inadequacy. We are concerned with physical wellbeing and proper nourishment of people. We should not lament over some shortfall in calorie as came to light in the NSS survey, if other nutrients make good the losses. The distinction between gross caloric intake and net caloric absorption is important in the caloric based discourse on poverty. Gastro intestinal disorder primarily caused by impure drinking water, unhealthy living condition characterized by lack of sanitation and hygienic can impede the absorption process. Malnourishment is thus natural occurrence in these situations. It is quite possible that a lower gross caloric intake could be associated with superior nutritional outcome due to better absorption of nutrients. Some nutritionists have recently observed that Indian poverty line insists too much on calory. It could have emphasized on lower calories to be supplemented by other micro-nutrients.

However, the objection to caloric fetishism and recommendation for balanced diet containing micronutrients, fats and proteins are welcome. It certainly paves the way for rethinking on the construction of poverty line in Indian context. But it is problematic to accommodate it in operational methodology and poverty measurement. Food consumption among general population is never driven by scientific knowledge of balancing micro-nutrients; on the contrary this is rather driven by taste, preference and dietary habits. The balancing of diet as required for optimum health outcome is not the practice even among richer classes not to speak of their poorer brethren. In such a situation of missing linkage between nutritional adequacy and purchasing power of households, nutritional poverty becomes hard to define and measure. Policy planners are increasingly looking for other measure for deprivation. Calorie based poverty figure is always beset with the problem of underestimation or over-estimation about the number of poor.

However, from 1973-74 to 1999-2000, a long period spanning around three decades, consumption behaviour in Indian population has undergone changes among all expenditure classes. The average caloric consumption has declined from 1993-94 to 1999-2000 both for urban and rural areas. The pace of decrease during this period does not appear to be out of line with the longer run trend beginning from 1973-74 (Sen, 2009). The average real expenditure of the poor has not evidently declined over the same period. It explicitly indicates that poor people are increasingly substituting calorie by proteins and fats.

Food habits have considerably changed among all classes, share of cereals in the diet is gradually waning and the deficits are met by non-cereals proteins and fats. Decreased intake of cereals does not seem to damage physical wellbeing of the poor. Poverty line was constructed on the basis of recommendations of nutritionists in India during the commencement of our planned development. The poverty line income must allow the people to buy consumption goods that would provide the minimum prescribed calories and that calories intake is a must to maintain a reasonable good health. But in India, interestingly, people have been found to maintain good health, capable of work for livelihood, living on food that contains lesser calorie than what prescribed in the poverty line. The southern States in India exhibit lower calories intake than the specified norm, but they also consistently display better health indicators. Thus the like between gross caloric intake and health outcome is not obvious at all (Sen, 2005). Thus while poor are moving away from coarse cereals evidently caused by changes in tastes and preference for food, the argument for continuing with subsidized food programme of the government is weakened in the challenged realities. Course cereals are now turned out to be inferior goods. It appears that government is spending huge public money for the sake of health and welfare of the underpriveleged people whose positive outcome is eluding us. The direct provision of coarse cereals to the poor runs the risk of wastage as inferior goods are abandoned by the consumer as has been empirically established in the consumer behaviour theory. The targeted public distribution system provides subsidized cereals to below poverty line people. Integrated Child Development Schemes, Antodaya Anna Yojana and Midday meal scheme for primary school-going children are prominent direct food programme currently in operation in India. The evidences of changed dietary preferences and consumption among poor calls for redesigning or even scrapping of theirs food subsidy programme. Time has come to reflect on our existing food intervention programme as an instrument for poverty eradication. Direct income transfer can be tried on experimental basis in selected locations. The income recipient poor can exercise their option in choice of foods according to their aspirations, tastes and preferences which they can get in the local market. Wastage of public money in procuring and distributing coarse cereals among poor at subsidized prices or free of cost should be an issue that calls for deeper debate.

4.4 Poverty Statistics in India: The Contested Terrain

The official statistics on poverty announced in India at a certain point of time that coincides with the publication of the results of N.S.S. consumption expenditure survey is published by the Planning Commission for public consumption. The Commission's poverty figures are head count ratios, separately published for urban as well as for rural areas of the country. India's constituent states and union territories can also have the statistics on the number of poor in their respective territories. In addition to that, they can also measure the relative contribution of their respective sub-national area's poverty towards its national magnitude. While states in India's 'Hindi Heartland' can contribute in a massive way, but the prosperous States like Gujarat, Punjab and Haryana can contribute very little toward national poverty figures. Some States can rejoice over the figures while others can be let down and make them reflect over the dismal performance.

The National Council for Applied Economic Research also conducts household survey all over India to collect income data and level of living occasionally. They did one such survey in 2004-2005. But most comprehensive head count estimate of poverty is provided by the National Sample Survey organization consistently every five years. The Planning Commission makes use of the survey results and calculates the poverty figures. The NSS poverty data published in recent times is quite satisfying. The government drumbeats its achievement, the party in power takes the credit and the public at large are fed with the heartening news. The estimate of poverty produced on the basis of the 55th round NSS survey published in 2001, showed a marked reduction in the head count poverty in India. It fell from 37.1 per cent in 1993-94 to 26.8 per cent in 1999-2000 in rural areas. In urban areas it fell from 32.9 per cent to 24.1 per cent during the same period. But this period is not ordinary in India's contemporary history. This was a turning point, a paradigm shift in India's development strategy a shift from Fabians' socialism to free play of market. This shift took place under duress to come out of the grave situation of severe balance of payment crisis in the external sectors and fiscal crisis of massive proportion. India undertook economic reform measures in 1991.

The reform measures adopted in India at the behest of the I.M.F. and World Bank were hailed by many who had sided with the government for the radical steps which were overdue for many years. The opponents dominated by people having socialist leanings dubbed this string of measure as a total surrender to the global capital. They began to remind the people of impending onslaught of poverty in India of unprecedented scale. They began to ventilate this apprehension of danger that lurks not only through street protest but also through academic writing in journals as well as in newspapers for wider audience. The opponents were convinced that economic reforms measures that paved the way for neo-liberal regime would deepen poverty and intensify vulnerability among the underprivileged people who will be disempowered in the wake of thoughtless globalization. Therefore, the poverty figure that came out and expressed in head count ratio in 2000 made available by NSS, 55th round survey of consumption expenditure evoked interest for the groups, the advocates and the opponents. The NSS report came in handy for liberalization advocates, who began to take pleasure in invoking the remarkable reduction in poverty by little more than 10 per cent during a very short period of five to six years. They claim that this miracle was possible only because of the economic reform measures. Liberalization has reduced poverty (Deaton and Kozell, 2004).

The opponent group puts forward the argument that trickle down effect of the so called growth in India is miserably missing. They point to the growing divergence between expenditure poverty and caloric poverty (Patnaik, 2004; Meenakshi and Vishwanath, 2004). They further agree that this fall in poverty as revealed in the NSS 55th round consumption expenditure survey is actually over stated because the previous rounds of survey do not stand to comparison with the 55th round as the latter was based on altogether different methodology. They rejected the claim of this sharp fall in poverty. There are disagreements across the board on the definition of poverty. Thus when the concept of poverty widely differs, the methodology for counting of poor would automatically differ among different agencies who conduct the survey. It can differ as a result of the variation in sample size of the households in a region. For example, the National Council for Applied Economic Research (NCAER) through its studying in India in 2005 entitled National Survey of Household Income and Expenditure (NSHIE) came out with the poverty figure of 21 per cent. But the study reveals a high level of inequality in household income across India. This report also unfolds that the rural income inequality is on the rise and is on the way to catch up with the level of urban income inequalities. The Gini Coefficient calculated from this household income data shows that inequities level in contemporary India is comparable to China, Hong Kong, Singapore and U.S.A.

Thus the NCAER data on poverty incidence of 21 per cent just matches with the Planning Commission's Report of 21.8 per cent based on Mixed Recall Period in the NSS consumption expenditure survey. The National Commission for Employees in Unorganized Sector headed by Professor Arjun Sengupta exposed that 78 per cent India's population is surviving on ₹ 20 per day. The poverty ratio constructed on the basis of Monthly Per Capita Expenditure based on Mixed Recall Period has been found by the Commission to be 27.5 per cent. The World Bank has reported 42 per cent as India's incidence of poverty. The Tendulkar Committee constituted by the Planning Commission as an expert group to review the methodology for estimation poverty in India puts the figure of poverty at 41.8 per cent in rural areas and 25.7 per cent in urban areas during 2004-05. Poverty statistics is important in many ways. It has significance in electoral politics where the party in power have to feed the vast mass of electorates with the story of its achievement accomplished during its reign. Reduction in poverty is placed in the top of such list of achievement. Government everywhere uses and drum beats in referring to its own statistics provided by the Planning Commission.

CHAPTER 5

Overcoming Income Poverty Line

5.1 Tendulkar Committee Report

India's official poverty line expressed as monetary value at the prevailing market prices of goods and services that contain in the Poverty Line Basket (PLB). The basket, as has been said earlier consists of food as well as non-food items for household consumption. The food component in the poverty line basket has to conform to the Recommended Dietary Allowances (RDA) prescribed by the nutritionists in India. In the rural areas the food intake has to ensure 2400 kcal and the same for the urban areas is 2100 kcal. This line was constructed in India on the basis of age, sex and occupation composition of Indian population provided in the census estimate in 1971 and the consumption data to arrive at poverty line MPCE was made available by consumption expenditure survey of the NSS in 1972-73. Poverty line was thus caloric anchored and the line expressed in monetary value is subject to periodic revision and upgradation. In the absence of any upgradation the line loses its significance and makes way for underestimation of poverty. The poverty line has to be responsive to price changes over time. The poverty line varies across States also because within State price differentials are omnipresent.

Likewise urban price level also differs from rural price level that can substantially cause variation in the purchasing power and level of living. The Planning Commission is aware of this variation. They have provided for differential poverty line in such a diverse country like India where price situations widely varies.

The national poverty line in 1973-74 of the Task Force was disaggregated into State specific poverty line using State specific price indices and inter-State price differential. The State specific price indices are constructed by averaging the state specific food and non-food price indices of the Consumer Price Index of Agriculture Labourers (CPIAL) with their respective weights in the consumption basket of the poor at the national level. Likewise, for urban areas, the state specific price indices are constructed by with the help of State Specific Consumer Price Index for Industrial Workers (CPIIW) with their respective weights in the national consumption basket of the poor in 1973-74. The inter-State price differential is captured through Fisher's index. Thus poverty line in India is always updated and upgraded to take into account the inflation that impinges on the purchasing capacity of the poor. The Planning Commission understands the significance of the periodic review and critical assessment of the methodology adopted for constructing poverty line. The poverty line basket for goods and services that can meet the basic minimum needs for life in a civilized society needs to be reviewed from time to time. The commission constitutes an expert committee headed by an eminent development economist to review the current methodology and suggest an improved methodology to incorporate, if the situation demands, the altered consumption behaviour of the poor. The composition of food and non-food items in the poverty line basket might have changed during this period, necessitating a redefinition of the basket and of the poverty line. This task was assigned to an expert committee comprising of eminent economists. One such committee of experts was constituted by the Planning Commission in 1993 under the leadership of Professor Lakdawala. The latest one is headed by Prof. Suresh. D. Tendulkar. The committee was constituted in December 2005. One reason is the Commission's routine task undertaken every 10 to 15 years to peruse the poverty line and the poverty line basket in the light of the changes that have taken place with regard to food habits and consequent changes in the composition of poverty line basket. The timing of the constitution deserves attention. It coincides with the period when result of the 61st round of consumption expenditure survey conducted by the National Sample Survey came out. Tendulkar finds no fault with urban poverty ratio derived from the 1993 expert group definition. The official poverty line is derived from the Uniform Recall Period (URP) consumption distribution of the NSS. The URP is 30 days recall period for household consumption. Tendulkar committee has converted URP consumption based urban poverty line into Mixed Recall Period (MRP) based poverty line.

The MRP consumption data is collected using 365 days recall period for five infrequently purchased non-food items: clothing, footwear, durable goods, education and medical expenses and 30 recall consumption based urban poverty line is worked out as the level of per capita consumption distribution. That corresponds to the bottom 25.7 per cent of the population which is official urban poverty ratio on the basis of URP consumption. In the next stage, State specific urban poverty lines are obtained from MRP consumption based national urban poverty line using State relative to all-India index number. After that, State specific rural poverty lines are worked out from these State specific urban poverty lines by applying State specific urban to rural price relatives. The quantity and value of different items of consumer expenditure collected by the National Sample Survey during the consumption expenditure survey provides the data for construction of State relative to all-India index urban to rural price relatives. At the end, State specific poverty percentages are estimated from State specific class distribution of persons obtained from MRP consumption distribution of the NSS consumption data Tendulkar Method can be presented below for the sake of clearer understanding the steps.

(1) He exclusively focuses on 25.7 per cent figure. This is the urban poverty ratio consumption expenditure survey
(2) This poverty percentage was obtained by using URP-consumption data.
(3) Professor Tendulkar converted this URP based poverty line into MRP poverty line.
(4) He converted MRP based national poverty line into state

specific urban poverty lines by using State specific price relatives.

(5) He estimated State specific poverty ratio from these State specific poverty lines and the class distribution of MRP consumption.

At the end, we get are this new poverty data on the basis of the Tendulkar Methodology. The urban poverty estimated at 25.7 per cent remains unchanged but the national rural poverty now goes up from 28.3 per cent to 41.8 per cent. The Planning Commission in a recent press statement announces that poverty ratio has come down to 32 per cent in 2009-2010 from 37 per cent in 2004-2005. The estimation was done on the basis of new methodology developed by Professor Tendulkar and his team.

The New Methodology

Tendulkar's methodology is certainly an improved tool for measuring head count ratio of poverty in India. Its finer points should not be overlooked and must receive mention and applause in poverty discourse. For the first time, this new methodology has abrogated caloric obsession in the measurement of poverty. Calorie anchored poverty line came under scathing attack from different corners. The allegation voiced mainly by opponents of neo-liberal policy reforms filled the air and reached the office of the Planning Commission in New Delhi. By keeping poverty line at such a low level, the centre would drumbeat the magnificent impact of reforms measures. They justify these actions by invoking India's remarkable success in reducing poverty. The allegation was straight forward against the government that the poverty statistics released by the Commission for public consumption is terribly underestimated. The constitution of expert committee under Prof. Tendulkar was basically a gesture to keep the House in order. The government rose to the occasion to comply immediately. The Commission was asked to redefine and reconstruct the poverty line in view of the changed circumstances.

The Poverty Line Basket (PIB) which makes the poverty line in India was fixed according to composition of food and non-food items of Indians as released in the consumption expenditure survey by NSS in 1792-73. Census Report of 1971 provided the demographic characteristics of our citizens relating to age, gender and nature of work that ultimately decides that level of calorie requirement of all individuals on the basis of those characteristic. For example, a young person of 10 years of age, doing no work, would not need the amount of calorie as might be needed by an adult of 30 years in age doing manual work in the agricultural field for 10 hours in a day. The poverty line basket, the expenditure for which defines the poverty line income has undergone changes during the period spanning more than three decades. Tastes and preferences have changed during this time. Rural people are increasingly coming closer to urban society and this proximity is brought about by improved communication and exposure to television. Rural people are imitating the culinary habits of their urban counterparts. Thus many food items that made poverty line food basket in the early seventies in India are missing right now. Even poor people might be consuming more pulses now in place of cereals. Reflection and redefinition of the poverty line basket are warranted for making this relevant for the present time so that it can precisely reflect the basic needs of the present time. The attainments which constitute basic needs are subject to alterations over a long period of time. It varies across space and times. For example, the commodities and services that constituted basic needs in East Africa might be altogether different in Scandinavian countries. Likewise, in an affluent nation in the Scandinavian, Sweden, for example, the basic needs as considered hundred years ago are no longer basic now. Some new necessities must have been included and some old be excluded.

In our country where basic needs approach went into construction of poverty line and poverty line basket for goods and services, education and health care service were kept outside that basket. It was taken for granted that these two vital basic needs were public goods and, therefore, entails no private expenditure. The excellence of the Tendulkar Committee lies in its rejection of public goods provisioning of these two vital basic needs. The arguments put forward by the expert committee are intrinsically irrefutable. Poor people are spending on health care and on education for children. There are plenty of studies on household expenditure pattern even for poor families in rural areas. The National Sample Survey has been conducting household survey to investigate the extent of private expenditure on health and education. All these studies have revealed that private expenditure even by poor families on medical treatment and education is inescapable. The Tendulkar Committee switches from Uniform Recall Period (URP) to Mixed Recall Period (MRP) and accepted poverty line basket for urban area to get the poverty ratio for the rural area. The MRP consumption based urban poverty basket is nearest to the actual consumption expenditure of the poor in the rural area.

5.2 Moving Away from Calorie Norm

Tendulkar Committee has obviously moved away from the usual practice of calorie anchoring in defining poverty line. The arguments put forward by the Expert Committee in favour of deviating from calorie anchoring seem to have essence. The committee observes that calorie anchored official poverty estimate in India is just music to the ears of the Planning Commission and to the Government under which the Commission works. Head count poverty ratio as per Planning Commission estimation has come down to 25.7 per cent in urban area and 28 per cent in rural area. But the head count poverty reduction does not tally with nutritional outcome as revealed in the National Family Health Survey findings reports published in 2005-2006. The survey reveals that one in three women in 15-49 years age group has Body Mass Index (B.M.I.) below 18.5 indicating severe nutritional deficiency and under-nutrition. The same survey also brings to light severe malnutrition among children below 3 years of age. For example, the proportion of children wasted was 16 per cent in 1998-99; it has gone up to 19 per cent in 2005-2006. The second Family Health Survey published in 1998-99 found that 47 per cent of India's children were underweight; the incidence remained almost same at 46 per cent in 2005-2006. Thus calorie anchored poverty line, as pointed out by the Tendulkar Committee, fails to explain the mismatch between reduction of poverty and increase or stagnation in malnutrition among women and children. The other reason for abrogating calorie norm by the expert committee is the recent prescription of the Food and Agricultural Organizations (FAO) about minimum calorie need for Indians in present time. FAO has prescribed 1800 kcal which is rather close to urban calorie need of 2100 kcal prescribed by nutritionists in India in 1979. The new poverty line developed by the Tendulkar Committee was close to 2005 Purchasing Power Parity (PPP) $ 1.25 per day as used by the World Bank for conducting international comparison of poverty. The Tendulkar Committee while recommending the new poverty line for India invokes those arguments to justify this new measure.

5.3 Against Tendulkar Committee

Updating of poverty line basket and upward movement of rural poverty line for Indians to obtain the actual poverty measure are upbeaten development. It was hailed from many corners as a radical shift in India's poverty assessment as step towards multidimensional approach in conceptualization of poverty. But despite all the finer points of the new poverty line, the methodology of the new lines is being subject to disapproval in different corners. The expert group asserts that the deviation from the caloric anchoring is driven by observed disjunction between caloric anchored poverty and prevalence of widespread malnutrition. The critics argue that abrogation of caloric anchoring on the ground of observed disjunction is not empirically sound proposition. There is no one to one correspondence between caloric consumption and attainment of nutrition. There are so many factors like body metabolic system, safe drinking water, hygiene and sanitation that go in between the inputs and body outcome. There cannot be any linear correspondence between them. Secondly, the critics also object to the presumption of the expert committee about the reduced caloric need in rural area in consequence changes in life style that has occurred in the landscape of rural India. They make it a point that the Committee does not refer to any research study to justify their premise of reduced caloric need. The expert committee has adopted F.A.O. recommendation of 1800 kcal. They did not try to verify the justification of reduction through the Employment and Unemployment Survey and Consumption Expenditure survey whether the nature of employment in rural area has really moved away from heavy work to light work. The last argument of the expert committee in favour of their new poverty line's closeness of the new line with the World Bank international bench mark poverty line is also objected. The World Bank has recently updated the same from one dollar per capita per day to 1.25 dollar per capita per day and the Purchasing Power Parity (PPP) dollar conversion rate from 11 rupees to 16 rupees. One can easily find that the stated closeness is seen only in the case of the urban poverty line.

CHAPTER 6

Who are Poor in India?

6.1 Identification of Poor

So far, throughout the preceding sections, we were engaged with the definition and measurement of poverty in India. Poverty is defined in purely commodity space where the precarious condition of living is characterized by deprivations of material endowment. Some people in the human society cannot access the poverty line basket of goods and services which is earmarked by the development authority as minimum. Those people are poor and the number of people who populate this category is very important. For a democratic country committed to welfare of the subjects, the number or one may call us as head count poverty ratio is the crucial yardstick for assessing the efficacy of the democratic governance. Bringing down the ratio over a period of time is considered a feat accomplished by the government. Democracy, in its letter and spirit, cannot survive and flourish when a large number of people go to bed every night without food. To every democratic government in the world, eradication of poverty and elimination of economic inequality is the primary task. Deployment policies have to be framed to improve the lives of the poor. In purely technical language these people have to be lifted above the poverty line. The latter is money metric. Any person who does not have income or purchasing capacity to buy this bundle of goods is poor.

The planners need to know how many poor do inhabit certain region, the latter may be a village, or district or a State even the entire country. But 'how many?' is quite different from who are they? How can we identify poor households among clusters of households in a locality? The government's duty is not confined to getting the data on magnitude of the poor. It has to identify them. This identification is necessary for the sake of targeting the beneficiaries for anti-poverty programme and social security benefits. Economic growth of a country that results in the development process may bypass the millions of poor. The trickle down effect of the growth process may be missing for a substantial section of the population as a consequence of inability to access the opportunity. Anti-poverty programmes obviously include a wide variety of specific programme ranging from wage employment to subsidized food programme for the poor. The targeted public distribution system for distribution of foodgrains, rice or wheat is currently underway in our country. Under this scheme, families below poverty line will be allocated 35 kilos of rice or wheat at ₹ 3 per kilo every month through PDS centre. ***The Antyodaya Anna Yojna*** and ***Annapurna Yojna*** are also food programme for the targeted beneficiaries who comprise of the households headed by ailing adults, widows with no income support and many other such vulnerable families who need food support for their survival.

6.2 BPL Survey and Saxena Committee

Household survey to identify the poor in a particular locality is undertaken by the local government at the behest of the Centre. The Ministry of Rural Development of the Government of India gets the work done periodically by the *Panchayats* at the village level. The list is made after the survey and is widely known as Below Poverty Line (BPL) list. The list once made remains valid for five years and thereafter a fresh list has to be made on undertaking fresh survey. The list of poor loses its relevance after certain point of time because some of the enlisted families might have improved their economic standing and thereby moved above the poverty line. Likewise, a few of families might have slipped down by this time. It may always happen that during the period of the household survey these families were placed above poverty line because of relatively better income position at the point of time. But income volatility and fragility of these families even though placed above the poverty line render them vulnerable to unforeseen shocks. For example, the family which were placed above the line might slip down to the bottom very soon as a result of unforeseen medical expenditure. These kinds of impoverishing shocks befall on families suddenly. The only earning members may fall ill and this sudden illness might have stripped the families of a little land or cattle.

The reference family should be included in the BPL list. This family must be allowed to access opportunities provided by the state to cope with the adversities brought about such shocks. There is equal possibility also of exclusion because some families might improve economically during the inter-survey period. They have been able to lift themselves above the poverty line. This periodic inclusion and excluding on conducting survey are necessary for the sake of the list itself to be worthy of its purpose and values. The social security benefits must reach the poor who actually deserve it. Here lies the significance of the updated and correct list. The purpose of the social security benefits in the form of subsidized sale of foodgrains at a nominal price, free health care benefits, and school stipends for children for the poor is thwarted if the substantial portion of the same is cornered by the non-poor citizens. The household survey to identify the poor households in the rural area is not a new exercise in India. This task was undertaken in 1980 to select the households eligible for loan-cum-subsidy programme launched in the name of IRDP (Integrated Rural Development Programme). This was a targeted anti-poverty programme undertaken to lift the poor above poverty line. This lifting will be effected by generation of income through undertaking economically productive activities by the members of the families. The selected poor households would acquire productive assets with the help of bank loan and government's matching subsidy.

The line between poor and non-poor was drawn in 1980 exclusively on the basic of family income. The ceiling was fixed at ₹ 4,800 per family per year below which all were eligible for receiving IRDP benefits. All the poor are not alike. Poverty is not uniform among poor, horrible for someone and less horrible for others. Some of the poor family may be living very close to poverty line and some are too far. Those who are too far are poorest of the poor. It was decided that families with ₹ 35,000 as income per year would be assisted first in the IRDP. BPL census was carried out, thereafter in 1992. Income as a sole criterion to be considered for inclusion in the BPL list prevailed this time also. The upper ceiling of annual income per family was substantially raised; more than two fold this time. Poverty line income was fixed at ₹ 11,000. The poor households were categorized in four broad income groups. In ascending order those four groups are; destitute (up to ₹ 4,000), very very poor (₹ 4,000 – ₹ 6,000), very poor (₹ 6,000 – ₹ 8,500), poor (₹ 8,5,00 – ₹ 11,000). The priority groups would obviously be the destitute who are placed in the lowest rung of the poverty categories. This categorization was certainly a welcome gesture to prioritize the neediest poor when number of seekers of IRDP assistance far exceeds the amount of financial provision.

But the number of poor households identified on the basis of the household survey collided with the number reported by the Planning Commission. The very basis of this kind of survey began to be questioned. The data on household actual income is hard to come by. A single point household survey to gather data on income earned by a reference household during the last reference period cannot gather precise information about income. Because, almost all families, barring very few, in the rural areas earn income through participating in informal economic activities in agriculture or in allied sector. Income from self employment is very hard to calculate as they do not keep any written records of income they earned in the past. Recall lapses are most likely. For those families who exclusively survive on wage income or salary income throughout the year, income data can easily come by if reported properly. The poor in the rural area draw their sustenance from a wide variety of sources. She may be a marginal farmer, raises food crop that can sustain her family for a few months. The same person works as agricultural labour in the peak season of agriculture in her neighbourhood when he is not working in his own farm. He may work as unskilled manual labour in the neighbouring village in the lean season. Incomes from all these activities have to be correctly recorded and then added up to get at the annual family income. How to measure income from self employment like peasant farming? The procedure is not smooth when the vegetables and grains raised in the field go to the farmer's kitchen instead of the market. We have to get the market value of the farmer's agricultural produce from which cost of production including the market value of all farm hands are to be deducted to arrive at income from the own farm for the whole year. Calculation of annual family income is thus problematic because the nature of income earning is not linear and simple. The problem lies also with family income as a variable rather than per capita income within a family. Family income as a measure of economic affluence suffers from a major shortcomings as it does not reveal the distribution of income among members. Per capita income would have been a better indicator. A large family with certain level of income is worse than a small family with the same level of income. Size of family is as important as the size of income. The identification of poor households on the basis of income alone came to an end after 1997. The BPL survey conducted in 1997, for the first time, had deviated from the age old practice of recording family income as the sole criterion.

It incorporated other vital indicators of economic wellbeing of families in addition to income. The methodology adopted this time was innovative in its own right. The family would be automatically excluded from the BPL list if it owns anyone of the following assets; (1) the family owns and operates more than 2 hectares of land; (2) the family owns a *pucca* house; (3) any member of the family earns at least ₹ 20,000 per annum as salary or as fixed wage; (4) family own consumer durables like T.V., Refrigerator, Ceiling Fan, Motor Cycle; and (5) the family owns tractor or a power tiller. After exclusion of family on the basis of their criterion, the survey will be conducted for the rest of the households in the villages. Instead of income, consumption data was recorded for each household during the survey. Per capita consumption expenditure was calculated on completion of the survey. Per capita consumption expenditure was compared with the State level poverty line. Those below the poverty line were included in the BPL list. The latter was certainly an improvement over the last list made in 1992 but further improvement was called for to look at multi-dimensional poverty. Five years later, in 2002 a broad based survey schedule was designed by the Ministry of

Rural Development of the Central Government. The survey schedule captured different and much wider aspects of poverty and deprivations. Score based ranking of the households on the basis of 13 socio-economic parameters was undertaken to prepare the BPL list. An individual household can score from 0 to 4 in each of the 13 parameters. It can obtain 52 as highest marks in the allotment of score, and '0' as lowest marks. The 13 parameters are as follows: (1) Land holdings, (2) Type of houses, (3) Clothing, (4) Food security, (5) Sanitation, (6) Consumer durables, (7) Literacy status of highest literate, (8) Status of household labour, (9) Means of livelihood, (10) Status of children, (11) Type of indebtedness, (12) Reason for migration, and (13) Preference for assistance. Each of the surveyed households will be allotted individual score on the basis of the aforesaid attributes. Families obtaining lower score obviously stand the chance of getting in the coveted list.

There was perceptible rat race among the families to procure the BPL card as passport for entry to the haven of government benefits. The number of central schemes for the poor went up manifold by the time. Only the BPL card holders are eligible to access those benefits. How this survey that provided scores obtained by each of the aspiring households could settle the very sensitive issue of identification? The cut off score was decided and each of households below the cut off score will be allotted the coveted BPL card. The cut-off score will be decided on the basis of head count poverty ratio prevailing at that particular moment in the State down at the district level. The percentage of households identified as poor to be eligible for BPL card should not exceed the percentage of poor in each State and in each district, the report of which is provided by the Planning Commission. So there is always a cap set by the Central Government beyond which the State government or the local government cannot go. Therefore, the cut off score adopted by the different State governments at the local level widely varied. Some of the aspects of this new selection process were of course radical turn as it put money income as indicator in the back seat. It was a comprehensive attempt for the first time to reveal the multidimensional deprivation for which the destitute households lead precarious life in the society.

Despite its finer points and improvement over the earlier methodology, its deficiencies also came to the surface after the same was put to practical use. Some of prominent criticism raised against the methodology deserves mention. It was pointed out by the critics is that some parameters for scoring has ***disincentivising*** syndrome. For example, the household would be reluctant to install own latrine at home despite having capacity to do so for fear of exclusion from the BPL list. There is another disincentivising syndrome that most likely to appear in the parental decision about sending children to school. If the household keep their children out of school they would obtain high score. Thus, there is a possibility that parent may not send their children to school for fear or exclusion from the BPL list. Some of the parameters are not directly verifiable but carries handsome score. Clothing, food security and preference for assistances are not verifiable outwardly as opposed to parameters like housing and lands. The grey area also generates corruption. The ruling party in power at the local self government find it as an opportunity to create vote banks through inclusion of the ineligible but party loyal in the BPL list. Thus the BPL list made on the basis of this methodology adopted in 2002 triggered much controversy and ignited opposition in different parts of the country. Evidences of exclusion of genuine poor and inclusion of ineligible non-poor in the rural areas began to reverberate everywhere. Voices were raised in different corners to review the methodology to keep corruption and manipulation at bay.

Some of the inaccuracies and deficiencies in the individual parameters for economic wellbeing measure can be presented here. Let us start with 'land holding' as indicator of economic empowerment. But this new methodology and improved identification exercise do not differentiate between irrigated land and non-irrigated land. No one can deny that quality of land contributes more to productivity. Ownership of housing or dwelling units as a parameter is also problematic under housing scheme for the rural poor by the name of *Indira Awas Yojna* (IAY). Pucca living room for each selected beneficiaries is built. These poor people living in IAY houses stand the chance of being excluded from the BPL list. Availability of clothing for household members is also confusing as indicator of wellbeing. Number of clothes and quality of clothes vary according to climatic condition. A single measuring scale for ownership of clothing may exclude the poor residing in hilly and cold climatic regions in India. The food security indicator does not spell out clearly on quality aspect of foods: two square meals in a day. The survey schedule that captures this 'food' data does not enquire whether those meals are balanced, containing the minimum supply of proteins, vitamins and other micronutrients. Here also quality aspect has been way laid which is incorrect from the point of view of outcome

Similarly, the issue of sanitation as one of the indicators of living conditions of the poor, can have discouraging effect on them. For fear of exclusion, the poor would be reluctant to build their own toilet. The same disincentivising effect will also work in case of pursuit of education in poor families. This is because; going to school and gaining literacy will have negative side according to their perceptions. The chance of exclusion from the list may rise in future if they pursue education. While recording the status of household workers, the survey does not record the status of women's unpaid labour and child labour within the family. The extent of indebtedness of a family in the rural area can hardly be an indicator of distress. The poorest of the poor without any asset to be used as collateral can never be indebted. They cannot access any credit from institutional source nor can they avail any loan from private sources. They will score good marks on this particular point of indicator and will be excluded from the BPL list. The question on migration in rural area also suffers from incompleteness. First it does not make it clear whether one or more than one migrates. Secondly migration does not always indicate economic precariousness. Some member may go to cities for better income prospect and good amount of money can be received by the family. Still this family will be identified as poor even after earning more income now than before. The question on preference for assistance serves a negative purpose. The respondents may furnish reply in such a way that begets high score.

Saxena Committee was constituted by the Ministry of Rural Development and the report of the Committee was submitted in 2009. The Committee was asked by the Government to look into the inaccuracies, inadequacies and misjudgement as pointed out by development planners and economists from time to time. The methodology needs further improvement to consider only objective conditions present in the households rather than questioning on subjective issues. In the background of lingering public outcry on the issue of wrongful BPL list in many areas of

Table 6.1: Chart of Credit Score

Parameters	*Categories*	*Credit*
Social parameter	SC/ST Households	3 points
	Denotified Tribes/Most Backward caste	2 points
	Muslim	1 point
	OBC	1 point
Livelihood parameters	Landless agricultural workers	4 points
	Agricultural labourer with some lands	3 points
	Casual workers	2 points
	Self employed	2 points
Educational attainment parameter	No adult in the family has studied up to class 5	
Medical condition parameter	Any member of the household has TB/Leprosy/Disability/HIV/AIDS	1 point
Household head parameter	Household headed by old person aged 60 years and above	

the country. The committee developed the methodology and indicators those were easily verifiable and nothing to hide under the carpet. Saxena Committee deserves applause for devising an innovative and path breaking approach in identification of really poor. As a first step towards making the list it excluded forthwith the families characterized by the following attributes. Family who are liable to be excluded automatically are, (1) Families who own double the land of the district average of the agricultural land per agricultural household, (2) Families who own three wheeled or four wheeled vehicles, (3) Families having at least one mechanized farm equipment, (4) Families having a person who draws a salary over ₹ 10,000 per month, and (5) Income Tax payers. While the committee has explicitly laid out types of families endowed with better economic predicaments to be automatically excluded from the BPL List, it has in the same vein, has earmarked some distraught types of families to be included forthwith in the list. The automatic inclusion list includes the following:

(1) Designated primitive Tribes;
(2) Maha *dalit* – discriminated SC groups;
(3) Single woman headed household;
(4) Household with disabled person as bread winner;
(5) Household headed by minor;
(6) Beggars;
(7) Homeless; and

(8) Bonded labour household.

The BPL list to be prepared must contain these groups or families characterized by acute defencelessness. The rest of the list would be filled by household survey. Each of the survey household would be allotted scores, the total of which may be 1 at the lowest and 10 at the highest. The cut-off will be fixed in such a way that the number of BPL households should not exceed 50 per cent as recommended by the Saxena Committee. The proposed scoring for ranking is given in Table 6.1.

The Sexena Committee recommendations to identify the eligible poor as prospective recipients of social security benefits evidently are remarkable measures that intend to dispel misgivings generated around the preparation of the list. The 2002 BPL Census, despite its inclusion of so many factors of relative deprivation, did not escape the scathing attack on its foundation. The method of information gathering was flawed and many questions set for asking were incapable of revealing the State of deprivations. Many poor households were excluded because of the grey area in the information collected through the survey. Large scale manipulation, nepotism and creation of vote banks for the ruling party by distributing undue privileges in putting these names in the list of newspaper headlines. Unfairness in the preparation of the list on the basis of 2002 BPL Census was corroborated by NSSO consumption expenditure survey 61st round onward. The survey revealed that BPL listing and their findings did not match.

It was found that many families with lower MPCE and below the poverty line did not get BPL card. On the other hand, some families with higher MPCE and far above the poverty line were found to have procured BPL card. Saxena Committee was well aware of the fundamental lacuna in the methodology of the previous survey. The government had tasked the Committee to devise a methodology by which error of identification could be brought down to nil as far as practicable and the Committee stood up to the expectation. Most remarkable aspect of the recommendation of the Saxena Committee is its transparency in approach. All the parameters are verifiable unlike its predecessors that contained many foggy areas of parameters providing ample scope for manipulation with immunity. Secondly, the scoring exercise is far less cumbersome. The survey schedule is terse, simple and easy to use. It saves time and energy but gathers relevant information on living condition. The committee recommended the upward revision of the ceiling to 50 per cent deviating from the usual practice of concurring with Planning Commission estimate of head count poverty ratio reported from time to time. The committee deserves appreciation for enhancing the entitlement for the poor in respect of food security coverage for the poor. The recent spurt in food inflation has deepened the poverty. Expanded food security coverage goes a long way in protecting the poor.

6.3 Saxena and Multidimensional Poverty

Material poverty is defined world over in the same way. It is a condition of life for a section of population marked by want of basic goods and services. The latter two words are important in understanding what exactly is meant by poverty as a state of being by humankind. The word 'basic' needs elaboration to understand its connection with conceptualization of poverty. The basic is minimum needs to be met by an individual for social participation. An individual must have command over the goods and services to lead a healthy life free from mental and physical distress. To put in different way, an effective social life requires meeting basic needs. The person who fails to meet the basic needs is poor. But what bundle of commodities and services constitute basic need is much contested. The composition of goods and services in the bundle widely varies. This variance is inevitable as value judgment in every society differs substantially. The bundle that contains the basic needs in a particular society is exclusively its own. How a society views the particular State of being as poor for its members is constructed within that society and, therefore, it is exclusive. It not only varies across societies and regions but it also varies over time. The bundle that made poverty line basket hundred years ago in the society no longer holds good now in the present time in the same society.

Social values and world view go on changing with the passage of time. When bare necessities of life were confined to bread, shelter and clothing, poverty was defined as a state of living in which one or all of this triad were missing. The list of 'missing' that characterizes economic poverty is now long. It includes the vital driver of human capital formation: health and education. There is increasing recognition worldwide that poverty is multidimensional. It encompasses many other deprivations in addition to income deficits. The one-dimensional approach for poverty focuses exclusively on purchasing power or earning ability. The customary practice has been to look at per capita G.N.P. at the national or sub national level to gauge the incidence of poverty. Income poverty is still a dominant measure of poverty world over. The world Bank used its one dollar per capita per day as an international benchmark to gain idea not only about global poverty but also can undertake inter-country comparison on the depth and reach of poverty across nations. The Bank also put $ 2 per capita per day as threshold limit for identifying vulnerable population. The last category of people identified on the basis of per capita daily income is better placed than the poor but they always run the risk of slipping into poverty. The Bank, therefore, insists on governments of poorer nations to enlarge the coverage of anti-poverty programmes to include these vulnerable groups.

6.4 Multidimensional Poverty *versus* One Dimensional Poverty

Poverty is the state of being of persons beset by scarcity of commodities. How much of commodities and what types of them would be required for living in a society is always context specific and value-laden. The characteristics of poverty are not uniform and universal across diverse societies in the world. A person may be poor as she is dubbed by her society and she may not be so in other society where she visits or emigrate for permanent living. The question that naturally haunts one's mind is why a particular society characterizes a living condition as state of poverty while other society may not do the same. This differential characterization is fundamentally driven by differentiated benchmark of variation across societies relating to bundle of commodities, the access or denial of which makes a person poor or non-poor. Poverty as defined by inability to purchase or to consume these basic commodities by the individual has been the problem of human civilization for thousand of years. This is not a modern malady. But it has captured global attention in the aftermath of the Second World War. The destruction and the holocaust brought about by the devastating war imperilled the world never seen before. Starvation, chronic hunger, infant mortality, epidemics, persistent mortality, widespread morbidity, civil war, communal riot and many other varieties of social ills besieged the humanity but befell overwhelmingly on the underdeveloped world. Poverty was considered as global challenges to be fought collectively.

The world community began to conceive the condition of poverty as income shortfall of a section of citizens. The poor lacks the purchasing power to have command over commodities the consumption of which is a must for physical living in a society. The prosperity of nation has been gauged by per capita Gross National Product or per capita income in a mundane sense. Nations of the world began to be classified in three categories: High income countries, middle income countries and low income countries. The first group comprises of industrially developed countries mostly located in the North America and in European continent joined much later by South East Asian nations notably Japan, Korea and Singapore. Middle income countries are located mostly in Latin America and low income countries are situated predominantly in Africa, South Asia as well as in Middle America. The World Bank collects the per capita income data to gain idea about their accomplishment and task ahead for removal of poverty from the world. The Bank publishes World Development Report where it presents the per capita income of the world nations in terms of purchasing power parity in United States dollars. The report also provides a picture of income inequality within each of the countries. It was revealed by the report for 1995 that income inequality is more prominent in middle income countries of Latin America than that in high income countries of the western world.

Persistence of inequality in income distribution within a country and its growing extent over time is an indication that economic development process bypasses a significant section of its population. Increasing per capita GNP over a period of time in a country may be coterminous with swelling magnitude of poor. Thus per capita income fails to reveal the real economic predicament of citizens where income-inequality is very high. Thus per capita income as a measure of economic wellbeing in particular and overall wellbeing in general was subject to questioning from many corners. Development economists particularly were uncomfortable with this measure. Many of them were pressing for a new and broad based measure to gauge human welfare that would capture not only income but also other two dimensions of quarterly of life: health and education. Human Development Index (HDI) incorporating achievements in per capita income, health and education attainments in a single scale for measurement was developed by leading economist at the behest of the United Nations and under the auspices of the World Bank. Human Development Report began to be prepared for each nation by the leading experts on the basis of the data available to them relating to these three aspects of human prosperity. Suitable formula was devised to obtain a score between 0 to 1 for each country. A list of the countries in accordance with the score obtained by them, beginning from the highest score and ending up to lowest score is prepared. A country's performance with regard to human development of her citizens can be gauged by the rank or relative position in the list. For example, in 2006 India was ranked 126th out of 117 with a human development score of 0.611. China's rank was 81 with HDL score of 0.768. Norway stood first in the world with HDI of 0.965.

Thus the advent of Human Development Index as a yardstick for human progress in each nation was a landmark change in the worldview about poverty. It was a pioneering move in conceiving poverty as multidimensional rather than one-dimensional in only income accrual. This was a remarkable turnaround and was applauded by all. Income poverty is just one part of human poverty and the latter is a broader concept that entails lacks of other means to achieve fulfilment of life. Thus it goes beyond the purchasing power of people to have command over minimum bundle of commodities to keep the body and soul together. It has been observed for quite a long time that a country with relatively higher per capita income can be discredited with lower life expectancy. Citizens cannot survive beyond 40 to 45 years on an average in this relatively affluent country. However it is possible to live a healthy and active life up to 85 or even 90 years in this world and this has been proved by Scandinavian countries followed closely by a many other countries in Europe. These countries having very high longevity of people are also high income countries and lower income inequality. The examples of high income countries should not be invoked as instances of high longevity. Incomparable examples are futile exercises. Examples of longer life expectancy in low income countries unequivocally tell that income is not only condition to lead a fuller life. It is interesting to observe that two countries might have similar per capita income but life expectancy in one is higher than the other. Higher life expectancy is an important achievement for any nation and historically it is a veritable outcome of development process like better education, nutritious diets, health, care, sanitation and many other provisions in society that prevents untimely death and reduces child mortality rate. Thus a country can be 'income poor' in the sense that her per capita GNP is on the lower side but this same country is comparatively richer in one aspect of human development, i.e., health. Physical wellbeing of citizens in this reference country is much better than its neighbour whose per capita income is higher. Therefore poverty in the broader sense should encompass, not only lack of income but also ill-health resulting in shorter life span of citizens. Let us take the example of Sri Lanka and Guatemala to illustrate what has been said. The World Development Report of 1995 revealed that per capita incomes in PPP dollar was 2,990 in Sri Lanka and 3,350 in Guatemala but life expectancy in Sri Lanka was 72 years and the same in Guatemala is 65 years. The most astounding aspect of Sri Lanka's human development performance relates to infant mortality rate (IMR) per 1000 live births. IMR was as low as 18 in Sri Lanka and it was as high as 48 in Guatemala. Adult literacy rate in Sri Lanka was almost 90 per cent and in Guatemala the same is just 54 per cent.

This instance is pointing out to the inadequacy and hollowness of income poverty as measure of wellbeing. The one-dimensional approach of income as measure of poverty falls short of what is globally accepted as human poverty. Multidimensional Poverty Index (MPI) is comprehensive tool widely accepted for measuring human poverty. MPI measures three attainments: Education, Health and Standard of Living. Education includes two indicator years of schooling and school attendance where each of the indicators is weighted equally at 1/6. Likewise, health has two indicators: child mortality and nutrition. Each indicator is weighted equally at 1/6. A family will be treated as deprived if at least a child had died. Likewise, a family will be deprived if any adult or child is malnourished. Standard of living has six components: electricity, drinking water, sanitation, flooring, cooking fuel, household assets. During 2007, MPI was estimated for 104 countries and 78.5 per cent of world's population. It came out that 32 per cent were identified as multidimensional poor. It was also revealed that 51 per cent of MPI poor live in South Asia. Thus MPI which captures broader aspects of poverty is an improved measure of human deprivation. Measurement and identification of poor are important tasks of the state that commits itself for eradication of poverty through state action. A democratic state as has been said earlier is accountable to the people. Failure to deliver goods during the term of office results in rejection by people when the election comes every five years. The poor themselves make a solid voters' group and poverty can be turned in a pivotal electoral issue. The poor can exert pressure on the government for formulating and implementing pro-poor policies.

CHAPTER 7

Facets of Poverty

7.1 Why Poverty is an Issue of Concern?

The persistence of poverty among a substantial section of human population in the contemporary world is the greatest threat to humanity. Many regions in the world, particularly the region in sub-Saharan Africa and South Asia are afflicted with endemic poverty. This regional concentration of poverty is not only an outcome of uneven progress across the globe but poses a serious threat to world progress and global prosperity. Poverty cannot only be defining feature of many world regions but it can be widespread in certain regions within the same country. The latter is also the manifestation of lopsided development within the national boundary. The development has to be balanced and even where no part or no regions should be left behind to grapple with poverty. This uneven development that results in concentration of poverty and deprivation in certain regions within the country provide fertile field for cultivating separatist politics. The contemporary Maoist violence in the tribal inhabited forest regions comprising of around one hundred districts in India's heartland has erupted largely due to development deficits in this area. If government attention is diverted from development initiative for focusing on law and order and for suppressing divisive uprising, then this investment of public resources for non-development agenda deepens poverty rather than mitigates it.

The armed rebellion against the state spearheaded by the Maoist groups in the tribal region encompassing the heartland of India is often passed on as law and order problem. The latter, thus, calls for the deployment of paramilitary forces to assist and strengthen the state police to reign on naxalite insurgency. This gesture of the state is akin to fighting the disease only without trying to root out the causes that continuously generate the disease. Thus endemic poverty can cause social destabilization and unrest when the poverty and deprivation are used as weapons for fomenting collective grievances against the state system accusing it as only agent creating development deficits. Thus persistent poverty in a region can help in generating divisive forces in the country. Therefore, poverty is a social malaise of concern as a progenitor of social chaos and disequilibrium. The foot soldiers of religious terrorism are recruited from poverty stricken areas and from poor families of urban and semi urban areas. This lends credence to the argument that poverty not only affects the poor by depriving her of basic needs for a decent living in a society, it creates an unwelcome situation where social living even by rich is threatened. The social instability and chaos have their own cost. It makes living conditions of the rich more strenuous and stressful where peace is lost and social living is stained and distressed. The social harmony is likely to be elusive in a situation where a significant number of people live in perpetual penuries.

7.2 Poverty and Democracy

Poverty is anathema to democracy the pursuit of which is hindered by economic adversity suffered by a section of population. Poverty stands in the way of political participation of the poor in the democratic state. Democracy is devoid of its essence when a selection of people does not take part in active political process. Democracy as a form of governance is always people-centric. The government is formed by the people, the government is run by the people and government is assessed by the people. Each and every person has equal stake in the polity and in the formation of system that governs. Every citizen has say in framing policies and enacting legislation that affect him. So citizens have to be proactive to ensure that right policies are framed and policies are implemented in its true spirits that aim at highest attainable welfare of the citizens. Citizens' active and informed participation in democratic process is the only key to success of democratic polity.

But that participation and making informed choices by citizens can be confounded by many unfreedom like illiteracy and poverty. The unlettered citizen is constrained to make informed choice in political judgment. The making of choice is the function of flow of information that citizen can access and assimilate. The citizen has to read and understand the written information to make autonomous decision and choice. Illiteracy stands in the way of forming informed opinion, for example, which party to vote for in multiparty electoral battle. Denial of entry to the world of written information for a section of citizenry is same as denial to democratic participation. Thus participatory democracy, as a basic premise of democratic practice and principles, demands that literacy must be universal. The foundation of education and delivery system must be inclusive. The essence of democracy as an overriding principle can be missing where illiteracy persists. People can be swayed by misinformation provided by others. Educated citizens are less likely to be swayed as they can verify the veracity of information by accessing the written sources which unlettered cannot do. There is always a yawning gap between the understanding power of educated citizens and those of uneducated ones in the conduct of interacting and negotiating with the literate world. The unlettered are denied of the development opportunities. Education instils the capability to judge. It imparts the training of minds to undertake critical judgment about the happenings around them to make right choice and opinion. Education can empower the citizens through enhancing intellectual capacity. Citizens are trained to argue and protest in case government fails to deliver or when government takes recourse to undemocratic policies to serve the interest of the few, neglecting others. Put in other words, the citizens must have power to dissent and oppose when governance turns out to be exclusionary. Thus, democracy in its letter and spirit, cannot flourish in the society where educational opportunities have eluded a significant section of the citizenry.

Poverty can curtail even strip the poor of the power or autonomy to vote for the right candidate or right political party whom she think serves them the best. The poor is subject to constraint while exercising his choice through casting vote at election that takes place at regular intervals in the democratic polity. Quality of democracy is compromised when poor electors are wooed and are forced to vote for a party which have control on them. The poor are susceptible to influence that turn them virtually into pawn in the hands of political leaders. Economic empowerment of the electors is the key to exercising or creating the agencies of the poor. Thus while illiteracy imposes barrier in accessing written information to form informed views, endemic poverty and destitution restrict the autonomy and agency. Political parties in the absence of strict vigil by independent election authority, try to buy the voters' minds through gifts and payment in cash. These clandestine activities of political parties as well as of the contesting candidates during election have been exposed by the alert media. Money and muscle power still rule the roost where electors are economically distraught and for them the need of survival at the moment is more pressing than any other consideration.

There is no one-to-one correspondence between democracy and poverty which means that the presence of the former has nothing to do as such with the latter. Democracy as a form of governance neither generates poverty nor eliminates it on its own. There are 'poor democracies' in the world today. Many less developed countries, having democratic structure of governance, are steeped in endemic poverty and the pace of poverty reduction is also slow. While democracy and mass poverty can co-exist, non-democratic authoritarian regimes in many parts of African continent have equally deplorable record in eliminating poverty. Both of these regime structures can survive and flourish in the ambience of poverty and deprivation of masses. Singapore, Korea, Taiwan are examples of authoritarian governance but their respective record in eliminating poverty is remarkable which many democracies in the world today consider it as distant dream. China's exemplary achievement in reducing poverty and undernourishment during last fifty years should not be overlooked. It certainly deserves mention as the situations existed in both of our countries half a century ago were similar in many ways. The post-revolution China like our post-independent India had embarked on the journey on the thorny paths beset with problems of overpopulation, endemic poverty, mass illiteracy, malnutrition, economic backwardness and varieties of adversities. China's incidence of poverty has drastically come down now far faster than what India could achieve during the same time.

But the record of the Chinese regime in reducing poverty is stained with black spot of human rights violation, abuse and misuse of power and state oppression. India's performance on this score is certainly not robust as that of her giant neighbour but she has to cautiously tread on balance between fight against poverty and fostering of democracy as essential feature of her governance. Can the blame for slower rate of poverty reduction in India since her independence be put squarely on the shoulder of democracy as a basic feature of her polity? On the other hand no one can surely say that India could altogether eliminate her poverty, like her many counterparts in the South East Asian region if she follow their footsteps, i.e., embracing authoritarians instead of democracy. The secrets of success in fight against poverty in the South East Asian nations lie not in the form of their political regime but in the nature of public policies adopted at the right moment. The communist China in the sixties and many of her neighbours in the Southeast Asian region notably, Korea, Singapore, Taiwan, Hong Kong could implement universal health care and compulsory universal education for children. The fruits of this remarkable public policy were reaped by them decades later during 80s. These countries could embark on such drastic measures and allocated huge resources for development of human capital at a time when their economies were characterized by low growth, poverty, over population, low skill, backward agriculture and many other ills that hold back economic expansion. This was very radical measure for these nations to allocate so much public resources for health care and education which no other countries with comparable per capita income could dare to think of. The dividend for this bold public action began to shower from the beginnings of 80s when these economies began to open up to the outside worldly particularly to the western industrialized world. This was a historic change over from autarky to trade openness. New opportunities for trade and development began to show up. Industrial investment from the western world in the newly opened economies poured in. New industrial projects came up one after another built on new technology.

Technological collaboration and joint venture in industrial undertakings paved the way for emerging as developed industrial nation under the tutelage of authoritarian regime. These regions created and fostered such policy ambience through crafting trade and industrial policies in favour of privatization and openness. These emerging industrial economies began to target the world market for their industrial products, which include a vast range of products from computer chips, computer hardware, electronic gazettes, and consumer durables to stylish motor vehicles. The economies began to expand on the back of unprecedented industrial venture and export growth within very short time. Export policies were liberalized for further expansion of exports. Industries that met the demand for exports were promoted and favoured. These countries could make use of the opportunities of global trade and technology transfer for eradication of poverty. The spectacular economic growth that followed the radical policy changes was instrumental in raising the living standard of the people. The benefit of global trade and development in these nations did not pass on to a limited few rather it was more or less universal. This horizontal distribution was possible only because of universal education and health care pursued a couple of decades ago over there. People at large could easily join the economic activities in manufacturing that come up in large number in the wake of global integration and export expansion. The manufacturing activities in the emerging export industries. People were already equipped with basic skill in literacy and numeracy with further training for skill formation in specific jobs. They were already enjoying comparatively better health status, longer life expectancy, and reduced infant mortalities rate as a result of provisioning of universal free health care system for these citizens. Thus economic benefits were evenly distributed in these regions despite having authoritarian regime. Poverty was removed through work opportunities, higher wages, non-wage economic benefits like housing and other facilities that moves up standard of living of the workers.

Thus South East Asian nations stand on one side as examples of market-led economic growth percolating down to the common people because of better human resources created by the authoritarian regime. Poverty can be eliminated through two ways; direct and indirect. The cases of South East Asian nations illustrates the working of the indirect method where government need not adopt or implement anti-poverty social welfare programmes for the poor to lift them above poverty line. In contrast, the democracy in India has been flourishing with direct method for fighting poverty. Antipoverty programme in myriad forms and features are underway in poor democracies as well as in poor non-democracies in African as well as in Latin American regions. International Donor agencies and global charities have undertaken poverty alleviation projects directly in sub-Saharan African nations. In many cases, however, these agencies are working on joint venture providing resources and technical guidance leaving the onus of implementing to respective governments. The World Bank has several antipoverty programmes currently underway in Africa to comply the UN Millennium Development Goals to bring down the incidence of poverty to half of the present rate by 2015. Removal of poverty from the region characterized by the long history of its presence, weak or fragile political institutions, unstable governments, ethnic strife, corrupt leaderships are really challenging. One may cast doubt about the efficacy of World Bank aided antipoverty programme through any short cut method one of which is cash 'transfer' directly to the poor. This move often promoted by international agencies has come under severe criticism from many corners who dub it as an attempt to heal the wound rather than treating the root cause. Anti-poverty programmes are in vogue in India since the initiation of the First Five-Year Plan in various forms. New programmes are announced in each year's budget proposal either replacing some of the existing ones or something adding up to existing stock. Programmes are named after the architects of free India. The party in power tends to project itself as friend and protector of poor in the hope of creating assured support base by announcing such schemes mainly on the eve of election. Some of the programmes are social security benefits meant exclusively for the weaker sections, those who cannot fend for themselves. The defenceless citizens in India comprises of the widows, the elderly and frail people, disabled persons, nomadic tribes, chronically ill persons, the destitute living on alms, pavement dwellers, scavengers, and many such helpless people. Government, constitutionally bound as highest organ of welfare state, must appear as saviour for these hapless citizens. Ministry of Social Welfare, both at the Centre as well as State level, formulate and implement social welfare schemes for economically vulnerable section. Old age pensions schemes for the aged and ailing persons in the landless agricultural labour families is one such specific scheme for the rural areas.

The subsidized foodgrain sale under Public Distribution System exclusively for the BPL families is India's most controversial and massive food based anti-poverty programme. Each identified BPL families are entitled to get 25 kilos of rice or wheat at rupees 3 per kilo from the nearest PDS shop. Mid day meal scheme for the school-going children and 'Sahaya' scheme for providing cooked meal for the disabled and old persons are instances of direct 'feeding' programme. BPL family members are also entitled to free health care services in the government run hospitals on production of BPL cards. This health care benefits is also an obverse of anti-poverty programme as it relieves the poor of burdensome health expenditure. Subsidized food for the poor, direct dole or provision for the destitute, low cost housing for the poor and even free health care for them is all survival assistance by nature. These distraught people who fail to arrange for themselves the bare minimum for living in a society are always beleaguered by survival or living deficits. The social welfare programmes are meant for filling these 'survival' deficits. Life could by further pushed to destitution even starvation if government does not take care of them through provision of survival necessities or essentials. Each and every ministries and departments of the Union Government as well as of the State governments has social welfare programmes for the benefit and better life for the poors.

Social welfare programmes in India meant for disadvantageous people are different from other poverty alleviation projects aiming at creating opportunities for economic activity. The difference between the former and the latter relates to approach and goal of them. The healthy adults can be employed in income generation economic activities if such opportunities are created by the State. This action, however, cannot be effected for people who are frail, old or disabled. Thus a distinct demarcation is present between adult and able bodied poor and the dependent incapable poor. The latter can hardly fend for themselves. The state has to come forward to protect her defenceless citizens in a manner that different from what it undertakes for the able bodied poor. The poor while physically able is constrained by lack of skill and other means to take part in gainful economic activities. Government can provide training for the unskilled poor for taking up income generating project along with subsidized credit.

7.3 Poverty Alleviation Programmes in Democratic India

India has had a number of antipoverty programmes since the early 1960s. These include, among others, the National Rural Employment Programme (NREP) and the Rural Landless Employment Guarantee Programme. The National Rural Employment Programme came into effect in 1980 replacing the earlier Food for Work Programme. The objective was to use unemployed and underemployed workers to build productive community assets. The Rural Landless Employment Guarantee Programme was adopted in 1983 to address the plight of the poorest of the rural poor by expanding employment opportunities through creating the rural infrastructure as a means of promoting rapid economic growth. There were many problems with the implementation of these and other schemes, but observers credit them with helping reduce poverty. To improve the effectiveness of the National Rural Employment Programme, in 1989 it was combined with the Rural Landless Employment Guarantee Programme and renamed Jawahar Rozgar Yojana. Integrated Rural Development Programme (IRDP) was a grandiose scheme, introduced by the government of India during early 80s throughout length and breadth of the country. It incorporated many other schemes within its fold. Under this scheme, an adult member of the selected poor households in the rural area was provided with low cost credit coupled with government subsidy to acquire productive assets. He could choose one among a long list of projects designed and planned, taking into account the forward and backward linkage in the particular socio-economic setting. The District Rural Development Agency (DRDA), as an apex body at the district level, was entrusted with the task for preparing such project list after careful study about the availability of inputs and market for outputs. IRDP was hailed as a remarkable instrument for alleviating poverty through creating self employment and by promoting entrepreneurship among the rural poor. The fundamental objective of this massive self-employment programme involving thousands of crores of budgetary resources was to lift a significant section of the poor above the poverty line. Economic growth itself could not accomplish this task. The 'trickle down effect' of the growth process was missing. India's economy, in the beginning of the 80s began to exhibit a higher growth rate and upward turn from what is known as 'Hindu' rate of growth. But the expansion of the national economy eluded the millions of poor, which turned into serious issue for the government. Even the World Bank conceded the absence of trickle down in the developing world. Poverty alleviation programmes were formulated in many developing countries at the behest of the World Bank. IRDP became a global movement to fight poverty. It remained India's massive anti-poverty programme for very long years until the advent of (Swarna Jayanti Swarojgar Yojana) SGSY which was another form of self employment programme that focused on forming self help groups for undertaking income earning projects.

The fundamental difference between the self-help group scheme under SGSY and IRDP pertains to organizational structure for productive activities. While IRDP was meant for individual beneficiary who is liable to repay loans taken from the bank, his or her own efforts, entrepreneurial skill, business acumen, tenacity and dynamism are collection of qualities required for success of the project. The latter is measured by the ability to repay the loan out of incremental income generated through the project he has taken up. Self-help groups on the other hand are collective body of at least twenty members of the same neighbourhoods coming together for the sake of undertaking income generating activities collectively on the principle of mutual co-operation and trust. There is other difference between them that should not be missed out while comparison is being done. IRDP projects where allocated primarily to male members of the households while SHGs are elementarily female dominated body. Therefore, there is collective liability and group involvement where profits are shared equally and losses also if occurs and have to be faced in equal amount. Rural women do not spontaneously form their groups and perform all official formalities to give effect to the formation. The local government engages local youth to mobilize the women to form groups and assist in the formative process. A leader is elected in the first meeting of the group after naming the group for the sake of its identity. Later, an account has to be opened in the name of the group at the nearest bank. This collective responsibility and group liability have enormous impact. IRDP failed to achieve the desired result and its failure is largely due to the lack of commitment on the part of the recipients of the benefits of self-employment programme. Studies undertaken to evaluate IRDP have revealed that there were fundamental lacuna in the implementation of the projects in India. Firstly, the recipients were not motivated and trained to take up a project. Projects were assigned to the beneficiaries by the government officials in a lackadaisical way without imparting training necessary for undertaking particular project. A landless agricultural labourer, for example, was given a sewing machine to make readymade shirts to be sold in the local market. The usual practice was to disburse subsidy within the quarter of the year to comply the directive from above. The said labourer without any prior knowledge about the trade, without the knowledge about the titbits of the business would be pushed to the wall. He would neither be able to repay the loan nor can earn enough income for the family. He would eventually discontinue the business and would sell off the assets. There was hardly any check and balance in the system. Default rate was too high; subsidy money was spent on conspicuous consumption as well as on other non-productive purpose instead of making use for the business.

Both IRDP and SHGs under SGSY are self employment programmes for the unemployed youths. They undertake business activities. The capital and the skill have to be wholly or partly provided by the government. The provision of subsidized capital to the little enterprises was to help them in the formative years in business. This is akin to watering a newly planted sapling in the courtyard because it is incapable on its own to extract water from the soil under it. The government is committed to the people and is accountable to them in a democratic polity. People's welfare to the maximum extent possible, should be the only concern and priority task of the democratic government. Human welfare can not be effected and sustained without removing poverty and associated adversities in life. The government not only takes care of the old and feeble, disabled and the defenceless women and the children as their protector but also must endeavour to improve the economic situation of the poor endowed with capacity but constrained by means to overcome poverty. The government must provide the necessary means through appropriate measure to the poor so that they can pursue self-employment projects to generate income. Since India's First Five Year Plan down to the ongoing Plan, self- employment programmes as a means for poverty alleviation remain in the forefront of priorities. Its deficiencies were pointed out in evaluative exercises by its pre-eminence as an instrument was never belittled.

The direct approach, in case of India to eliminate poverty, consists grossly of three measures: social welfare benefits, self-employment programmes and wage employment programmes. Our planners could understand that the three methods have to be combined to end massive poverty in India. Wage employment programmes unlike self-employment do not demand any skill in trade or initial capital on the part of the poor adults. Thus wage employment provision by the government for the teeming millions of unskilled poor adults holds the key for eradication of poverty. The significance of wage employment programme in the armoury of anti-poverty shells cannot be belittled. Out planners have been trying with this instrument for quite some time from now. Food for work programme, introduced during 70s, as a pioneer in this genre came into being in the background of endemic undernourishment particularly in the rural areas. The idea behind the framing of this national programme was to provide foodgrains directly to the workers instead of payment in cash. It had twin objectives to achieve. One was to create rural infrastructure through provision of public works in villages. The other one was to fight malnutrition and sporadic hunger among poor households that not only began to be condemned by international community but was also posing serious challenge to our government. This programme later renamed as National Rural Employment Programme (NREP) later with some modifications structure of the scheme.

The ongoing wage employment programme by the name of N.R.E.G.S. prefixed with the name of the father of our nation, Mahatma Gandhi, is unique and second to none in the world in many ways. Firstly, it is the largest in the contemporary world by its size, coverage and financial provisioning. The targeted beneficiaries of this mammoth programme could easily outnumber the entire population of West Europe or the whole of Australia. Secondly, unlike its predecessor this programme is rights-based whereby the state in a general sense and the local self government in the practical sense are bound by law to provide job to the job seekers on demand within fifteen days of submitting prayer for job. National Rural Employment Guarantee act confers the right to employment for 100 days in a year to adults in the rural areas. This is an epoch making gesture on the part of the Central Government as a potent instrument for providing livelihoods during lean season in agriculture. The scheme also provides for unemployment allowances for job seekers in case of delay in assignment of work within 15 days of job application. As far as practicable the local government must provide job within the neighbourhoods of the workers. The scheme as far as practicable has been designed to make it transparent, participatory and broad-based. All job seekers have to register their names and express their willingness in writing to the Gram Panchayat office within whose jurisdictions they reside.

NREGS is thus an imposing example for direct poverty reduction measure undertaken in the largest democracy in the world. The programme is just few years in operation but it has drawn attention from all corners as a symbol of radical swift in the government policy towards wage employment. It has been hailed by right activists as a remarkable move towards fulfilment of right to life in India which encompassed right to adequate livelihoods for her citizens. The scheme came into effect at a time when concern began to be aired in different corners that India's spectacular economic growth momentum would evaporate in the face of global meltdown. India's cherished goal to build an egalitarian society on the pillars of social justice and democracy seems to have taken backseat in the euphoria to catch up with growth performance of neighbouring China. The programme was mooted and undertaken in right earnest to render the growth process inclusive so that the underdogs of the society can also obtain benefits on equal terms. The huge financial resources needed to run this employment guarantee programme was made available through higher tax revenue as a consequence of expansion of our economy. There are so many shortcomings that blight this massive employment scheme. Some of its loopholes have been detected. The target of 100 days for all the States and regions in India is yet to be fulfilled.

Thus a democratic nation-state can adopt pro-poor development policies that can strike directly at poverty or it can be less proactive. It can wait for national economic prosperity and expansion of economy, the fruits of which will trickle down. The economic growth will have indirect effect on poverty. But how the democratic state would tend to act on removal of poverty is a significant issue to reflect on. The party that forms the government on getting peoples' mandate have to remain committed to peoples' causes and popular aspirations during the term of its office. After the expiry of the term, the party has to face the electors for its return to power in the next term. This is the beauty of the parliamentary system of democracy based on adult franchise. People can indirectly participate in framing public policy and enacting laws in the legislature that best serve this interest. This popular participation and influence over decision making process are altogether missing in the non-democratic authoritarian regime that may not care peoples' concern and problems and still continue to stay in power through military might. However it does not lead us to the conclusion that authoritarian regime is always associated with repression and destitution of the subjects. Here is no hurdle on the way as such to adopting pro-poor public policies by such forms of governance.

The problem with India is that the vast sea of poor people is not organized as constituency of poor to exert influence on the public policy. The poor in India is not undifferentiated categories of people. They are put into different boxes of caste and communal identities. The presence of caste as social identity is very strong in India that people tend to honour and preserve. The bonding among a group of people on the basis of caste is so strong in India that it overpower others identities and affiliations. The poor, as a uniform electoral constituency, failed to emerge only because caste consideration predominate all other considerations in all social actions. Even the Panchayat system as a symbol of grass root democracy in rural India is being defiled by the self-styled caste leaders who are spreading communitarian message among the caste groups. *Khap* panchayat or caste panchayat are gaining unofficial status for dispensing disputes and delivering justice that go against the spirit of our Constitution.

This caste panchayats are encouraging honour killing as a form of brutal punishment for the action approved by this country's sacred Constitution but disapproved by the particular caste. The dominance of caste affinity impedes the emergence of collective voice of the poor in India beyond any other caste or communal identities. For example, reservations of job in government service for a particular caste can be a vibrant political issue in the electoral battle but the same zeal is absent in making land reform a priority political issue. The difference between populist job reservation for a particular caste and uniform radical measure of land reforms lies principally on the depth and reach of impact of these two programmes. Former is ornamental in nature having very little lasting impact for the caste group for which job reservation is granted. It has a very narrow focus while the latter has broader goal and has far reaching impact in improving the quality of life for the underprivileged. But the government seems to be more occupied with the task of effecting job reservation for a particular caste group rather than mulling over to enact land reforms for better life and livelihoods for the agricultural community. From the viewpoints of electoral benefits, effecting job reservation is more paying than land reform because caste group is more organized as solid constituencies of voters. Electoral gain is far bigger in case of caste-based reservation than any general anti-poverty programmes that does not target any specific caste group. Despite irritable pull of electoral gain for party in power, the Indian democracy has witnessed series of anti-poverty programme since her independence for ameliorating the economic predicament of the poor and vulnerable who constitute a majority of electors but not yet organized as a homogeneous group for exerting pressure on government to consider poverty eradication as a priority electoral agenda.

7.4 Child Poverty

Child poverty as a field of study has emerged in recent times but has succeeded in capturing the attention of policy planners, development economists and social activists. It is gaining currency as well. Removal of child poverty has been taken up as a priority task where child poverty is acute. Is this any particular variety of household poverty? Or certain measure? Child poverty is, in essence, different from household poverty in generic sense of the term. Any household in purely economic sense or any family in general sense can be poor but child poverty relates poverty with child, therefore, any poor household without any child as member of that unit does not experience or undergo child poverty. Therefore, not all poor households are 'child poor' some of them may be. The first symptom or indicator of child poverty is the presence of at least one or more children born to a poor household in a technical sense or to a family in general sense. A child is poor if she is a member of a poor household. Household poverty poses a serious bottleneck to child's harmonious growth and development. There is a marked difference in opportunities to growth between children born to an impoverished family and their counterpart born to a relatively better off family. The sufferings start from the birth of child. The child born to an impoverished family is also likely to be begotten by the malnourished mother. Gender discrimination in the matter of food and nutrition even in poor families has been found to exist in a massive way. Prenatal care and nutrition for the pregnant mother as condition for the healthy growth of baby is conspicuously absent in poor households. The poor cannot afford such balanced diet, expensive prenatal medical attention and care for the pregnant women in the family. She cannot even indulge in the luxury of taking sufficient rest, staying away from onerous tasks in the household. The poor family cannot afford to engage others to substitute for the ailing and frail woman members. The women in the poor households not only perform household chores but also take part in productive work in the field as wage workers. Thus stoppage of wage work for the sake of taking rest by the pregnant mother is just cessation of income to the family and it heralds the onset of further misery associated with reduced income. The household poverty brings blow to the child when she is in the womb. She does not get needed nutrition from her mother's measly diet. Prenatal care is emphasised now worldwide as only way out to ensure the birth of healthy babies. The malnourished mother is most likely to give birth to crippled child.

Low Birth Weight (LBW) is the leading indicator of ill health among children. The incidence of LBW is alarmingly high in India largely because of neglect of health care of pregnant mother. Stressful life, overwork and lack of nutritious diet, lack of medical monitoring during pregnancy are associated with unwell offsprings. All kinds of physical disabilities and mental retardation detected in the infants are attributed mostly to prenatal health care neglect although genetic disorder is also dominant factor. Physical disability, deformation or absence of vital limbs of the body is not the only impediments to healthy and active life. Mental illnesses, learning incapacity, cognitive disorder, attention volatility, short temperedness, memory lapse are major mental disorders that can affect the new born if parental care and attention is altogether ignored. Growth stunting and growth wasting in children are not altogether unconnected with prenatal health care. Although postnatal health care of basic and lactating mothers are also equally important. Full course of immunization for the child is now accepted as key to child health and prevention of deformities that can afflict the child. The plight of polio affected children needs no description. Therefore, polio vaccination for all children is the only way out to prevent affliction of polio. Polio is preventable. Thus crippled health of the child is not only the manifestation of child poverty but also an outcome of it. Child poverty is not notionally confined to belonging of a child to a poverty ridden family. It encompassed a broad range of deprivation that holds back the child in attaining perfect childhood. Physical deformities and persistent illness impedes normal growth of the child. Child poverty is not income poverty or consumption poverty of the children' households, it includes deprivation and impediments that restrains child well-being.

7.5 Feminization of Poverty

Poverty as a cause of human distress has been plaguing the human race almost since its birth on this planet. It was widespread during the pre-modern phase of human history. Material scarcity was usual feature of human existence when human life was nasty, short and brutish. However, the depth of and spread of poverty could not be perfectly ascertained, primarily for two reasons. One is the absence of the concept of poverty as a symptom of distressed state of human living. The other is the absence of any descriptions chronicled in any written text that could turn out to be any authentic source of information. The period preceding the Renaissance and Enlightenment is a dark era for which construction of the concept of poverty is deeply problematic. Enlightenment thinkers began to view human distress caused by scarcity of material goods comprising of food, clothing and shelter was unacceptable. They began to argue that this miserable state of human living could be altered by appropriate public action. The advent of the age of reasoning gave birth to critical thinking among the forerunners that poverty was not preordained state or curse or any handiwork of any invisible superpower beyond our reach and comprehension. The reasons for poverty could be easily located. Logical understanding of poverty among masses took root gradually.

Poverty is no longer an issue of concern for the national government only. The international community is equally if not more concerned. The United Nations Development Programme is a special UN organ created to eradicate poverty from the poor regions of the world. The UNDP would support the national governments in their effort to eliminate extreme poverty in the respective countries. The UNDP has recently introduced Multi-Dimensional Poverty Index that tries to look at poverty beyond income shortfalls. Contemporary concept of poverty is much more comprehensive as it views it from the angle of human deprivation. Income shortfall is unidimensional view of poverty. This short-sighted description is replaced by broader outlook on poverty. Gender dimension of poverty is rather contemporary proposition in line with the thoughtful effort on global scale to rescue poverty from the long confinement in the box of income shortfalls of human persons.

Question is being posed whether male persons and female persons bear brunt of poverty on equal terms. Feminists argue that women suffer more than the men by the onslaught of poverty. They tend to accuse global economic integration and neoliberal economic policies for the differential impact of poverty on women. National governments everywhere publish poverty statistics for the entire country. Segregated statistics on the basis of caste, gender, religion, circumstantial distinctiveness and disability are hard to come by. India in this regard is ahead of others in the group of developing countries. India's accomplishment in collecting and compilation of socio-economic data is commendable considering the huge population size, vast geographical area and remote locations inhabited by tribes or forest people isolated from the mainstream society. Classificatory statistics on poverty is, therefore, hard to come by. Still India has gone a long way in the preparation and presentations of demographic data classified on the basis of various categorizing features. Gendered dimension of poverty is a recent proposition which has gained currency after the fourth world conference on women held in Beijing in 1995. The UN has been insisting vigorously on mainstreaming gender perspective in all poverty eradication programmes. A group of persons comprising mainly of women's rights activists and feminists coined this pauperization of women as feminization of poverty which conveys the serious concern that women are hit more by poverty than the men. This accentuation is caused by the neoliberal economic policies adopted by the governments during the early 90s to conform the terms laid down by the Breton Woods institutions.

In line with disparities in the distribution of economic prosperities, disparities in deprivation among the poor on the basis of gender overwhelmingly prevail in the developing world. While concern is aired, the problem is diagnosed; there is sincere effort to locate the reason among the economists. The root can be traced to the unequal status of women in families from birth to death. The cycle of discrimination binds the women folk all throughout her life. It is said that in India, women are dependant on fathers until they are married off. They are dependant on husbands during entire conjugal life. During widowhood, until death, they are dependant on sons. Women depend on nearest male kin for shelter, food clothing and care. This dependence makes them subservient to males. Females obey while male dictates. Intra-household allocation of resources in the poorer households is alarmingly large in the poorer regions of the world comprising of South Asia, sub-Saharan Africa and in some parts of Latin America. Women face restriction on their choices and opportunities *vis-à-vis* men in the families first then at the level of society at large. Women's autonomy which is coined now as women's agency is either missing or strikingly restricted

However, it would be gross mistake to identify women's subjugation as a distinctive feature of third world society as if the latter is an organic whole without heterogeneity. This feature is neither irremovable permanent to third world nor the third world society is uniform in its organization and characters. Today's developed world has also inglorious part. They did not bestow equal state in every sphere of life to their women. Women's agency was missing there for a long time since emergence of modern nation-state in Europe and America. America, the oldest democracy in the world did not confer voting rights to women even in the early phase of twentieth century. Women certainly enjoy equal position over there but that was not accomplished overnight by a single action. That was the culmination for movement and triumph of humanity as a premise of social progress in the western world. It took many years to achieve the desired outcome of gender equality in all spheres of life in the developed world. India's record in the realm of women's emancipation is not altogether dismal. Indian women are participating and contributing in a bigger way now in nation building. Women in India are present in many fields: science, technology, business, industry, literature, education, politics and social service. But it would be erroneous to infer that the presence in these fields of a few women reflect gender equality in Indian society. The micro-credit movement in Bangladesh spearheaded by redoubtable economist and social activist Mr. Muhammad Yunus has greatly improved the women's position in underprivileged families. But the war is not won. Many miles are ahead to tread to reach the goal. Feminization of poverty is basically rooted in the unequal position of women. The statistics of deprivation for women worldwide is staggering: of the world's 800 million illiterate people more than two-thirds are women. Of the 110 million dropout children, three out of five are girls. In the field of politics, the statistics is also upsetting. Only 7.5 per cent of ministerial positions in governments in the world are occupied by women. These are just snapshots of women's political empowerment in the contemporary world. Feminization of poverty is also caused by lack of choice and opportunities to take part in political decision making process. Human poverty index and human development are important scale developed by the UN to measure human deprivation is gender neutral. They do not reveal the disparities in deprivations. The UN acted upon quickly to devise some instruments to gauge the extent of gender based poverty and development performance, Gender Development Index (GDI) and Gender Empowerment Index (GEN) were adopted.

Governments in many countries are now applying the formula to measure the women's position and relative deprivation occurring within the respective countries. Respective nations can take stock of their performance and devise action plans to improve the positions of women. The Beijing conference held under the auspices of the UN in 1995 is remarkable global event. It paved the way for a global thinking and action for women's empowerment. This was the first global gathering where the world leaders had converged not only to recognize feminization of poverty but also had pledged to undertake affirmative action to mitigate it. The world could realize that income poverty is not the ends but the means to achieve capability. Many African nations namely Uganda, Cameroon, Madagascar and Niger adopted women focussing anti poverty programme at the behest of the UN in the aftermath of the conference. Micro credit movement for the economic empowerment of underprivileged women in India and Bangladesh got fillip by the call aired from the conference. But the opponents of neo liberal global regime are vociferously pointing at the precarious plight of women created by liberalization and structural adjustment programmes. Economic reforms measures entails drastic cut in social sector expenditure which includes huge budgetary subsidies targeting the poor. Under neoliberal global regime developing countries have to keep their fiscal deficits in check. Withdrawal of subsidies and welfare programme for the poor as economic reform measures deepens poverty. Poor families are hit by the stoppage of social welfare programmes by the state. When scarcity invades a poor family, women and children are badly hit because they were already placed in weaker position *vis-à-vis* the male members. The meagre resources in the poor families are distributed in skewed way against the women. Further destitution leads to reducing of already skimpy resources comprising of food, clothes, shelter and health care for the women in the families. On the other hand economic reforms measures have been keeping away women from formal sector of employment. Lack of education among women folk has come on the way to learn skill to take part in formal employment. When formal sector employment characterized by job security and remunerative payments are keeping them off, they are drawn to informal sector as 'default activity' to earn a living to help their families. Informal sector of employment is not only volatile in nature; it pays little compared to the work load they take up. They are at the mercy of 'fly by night' employers who are beyond the control and reach of the government. Low pay, long hours of work and insecurity make the vulnerable women 'working poor' instead of only poor. Advocates of neoliberal policies, however, put the blame on the government for its failure to equip their citizens with appropriate skill to reap the benefits of global economic integration. Women rights activists point out towards the prevalence of extreme destitution among female headed households compared to male headed households.

7.6 Globalization and Poverty

Those who oppose neo-liberal economic doctrine tooth and nail straightway blames market reform for deepening poverty in the poor third world regions. The undertone is that poverty is generated by economic globalization. They put globalization and poverty in the same box as if they are inseparable companions cohabits all the time. The opponents in the fervour to attack neoliberal policies and their proponents do not tend to invest some thoughts on what exactly constitute globalization. Is it economic integration of the national economy with global economy in which flow of goods, services and technology between and among countries is unhindered? Trade, investment and transfer of technology between nations are being undertaken on unprecedented scale. Even intelligent people fail to differentiate between economic globalization currently underway and globalization in broader sense that began with the birth of humanity thousands of years ago. Globalization in that broader sense is an important feature of human civilization that goes beyond the limited realms of economic interconnection among countries. It has enriched the civilization and it will continue to be so in future. Free movement of people, of ideas, science, art, literature, and politics across nations characterizes the Globalization. This is very old and universally beneficial.

The spectacular advancement of science and technology over the last few centuries is largely due to the free flow of knowledge and ideas through global connection. The discoveries in medical science in western world during nineteenth and twentieth century have benefited people worldwide. The benefits of discoveries and new knowledge in medical science were not confined to the land of discovery. It reached far and wide subsequently. However the benefits could not be reaped by inhabitants of every location of the world. Two examples would suffice to demonstrate the far reaching beneficial effects of medical invention in the western world. Over the last hundred years, the average life span of people all over the world barring a few dark locations like Afghanistan and sub-Saharan countries has gone up significantly. In India, the life expectancy now stands at around 64 years which was 45 years during her independence, sixty plus years ago. Long and healthy life has always been a cherished target which has recently been incorporated in the human development index. Enhancement of life span over the years in India is undoubtedly a remarkable accomplishment. But did it happen? It has been possible in India through a combination of health awareness, sanitation, better nutrition, better health care, spread of literacy and education and most important among them is child immunisation programme. Better nutrition and improved living standard is always associated with longer life expectancy.

Scientific knowledge about hygienic living, sanitation and discoveries in medical sciences occurred in the western hemisphere but they reached the East by interconnection and exchange. Globalization thus helped not harmed. There is another instance of the far reaching impact of global inter-connection on the expanded life span of people. The world had helplessly witnessed elimination of population of a region in the event of the invasion of epidemic. Bubonic plague used to kill people periodically in fifteenth and sixteenth century Europe, malaria, Kalajar, Cholera visited India almost every year in the shape of man-eating demons even a few years back. The battle is not altogether won but the demons of horrifying epidemic is almost under leash. The diseases have been diagnosed by the medical community in the world through global interaction and exchange of ideas. Medical science has successfully found the way to prevent the onslaught of the killing epidemic. Mortality on a massive scale has been brought down significantly over the year. Speedy recovery is no longer out of reach. This is a significant step ahead in the advancement of humanity. The globalization that stands quite opposite of 'isolationist' existence of nations and the people are always welcome and beneficial. Globalization in the past not only helped the non-western world by the discoveries and scientific invention in the western world. It also worked other way round. The inventions of printing press, gun powder, wheel barrow and many other scientific and technological achievement occurred in the eastern world greatly helped the western world in the pursuit of their scientific progress.

Discoveries of decimal point and zero are India's immeasurable contribution to the humanity. Thus the world, east and west, gave and took through intercourse and exchange. Globalization is wrongly characterized and erroneously mentioned as something other than the broader meaning that it bears. Advocates of neoliberal economic policies argue that economic globalization reduces poverty. Poverty according to them is caused by lack of skill among the poor that stand on the way of taking of gainful employment in the economically productive activities. Globalization opens the door for investment within the country from abroad. Free movement of capital and technology in the wake of the removal of trade restriction have been helping local economy through initiation of productive activities. Foreign Technology would need new skill and knowledge in the productive activities. Transfer of technology follows transfer of new knowledge to the country not familiar with it. Dissemination of new knowledge in many fields of production would create demand among the local populace to learn the new skill needed for the industries and business. People would demand from the state for establishment of school and improvement of existing ones. Basic education is most likely to get boost. When the world is open to the people, they can evaluate their position *vis-à-vis* the outside.

Technology and foreign investment can efficiently use the natural resources of the home country that was never done before. Efficient allocation of resources for production of goods for the local as well as for global market would rejuvenate the domestic economy. Employment in the new areas of industries and business for the local people would certainly go up manifold. Increased earnings among the people would be spent on the local economy which would generate income and employment in turn. This beneficial impact is described by economist as 'trickle down' effect of development programme generally designed and funded by the external authority such as World Bank. Improved economic predicament even if for a few in the home country is characterized by demonstration effect. The others in the society would try to emulate them. Demand for better schooling to acquire skill would be built up paving the way for income and employment for larger section of society. Advocates of globalization press the point that economic interconnection reduces poverty by creating opportunities for employment in the emerging areas of productive undertakings. East Asian miracle is often referred by them as examples of beneficial outcome. Export-led growth of the East Asian countries have reduced poverty very fast from the period from 1960 to 1980. This is unprecedented in the contemporary history not only in Asian continent but also in the world. This rapid growth in these countries was possible in the wake of a bold step fraught with risk and uncertainty posed by global competition mainly from industrialist nations of the west. Globalization has helped in organizing production for export.

Proponents and opponents of globalization are at loggerheads hell-bent to argue out one another. The opposition is manifest in the protest movement in many parts of the world spearheaded by the anti-globalizers led mainly by left leaning intellectuals. The movements are organized not in third world regions going to be harmed by this economic phenomenon but in cities like Seattle, Paris, London and Geneva. Thousands of people in these affluent cities joined the rally decrying the neo-imperial regime under the tutelage of W.T.O. The birth of W.T.O. in the aftermath of GATT signed by almost all trading nation was hailed as reincarnation of western imperialism. It has come back in the new garb on the back of revolutionary advancement in communication technology. The west can now control the economy of the third world by remote control without physical presence in the former colonies. The protest movement in the west reached the shore of the developing world in no time. Advocacy for neo-liberal global order was muted by this vociferous street protest almost worldwide. It was depicted as demon on its way to maul the poor nations. Resistance or counter voice against the anti globalization movement was less exerting. Advocates confined themselves in the board meeting of the WTO unfazed by the street protest taking place during the meeting.

Opponents of globalization invoke the issue of deepening poverty in the third world nation. Global trade and investment run after profit anywhere in the world ignoring people and the poor in the regions of business activities. Multi-national corporations as global players are ruling the roost. Local government cannot reign on them. They can move anywhere in the country to do business blessed with neo liberal policies adopted in these countries at the behest of the WTO. Neo liberal policies also ensure remittance of profit generated in the home countries to the safe haven. This is a well laid arrangement for unhindered exploitations nothing less than plunder of the third world region, rich in natural resources and beset with unlimited labour supply. These are almost the hunting ground for the MNCs. The opponents smell design of doom for the working class in the domestic country. The MNCs, before their foray into business make sure that labour laws is sufficiently flexible amenable for tweaking to promote the pursuit for profit. The neo-liberal policies adopted in the home countries incorporates, as a condition of the multilateral trade agreement, the policy of hire and fire for the employees in the work places. Entry of the MNCs through the road paved by the opening of the external trade has jeopardized the livelihood security of the millions of workers. They work in enclave economy put in place by the MNCs protected from the red eyes of the state for violating labour laws. Special Economic Zone (SEZ) or Export Processing Zone (EPZ) is such production enclaves in developing countries where workers are at the mercy of the corporate employers.

They allege that MNCs bring obsolete technology long discarded in the west. Technology transfer does not accompany transfer of knowledge and skill for the destinations in the third world. They come to extract the mineral resources that cause environmental degradation. Mining business is most alluring for these giant corporations. They take advantage of the under-pricing of the rich national resources greatly helped by the corrupt politicians in the destination country. Areas rich in mineral resources, for example, iron and coal mines in India are inhabited for thousand of years by tribal people. Mining projects are evicting them from their traditional habitat. Displacement leads to deprivation of these indigenous people pushed to the brink of disaster. Thus globalization that paves the way for smooth entry of MNCs deepens poverty among the displaced people. Macroeconomic stabilization and structural adjustment programme are twin pillars of economic reforms measures that help global economic interconnection among nations. Opening of external trade to welcome foreign capital is the part of the globalization process. Nations cannot expect to receive enough foreign capital as and when they wish to have it to rescue the sagging economy. Foreign capital does not flow wherever they receive the invitation. Entry is always conditional pertaining to macro economic indicators. Satisfactory macro economic indicators are reflections of good economic health of the destination economy.

Foreign capital is not charity. The investors expect good return from the investment in the projects. The home country must ensure smooth remittance of profit from the business in dollars. Large fiscal deficit would dissuade the foreign investors. They read it as disastrous outcome of bad management of the economy. Run away inflation is another area, linked to the burgeoning fiscal deficits, that discourages the investors to step in. Physical infrastructure including of roads, rail, telecommunication, port, power and other such provision of public goods in the domestic economy is of much concern for them. Good governance that implies rules of law, work, culture and accountability of public servants comes in their considerations. Developing countries have to comply with their condition for reducing fiscal deficits as per cent of GDP below or certain benchmark as set by them. The first casualty of the reduction drive is the social welfare programme meant for the poor and powerless. Planners officially identify them as persons below poverty line or BPL in short. Democratic states committed to maximum welfare of the people spend heavily on health and education for the citizens who cannot afford to buy them in market. Poor lack the purchasing capacity. So the state has to provide goods for these people. Free and compulsory elementary education for all children in India has been enacted in India as rights of the children. State has to bear the entire expenditure to fulfil the goal to realize the rights. Universal free health care is still far away for almost all welfare states. India's accomplishment to that direction cannot be disparaged. Identified poor holding BPL card are entitled to government health care services free of cost.

Provision of subsidy for fertilizers used in Indian agriculture aims at helping the poor farmers. Subsidies on many essential items for use by the poor are extended as safety nets for the poor from the heat of the market. Government appears as a shield for the poor. Social welfare programmes for the underdogs of the Indian society are meant to promote social justice as goal set in the Constitution.

Welfare programme for the scheduled castes, scheduled tribes, forest people, women and children, disabled persons and for minority community in India came into being with the adoption of our Constitution. Our founding fathers while articulating the Constitution had laid emphasis on social equality. Social discrimination and social repression are baggage which India has been carrying for thousands of years. The free India must commit herself to remove discrimination. Positive discrimination was prescribed for the socially oppressed community in India's traditional caste-ridden society. Fiscal deficits swell if current government expenditure goes on increasing exceeding current revenue over the years. Fiscal deficit, the bigger size which is the villain to nab, can be brought down through reducing the budgetary spending on social welfare for the poor and vulnerable. Thus entry of global capital as an offshoot of globalization deepens rather than reduces poverty in the home country.

Is globalization an evil force, a neo-imperialist design of the developed west to exploit the rich natural resources and cheap manpower of the third world? Anti globalization tend to put the blame on globalization for all types economic adversities plaguing the third world. Globalizers while contradicting the allegation argue that global interconnectedness that paves the way for free flow of ideas, knowledge, technology and capital is always beneficial for the developing countries grappling with poverty. If poverty still persists in some region of the world this is due to obstruction on the way to genuine interconnection. Globalization is not responsible but less globalization is. Half-hearted globalization coupled with sloth economic reforms is doing away with fruits of globalization. One group of development economists who stand on between the polar opposite school of thought tries to reconcile the reigning debates. They regard globalization as an opportunity for economic transformation of the poor countries. But that is not unconditional and automatic. Globalization had remarkably helped the east Asian countries. That was possible there because people were ready to embrace the foreign technology to boost their exports. Universal elementary education and health care were in place in those countries years ahead of trade opening. Skilled manpower could reap the benefits of trade opening. Thus public policies and actions determine the outcome of globalization. Thus this is neither necessary evil nor unnecessary benefactor.

7.7 Poverty as Unfreedom

Freedom centric view of poverty is a relatively recent outlook that has gained currency worldwide after publication of the remarkable book "Development as Freedom" penned by Amartya Sen. The idea gained ground in the eighties of last century when World Bank began to publish Human Development Report. It accepted, through this exercise that development does not mean rise in real per capita income. It goes beyond the narrow income plane. Health and education are also driver of development along with ability to buy consumptions goods and services in the market. Poverty as gravest problem of humanity came to the fore after the end of the Second World War that also brought an end to western imperialism. The United Nations Organization was born in the aftermath of the global war. The International Bank for Reconstruction and Development later named as the World Bank came into being to help and reconstruct the war ravaged countries. The newly independent countries in Asia and Africa, freed from long colonial domination, were almost devastated. Development of the erstwhile colonies was the priority of the Bank. The message was clear. Forget the past and look forward to the future. The war has shattered the humanity. It has greatly jeopardized the human civilization. The world must come out of the ravages of war.

Peace cannot return in the war-torn world without prosperity to be shared equally among people everywhere in the world. Bank was tasked to assist the newly born free nations in the other world in their effort to transform their sagging economies. Poverty is the common enemy to confront and defeat. Humanity cannot move an inch forward with this baggage of extreme poverty. Leaders who came together to eliminate poverty from the face of the earth had a particular image about poverty. Definition of poverty was uniformly accepted by the scholars, statesman, planners and policy makers at the national levels as well as at supra national bodies. This is a state of material wants caused by low income or lack of it.

Income or expenditure based definition of poverty stayed firm for a long time until the emergence of capability approach pioneered and popularized by Professor Amartya Sen. Income is not the end but only the means to achieve higher quality of life. Income has to be translated into functioning. A disabled person, despite having enough monetary means, face constraints of various kinds. His freedom to participate in social and cultural activities in the society is seriously restricted. An old and ailing person is equally stripped of the freedom of social participation despite his enough affluence. His frailty is the unfreedom. The socially outcaste ***dalit*** in Indian's caste divided society are stripped of many other kinds of freedom in addition to freedom to live a decent living. Poverty is not the economic poverty or income poverty only it is unfreedom. Poverty keeps the poor incarcerated in the prison of scarcity of material goods and services.

The worst casualty of poverty is the freedom from hunger for section of people in the society. Poverty triggers hunger which in turn impedes one's ability to live an active life for a long period. Hunger takes away the freedom of active and healthy life. Freedom to lead a life enlightened by education to take informed decision in life is greatly jeopardized by the affliction of poverty. Freedom to think independently enriched by treasure of information and knowledge acquired through meaningful education all throughout is constrained by poverty. Poverty comes in the way of access to quality schooling for children. Education enhances not only freedom-oriented thinking, it promotes freedom by equipping the learners with knowledge and skill for a productive life. Poverty, as unfreedom, limits the access to quality health care for a significant section of the citizens. The poor cannot afford to buy health care services in the market. Inability to access health care surely result in preventable mortally or crippling morbidity. Freedom to vote for a candidate in elections without fear or intimidation is curtailed for the poor citizens in a democratic country. Freedom to take part in political process is contingent upon economic standing. The political vote or agency for effective participation in the government is almost absent in a poor democracy where poverty and extreme inequality simultaneously persists. Politics are dominated by the powerful. Powerless underdogs passively participate. Poverty thus is a restriction in all spheres of life.

7.8 Capability and Poverty

Capability as a means for good living was conceptualized in the long past during Aristotle's time. The idea of capability was born then but it did not flourish for long until it gained currency recently. Aristotle, during the third century B.C., opined that resources or means are nothing but means to achieve other goals. The great philosopher Aristotle noted in his ***Nicomachean Ethics***

> *"Wealth is evidently not the good we are seeking; for it is merely useful and for the sake of something else".*

Aristotelian observation on wealth or resources sowed the seed that grew as the present day tree of capability approach. The full grown tree of capability analysis as a tool to explore human distress in contemporary social thinking accommodates and promotes disparate ideas on poverty. Poverty analysis is much richer and reflective now because capability approach has revolutionised the thinking. What is capability? This is opportunity or ability for a person to do what she has reason to do. This is viewed as opportunity to lead a good life for any person. One should have the opportunity to become certain person in life in which she thinks reasonable. These doing and being are ***'functioning'*** which captures the basic premise of capability. Income or resource dose not automatically lead to good life. Poverty causes bad life. The person, who is poor, is leading a bad life and, therefore, capability deprived. The person who leading a good life is non-poor and, therefore, capability endowed.

Real life examples are aplenty to demonstrate that the gap formidable between means or income and the good life. The latter is characterized by substantive freedom to lead a life dictated by informed choice of her own. Enough means or handsome income cannot guarantee the freedom of choice or ability to do things or become someone as she has reasons. Take the example of a disabled person, or an aged or infirm person. Her ability or mobility is extremely restricted by her disability, age or debility. She cannot lead a good life despite having enough means or income. Income is the means and the good life is the end. Income has to be translated or converted into good life. The ability to convert is the capability. A disabled person even though is rich may be capability poor because of 'conversion handicap' in addition to **'physical handicap'**. But the **'conversion handicap'** is not uniformly present across all context and social environments. A disabled person living in Ethiopia is more capability poor than his counterpart in Sweden or in Australia despite owning same level of wealth or income. The disabled person in the developed countries having public arrangement for smooth mobility of the disabled is close to good life. Her conversion problem is minimal. Contrastingly her counterpart in the poorest countries in Africa has to confront insurmountable barrier of conversion handicap because her state has failed to provide the necessary arrangement.

The distinction between income poverty and capability poverty is manifestly sharp in this case. A visually challenged boy or girl in the western world finds less difficulty in learning through brail system at school. Schools provide all such arrangements for children with special needs in the rich nation. The poor nations in the developing world cannot provide schooling for normal children. Provision of kits and teaching aids for the disabled children is just beyond imagination at this stage of economic development. Thus, these two children born and raised in two contrasting social circumstances will face different conversion crisis situation on the same income plane. A disabled person in the US who lost his limbs in the accident would be provided with a wheel chair fitted with electronic gadgets. His mobility is far less restricted. He can enjoy and participate in life almost fully. His conversion problem is less acute. In contrast, the person in similar predicament in Congo or Liberia even in India is almost doomed to disastrous state of living. His conversion problem is acute. He cannot do with the handsome income whatever he has reason to do. Disability stands in the way for the smooth conversion. India, as a developing country constrained by adequate resources deserves credit for enacting rules for the disabled. India has provided for certain entitlement with regard to education, job training and facilities for the disabled person. But the conversion problem is present here also. Right are yet to be converted fully into reality for the disabled Indians. John Rawls's remarkable theory of justice highlights the endowments of primary goods which include income or wealth decides the distributional equity in a society. Just society is built on institutions that promote justice in the society constitution of individuals. He insisted on primary goods but he comes out less clear on capability that makes conversion possible. Primary goods have to convert into good living.

Before the advent of HDI as a tool for measuring human

development GNP, per capita was taken as index for poverty measurement. Countries were classified as poor or rich on the basis of per capita GNP or income. Manifestly per capita income hides capability failure. Family income earned by earners of a family unit is regarded as yardstick for economic standing of the family. Per capita income of the family manifestly hides the pervasive gender bias in intra-household allocation of resources. Gender discrimination in families overwhelmingly persists in South Asia as well as in Africa. Preference for boys over girls is the predominant fertility choice among eligible couple. Females are at the receiving end of allocation of family resources. Males receive the large share in food, nutrition, health, education and leisure *vis-à-vis* females of all ages. Family income divided among the members at par fails to reflect the gender based deprivation occurring in the family.

Thus the relationship between resources and poverty is both variable and deeply contingent on the characteristics of the respective people and the environment in which they live both natural and social (Amartya Sen). There are four important sources of variation: personal physical characteristics, physical environment, social condition, and relational perspectives. Consumption need. varies depending on the physical condition of people. A severely disabled person needs more income to lead a good life than a normal person of same age and sex. A chronically ill person in the family would need more income to do the same elementary things which normal person can do with less income. Likewise, a person living in flood prone or drought affected areas would need more income than her counterpart living in places with normal weather condition. Social condition prevailing in a polity marked by universal public health care and education makes a large difference in converting income into capability. Community relationship often described as social capital makes a difference also. Established culture and pattern of behaviour in a community that defines the decent living is also a factor. The inter-societal variation in the perspective on decent living influences the relative advantages.

7.9 Poverty as Violation of Human Rights

Poverty as a description of human distress marked by scarcity of material things encompassing food, clothing and shelters as primary need has been with the humanity since its birth. Our ancestors thousands of years ago in their place of origin in the present day Africa also lived with poverty. But the poverty of yester years during the beginning of humanity and that of the contemporary world differs on what constitute poverty. Many of our ancestors were poor in the sense that they could not gather enough food for themselves for the lack of physical ability. Altruism is conspicuously absent in the animal world in which human ancestors lived and survived. Nobody thought of it as a problem for human beings. The age of enlightenment brought to light the circumstances that lead to human distress caused by poverty. It was placed in the priority agenda for global action in the aftermath of the Second World War. The United Nations, born out of humanity's craving for peace and prosperity in war ravaged world, committed to end poverty. The Millennium Development Goal adopted at the UN before the beginning of the new millennium is the expression of global concern to take up with new vigour the unfinished task. But the exercise of linkage between and human rights was undertaken by selected scholars led by Amartya Sen. Sen's capability approach is the leading light in that direction.

The Universal Declaration of Human Rights was adopted at the UN in 1948. Rights as legal entitlement for the citizens of the state was conceived well before the UN adoption in a scattered way within the nations in the western world. Post-war scenario provided the opportunity for global leaders to articulate and adopt the Universal Human Rights. The holocaust triggered by the world war is a turning point in the history of mankind. The world had witnessed the brutal repression of the humanity. Racism spearheaded by fascist misadventure of dictators, hell bent on occupying the world by brutality, brought forth genocide on massive scale. Millions of people died within few days. Loss of lives and destruction of property caused by the war led the world leaders to reflect on the future course of humanity. The war had damaged the human civilization and this was to be repaired through collective action with minds filled with love and compassion for fellow beings all over the world. All of us are members of human family. Failure of the League of Nations to prevent the horrific war was realized very soon. Unspeakable torture of people by the racist forces stirred the sensible minds. The world, after the brutalizing war must place human dignity above all. Greatest good for human kind should be the underlying message in the policies adopted at the newly born UN. The UN Declaration of Rights considers that human rights are inalienable.

There is an emerging view that poverty constitutes a denial or non-fulfilment of human rights. Question is posed whether poverty leads to violation of certain kind of human right or entire gamut of human rights. The simplest approach is to define poverty as non-fulfilment of human rights. But understanding poverty as denial of human rights in totality is problematic if poverty implies material destitution. One example will not be out of place in this context to establish the fallacy in equating them. Suppose a tyrant dictator imprisons his subject not necessarily for any genuine fault of the victim. He is kept in a cramped cage. But the incarcerated subject is fed with sumptuous meals in time. Clothed in expensive dress and the shelter is protective that keeps him safe from rain, heat or any threat from nature. Is the prisoner poor? Deprivation has certainly occurred in this case. But is the deprivation can be termed as poverty? From one angle, this is not because poverty is the situation of lack of command over economic resources. The prisoner, in the above example gets everything for his physical survival. He is not poor despite his incarceration without right to mobility and free speech. Therefore, poverty should be defined as non-fulfilment of human rights but without delinking it from the constraints of economic resources.

Amartya Sen's 'capability approach' provides a concept of poverty that satisfies these twin requirements. The capability approach does not explicitly mention rights but it paves the way for smooth transition from capability to rights. Therefore, capability approach is the precursor of rights based approach to poverty. Let us reflect on, for a while, on the wellbeing of the subject in the above example. Does the prisoner lead a good life? Then, what is a good life? A good life is characterized by the ability of the person to do anything or to be anyone as she has reason to value. The person must have substantive opportunity to do anything he values out of informed decision. Wellbeing can be thought of as the quality or wellness of a person's being or living. Living can be seen as consisting of set of interrelated *"functioning"* the thing that a person can do or be. The level of wellbeing thus depends on the level of functioning. Capability is thus a person's freedom. This freedom from hunger, freedom from illiteracy, freedom from crippling diseases, freedom from preventable death, freedom from torture and freedom from press censorship. Wellness implies a person's freedom to express opinion, to participate political process, freedom of expression, freedom of association and freedom of mobility. The prisoner in question has freedom from hunger which means his right to food is realized. But other freedoms as stated above that make wellbeing or good living are stripped by the tyrant.

From the view point of adequacy of nutrition, the prisoner subject is not poor. But when we move from sense of food poverty or income poverty to a broad measure of capability, the person is poor. Capability approach understands poverty as defining feature of a poor person who has very restricted opportunity to pursue her wellbeing. Poverty implies very low level of capability. The concept of poverty is certainly relative but some basic capabilities are common to all. For example, being adequately nourished, being decently clothed and sheltered, avoiding preventable morbidity, taking part in life of the community and being able to appear in public with dignity and so on. The phenomenon of poverty has to be distinguished from low level of living. No all the cases of low level of living can be regarded as poverty. The absence of the capability to live a healthy life is a case of low level of wellbeing. Ill health caused by a genetic disorder for which no remedy is available does not manifestly constitute poverty. But the ill health caused by lack of access to basic health care resources is certainly the state of poverty. This means that low level of wellbeing caused by ill health as a result of lack of command over economic means is poverty.

Poverty does have an irreducible economic connection. Low income implies inadequate command over resources. Personal income constitutes a part of command over economic resources. The other sources or lack of them include insufficient command over public goods and services, inadequate access to communally owned and managed resources, etc. The capability approach defines poverty as the absence or inadequate realization of certain basic freedoms, such as the freedom to avoid hunger, diseases, illiteracy and so on. Freedom here encompasses negative freedom. A person's good health depends on both of these freedoms. The society must provide adequate health care facility. This provision is positive freedoms. No one will have the freedom to hurt or kill her. This restriction is negative freedom. The concept of poverty is concerned with basic freedom which is fundamentally valuable for minimum human dignity. This concern for human dignity motivates the human rights approach to poverty. The fundamental premise is that poverty is violation of human rights and these rights are inalienable. One particular right cannot be fulfilled while other rights are violated. When the state undertakes poverty alleviation programme through which the identified poor are to be provided with means or income, human right is particularly promoted. Disadvantages come not only from inadequate command over economic resources or inadequate income but other sources are omnipresent and omnipotent. The case of India as a democracy as well as overpopulated poor country is the prominent site for the breeding ground of multifarious source of disadvantages in life of common Indians. Gender, caste, community, place of birth and living conditions are such sources of disadvantage in India. Human rights is not partial, it connotes right to life for all citizens. Right to life encompasses right to full dignity, full participation in political and social life and, a life marked by highest attainable wellbeing of human person. Eradication of poverty in its narrow sense, is therefore, not the clue to fulfilment of human rights in its comprehensive sense.

CHAPTER 8

Debate on Poverty Reduction

8.1 Is Poverty on the Decline in India?

Poverty in India is on the wane if official poverty line is accepted. During last 20 years, the government takes pride in reducing rural poverty from 47 per cent in 1983 to 28 per cent. This amounts to almost 1 per cent reduction per year during this period. The urban poverty during the same period has declined from 42 per cent to 26 per cent. Evidently the rate of poverty reduction in urban landscape is a bit slower than its rural counterpart in India. Government has been trumpeting its remarkable success in war against poverty, the number of poor in 2005 was 300 million by Government's estimate. The magnitude of poor Indians is quite upsetting for the planners despite the reduction in headcount ratio (Fig. 8.1).

The decline was not sudden nor had it set off from 1983 onwards. It had started much earlier 1970 when rural poverty level reached a staggering level of nearly 65 per cent. Contrastingly, urban poverty was much less during the same time the data reveals considerable rural-urban gap in the incidence of poverty demonstrating a fast that an average villager in India is more likely to be poor than her counterpart in the urban locations (Fig. 8.2).

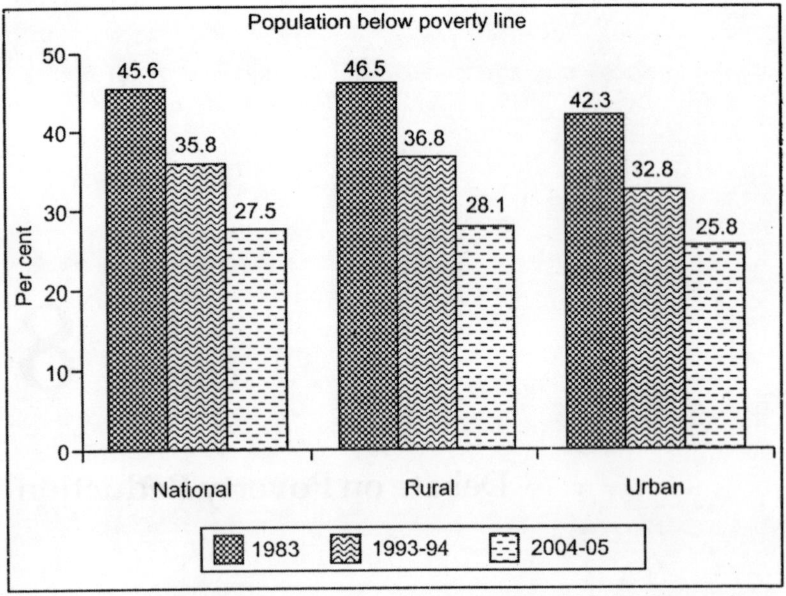

Source: Perspective on Poverty in India: Stylized Facts from Survey data, World Bank, 2011.

Note: Data based on uniform recall period consumption aggregates and official Planning Commission poverty line.

Fig. 8.1: Evolution of Poverty since the Early 1980s

The controversy surrounding the pace of poverty decline is further exacerbated by a recent report of an expert group constituted by the Planning Commission. The report takes up the issue of price index problem that beleaguers comparability over time. The same problem afflicts the comparability between urban poverty and rural poverty. The committee not only points out the inaccuracy of current method of constructing poverty lines it calls for revision in the light of the changed ground realities. The ground for claiming poverty reduction by the Planning Commission of India is further weakened by the growing divergence between mean consumption per person from the National Sample Survey (NSS) and the private per person consumption of the National Accounts Statistics (NAS) (Fig. 8.3).

The picture is widely clear that NSS household consumption is grossly underestimated in comparison to NAS consumption. The figure brings to light that NSS consumption is just half of the

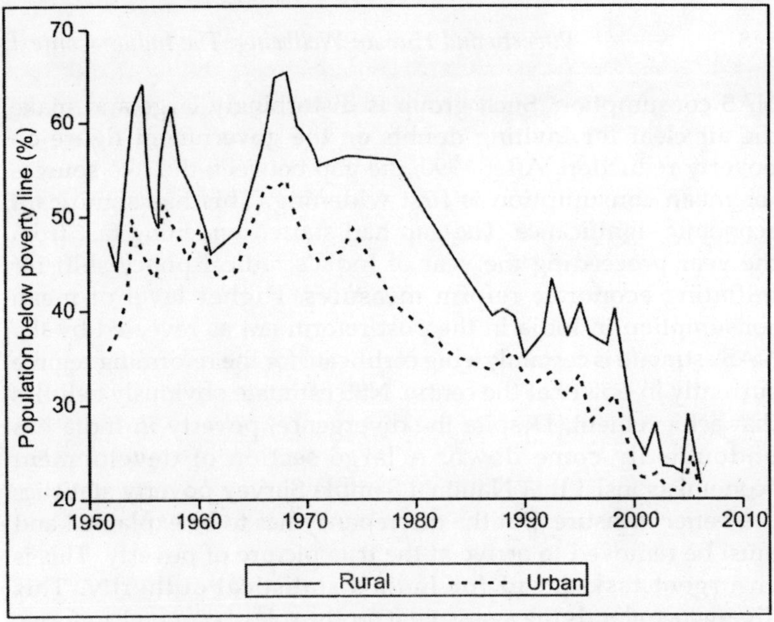

Source: Perspective on Poverty in India: Stylized Facts from Survey data, World Bank, 2011

Fig. 8.2: Evolution of Poverty, 1951-2006

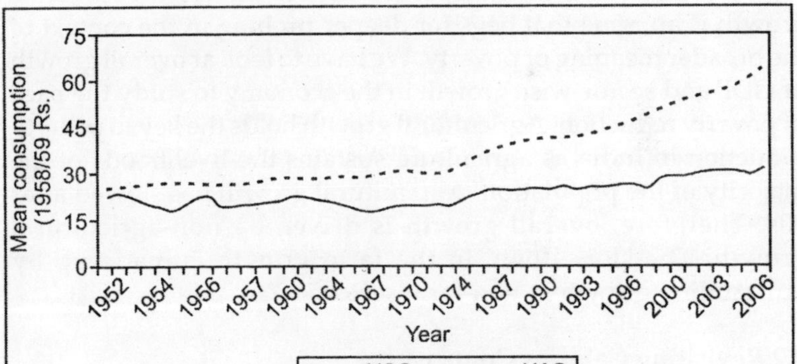

Source: Perspective on Poverty in India: Stylized Facts from Survey data, World Bank, 201(http://www-wds.worldbank.org)

Fig. 8.3: NSS and NAS Consumptions are Diverging

NAS consumption. Such group is disturbingly large and make the air clear for inviting doubts on the government figure on poverty reduction. After 1990, the gap between the two sources for mean consumption is first widening. This has significant economic significance. The gap had started widening fast from the year proceeding the year of India's radical policy shift for initiating economic reform measures. Higher level of mean consumption in India in the post-reform era as revealed by the NAS estimate is certainly a big certificate for the reforming regime currently in power at the centre. NSS estimate obviously belittles that achievement. Despite the divergence, poverty in India has undoubtedly come down. A large section of development economists insist that National Sample Survey poverty statistics is a better measure. But the discrepancy has to be explained and must be removed to arrive at the true picture of poverty. This is an urgent task ahead for India's statistical authority. This divergence clouds the assessment for the role of economic reforms in reducing poverty. Per capita income growth has evidently gone up. Per capita GDP grew by 1 per cent during 60s and 70s. During 80s, the same went up by 3 per cent and after 1991; it grew by 4 to 5 per cent. However, the responsiveness of poverty to economic growth is an issue that begs for deeper probing in the context of the broader meaning of poverty. We have to look at overall growth of GDP and sector-wise growth in the economy to study the pace of poverty reduction. Agricultural growth holds the key to poverty reduction in India as agriculture sustains the livelihoods of the majority of the population. Agricultural growth has slowed after 80s. Therefore, overall growth is driven by non-agricultural growth. The slow down in the farm growth is made up by outstanding growth in non-farm sector.

8.2 Revisiting Calories Controversy

Consumption poverty dose not seem to match up with calorie deficiency. It has been found in 2004-2005 that 80 per cent of rural households were calorie poor. The share of rural Indian's consuming food having 2400 calories has fallen. This is a paradoxical situation befuddling our planners. Opposition political parties led, mainly by left group, have been pooh-poohing government's claims of spectacular success in poverty reduction as a result of neo liberal economic policies. The explanation that is offered for quite some time seems to have cogency. Shift in food preference in the post-reform period is presented as explanation for the paradox. Households could buy more calories with their increased income but they are not going that way. Why? Indian's are abandoning cheaper sources of calories in favour of expensive food. The altered food preference is explained by two reasons. One pertaining to enhanced income and change in relative food prices. The other relates to non-economic factors like exposure to new food introduced by electronic media, imitation of food habits of wealthy neighbours, impact of advertisements, etc. (Fig. 8.4).

There is a significant reason that explains the diminished caloric consumption in post-reform India. Work activity that significantly determines caloric need has altered. Greater mechanization of agricultural operations and improved transportation have reduced the intensity of work. Safe drinking water coupled with better sanitation and hygiene in rural area has interfered with body metabolism to work hard with less calorie consumption. Therefore, as argued, caloric poverty as revealed in the caloric deficiencies in food consumption dose not imply rise in consumption poverty. This is corroborated by the data on perceived inadequacy of food in Indian households. In 1983, 17.3 per cent of individuals had reported inadequacy of food. The incidence came down to 2.5 per cent in 2004-2005. The reported decline in consumption poverty is further buttressed by self reported improvements in wellbeings. The World Gallup Poll Survey, conducted in 2006 for India reported that half of the respondents had expressed their feelings of 'getting better'. Only 12 per cent of the respondents were upset over deteriorating economic position.

India is a federation of 28 States and a few union territories. India is the replica of the world, characterized by huge diversities in various ways. The landscape is distinctively diverse where the great Himalayan imposingly stands on her vast stretch of Northern boundary. The great mountain influences our climatic conditions which in turn influences agricultural production. Monsoon still is the harbinger of happiness. But it does not shower its blessings unvaryingly all over Indian soil. Some places are blessed with fertile agricultural land watered by monsoon rain. With the

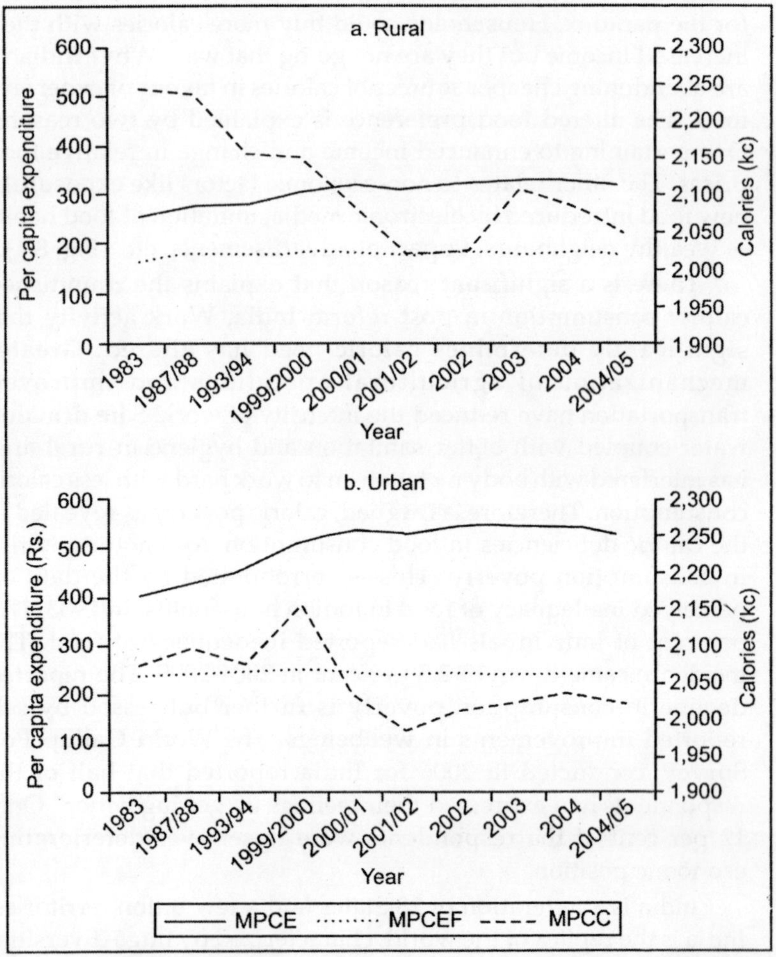

Note: MPCE = Monthly per capita (total) expenditure; MPCFE = Monthly per capita food expenditure; MPCC = Monthly per capita calorie consumption.

Source: Perspective on Poverty in India: Stylized Facts from Survey data, World Bank, 2011**http://www-wds.worldbank.org**

Fig. 8.4: The Calorie-Income Puzzle: Declining Calorie Consumption during a Period of Rising Per Capita Expenditure

advancement of irrigation technology, dependence on monsoon for crop farming has substantially lessened. Our green revolution belt comprising of Punjab, Haryana and western Uttar Pradesh had turned away from monsoon long ago. This region made history in independent India through demonstrating the reaping of huge harvest of wheat with the help of new agricultural technology. But the revolution that occurred in the sixties in this region did not reach everywhere. It did not come forward in the region where agricultural is still outmoded. It did not visit the places where infrastructure was not built up through public investment. This largely explains the vast variation in agricultural productivity across the States in India. This also explains why rural Punjab and rural Odisha differ so much in economic wellbeing.

Development disparity among States in India is longstanding, widespread and a formidable challenge to the Indian States. Incidence of poverty among States, therefore widely varies. Interestingly, rural poverty and urban poverty within the same state varies. India thus offers a fascinating contrast. Poverty rates in the rural areas of the poor states in India are comparable to those of the sub-Saharan African countries. For example, rural poverty rates in Odisha and Jharkhand are close to the poverty rate of Congo and Chad in Africa. Contrastingly, urban poverty rate in Assam or in Himachal Pradesh is comparable to the poverty rate in Brazil even less than that of Peru. Poorer States in India are burdened with overpopulation.

8.3 Urban Growth and Poverty

Economic growth in urban India is not only reducing poverty in the cities but also contributing to reduction in rural poverty. This has been happening for two reasons. First urban population has been on the rise faster than rural population since 1991. In 1950, 17 per cent of Indians lived in urban areas. The proportion rose very little to 26 per cent in 1990. During a long span of 40 years, urban population grow by 9 per cent. From 1990 to 2005, after a span of 15 years, the proportion stands at 29 per cent.

One noteworthy feature of trend in the trajectory of poverty is the manifest convergence of urban poverty and rural poverty on the basis of official poverty line.

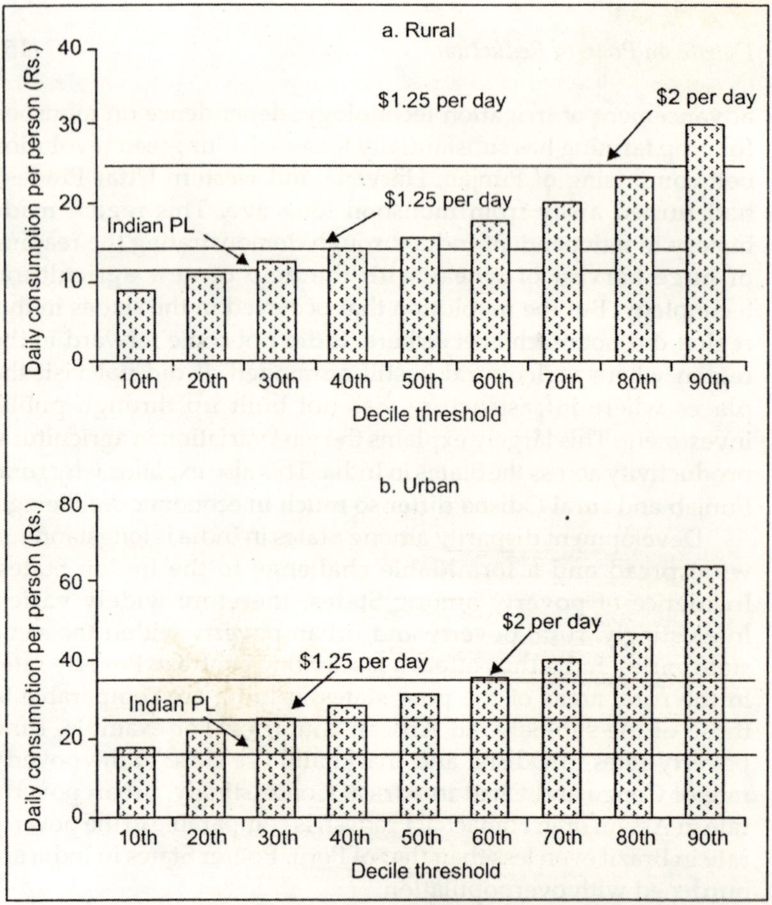

Note: Consumption estimates are in all-India rural or urban rupees and are corrected for cost-of-living differences between States using the official poverty lines. International poverty lines were converted to rupees using 2005 purchasing power parity rates of 11.4 ₹/$ in rural areas and 17.24 ₹/$ in urban areas.

Source: Perspective on Poverty in India: Stylized Facts from Survey data, World Bank, 2011http://www-wds.worldbank.org

Fig. 8.5: India's Middle Class Lives not far above poverty line

The data reveals that the gap between urban mean consumption and rural mean consumption is growing. Urban poverty reduction is lagging behind rural poverty reduction because income inequality in urban area is stalling the poverty reduction. This is quite obvious that urban economic growth contributes to lowering of urban poverty. But the impact of urban growth goes beyond the contour of urban location. Urban growth has been found to contribute in lowering rural poverty significantly.

The locations of the rural habitations certainly matters in reaping the benefits of urban growth. Villages surrounding the boundaries of the cities are beneficiaries of urban economic expansion. The benefits hardly percolate to remote villages. Proximity of villages to the urban centres can be advantageous where workers can easily commute without settling in the urban centres. The journey can be undertaken on foot. Simple mode of transport like bicycle can be used to commute daily. This is possible for villages not far from urban periphery. Villages little far from the cities can also reap the benefit of all-weather roads and public transport. Economic reform measures undertaken in 1991 had greatly helped in boosting the urban economy. Migration from rural to urban areas in search of livelihood went up for two reasons: push as well as pull. Agriculture as occupation has been failing to absorb surplus work force in the rural area. Seasonal unemployment in agriculture is added by disguised unemployment of the workers. Unskilled workers are compelled to move to cities to eke out living. Irrespective of size of cities, the urban areas need workers for the construction sites. The booming construction sector needs skilled, semi-skilled and unskilled workers. The distressed and displaced agricultural workers join the rank of construction workers in the distant cities. Service sector activities have gone up in the urban localities. The expanding service sector needs semi-killed workers for menial jobs like security, carrier, orderlies, and similar such jobs needed outside the core of the service production.

Economic growth and poverty reduction have not been uniform to all urban locations in India. Growth has bypassed smaller cities. Large cities and metropolitans are benefited much more than their smaller counterparts. City size largely matters and the size is measured by the size of the urban population not by any other characteristics. One dividing line is the population size of 1 million between large cities and medium or small cities. Cities above that dividing lines do not shelter that much poor within their areas as smaller cities have been doing. It has been

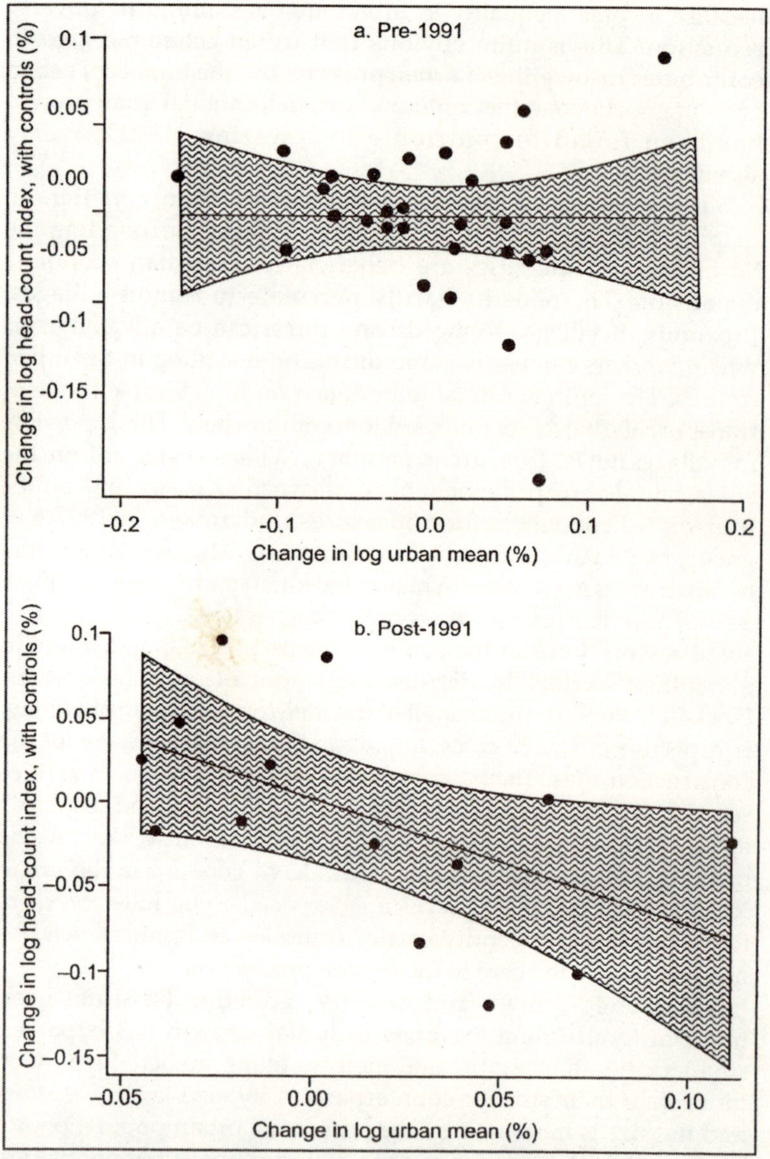

Source: Perspective on Poverty in India: Stylized Facts from Survey data, World Bank, 2011http://www-wds.worldbank.org

Note: The shaded areas show 95 per cent confidence intervals.

Fig. 8.6: Growing Poverty Impacts of Urban Economic Growth

found that 70 per cent of India's urban population lives in towns with a population of less than 1 million. Urban location in India below that dividing line is the living places for around 85 per cent of urban poor. As the sizes of the urban centres go down, the incidence of urban poverty goes up. There is an inverse relationship between them. But this does not imply that poverty reduction over the years is less in small towns. The reduction has been found to be uniform over the years across all city sizes. Smaller towns are not only effecting poverty reduction at par but they have spill over effect on rural poverty. On this count, the contribution of smaller towns in bringing down the incidence of poverty is quite commendable. The growth in small towns is helping rural poverty to come down. One can technically describe this spill over effect as an instance of positive externality.

8.4 Non-farm Employment in the Rural India

The conventional wisdom about rural India that rural prosperity is contingent on agricultural growth has lost its ground. Agricultural growth is no longer the sole driver of rural economic transformation (Fig. 8.7).

All the new entrants to the rural labour force are joining off-farm employment as per the data released by the National Sample Survey. The data on the nature of rural employment is collected through the employment unemployment survey from time to time. During last ten years non-farm employment has been growing at least four times faster than the on-farm employment. While the rank of non-farm workers in the rural areas has been swelling during the last three decades, the quality of employment has been on the wane. Some of the features of the burgeoning workforce in the non-farm jobs are worth noting. First, more than two-thirds of non-farm jobs are in the service sectors in the rural areas. We may be misled to understand that the predominance of service sector in the rural economy is an indication of higher income and consequent prosperity. We are under the false impression that service sector activities that have been paving the road for remarkable prosperity in India's southern metropolis are doing the same in villages. These cities are growing fast on the back of information technology service that boomed in the wake of trade liberalization. Software industries lined up one after another in

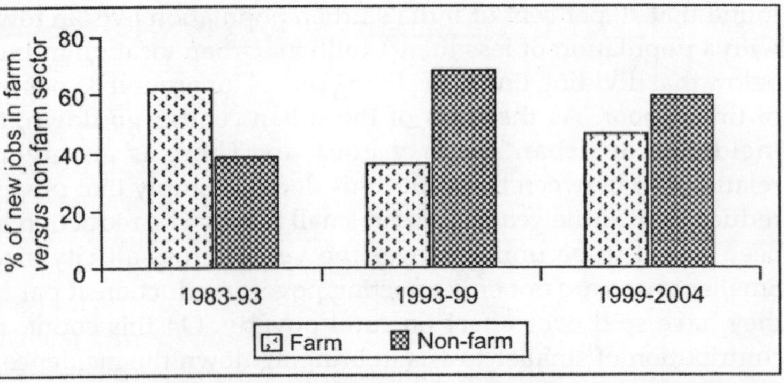

Note: Employment defined on the basis of principal-cum-subsidiary (usual) status. Farm *versus* non-farm assignment is based on workers' reported industry, occupation, and employment status. The number of farms and non-farm workers are calculated using (a) estimated proportions from unit-level data, and (b) total rural workforce as in Sundaram, 2007.

Source: Perspective on Poverty in India: Stylized Facts from Survey data, World Bank, 2011 *http://www-wds.worldbank.org*

Fig. 8.7: The Non-farm Sector is now the Source of Most New Rural Jobs

these cities are catering to the global demand for IT products. Foreign money has been pouring in as result of India's relative advantage of the abundance of skilled professional in these emerging areas.

The other prominent occupation in the contemporary rural India is construction work being undertaken to create rural infrastructure under various government rural infrastructure programmes, Food for Work programme and National Rural employment programmes were designed to create jobs for the unemployed workers in the villages during the lean season of agriculture. The ultimate goal of such project was to create and add to rural infrastructure that would help agriculture to flourish. The National Rural Employment Guarantee Scheme, NREGS in short and currently under way across length and breadth of the country is one such flagship programmes. It aims to kill two birds with a single throw of a stone. Paid employment for unemployed worker is provided during the period when they usually remain idle for lack of work opportunities in agriculture. In that sense, the programme is meant for removing poverty. The other end is the creation of rural infrastructure without which sustainable rural development is out of bounds. The data released by the NSS brings to the fore the fact that construction is the fastest growing rural non-farm activity. Construction works in rural area now engage 20 per cent a decade ago. The other defining features of the rural employment revealed in the NSS reports of different rounds relates to employment relation.

Self-employment in the non-farm occupation comprises 50 per cent of the total. The share of self employment in the work force has been more or less unchanged for last many years. Casualization of non-farm employment has become a distinct mark that speaks of helplessness of a large sections of rural workmen. The share of casual worker in total non-farm labour force has increased from 24 per cent in 1983 to 29 per cent in 2004. Growth in formal sector employment is confined to lower end jobs offering comparatively less payment. Higher paying formal sector employment in rural India is not growing over the years. Non-farm employment is held largely by young persons when the age breakup of non-farm employment has been brought to light by the NSS. Education level and social category determine the quality of employment in the non-farm work. The poor are most likely to join casual non-farm jobs. One is sure to land in casual job if she belongs to socially disadvantaged categories. Poverty and low caste tend to coincide. The double disadvantages deepen economic distress and entrap in perpetual cycle of social and economic disadvantage, one reinforcing the other. Regular employment seems to be the prerogative of the educated rural rich confined to upper castes in the rural society (Fig. 8.8).

The disadvantages are three-fold: poverty, low caste, and lack of education. They collectively put a barrier on the way to accessing regular employment. Despite the discredits hurled on the casual employment for paying much less compared to regular employment in rural non-farm jobs, the credit is equally due to reducing rural poverty. The wage rate in casual job in the rural area is higher than the agricultural wage. The premium of casual non-farm wages compared to farm wages has been increasing over the year. Non-farm casual wage is not only contributing to rural poverty reduction but also putting upward pressure on agricultural wage. Agricultural wage growth during 90s has slowed but it would have been much slower had there been no

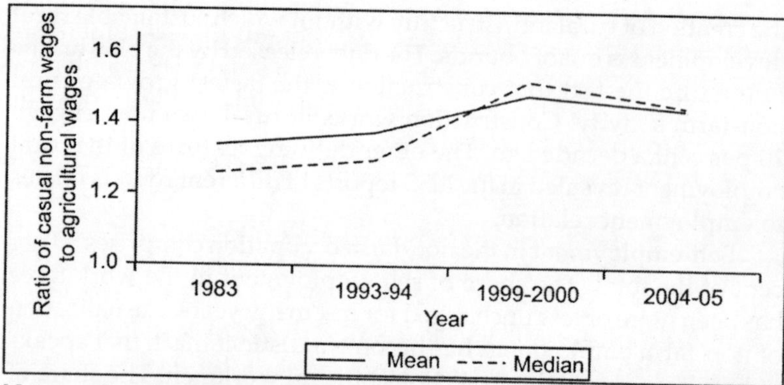

Note: Employment defined on the basis of principal-cum-subsidiary (usual) status. Farm *versus* non-farm assignment is based on workers' reported industry. Occupation, and employment status. The numbers of farm and non-farm workers are calculated using (a) estimated proportions from unit-level data; and (b) total rural workforce as in Sundaram 2007. Mean and median daily wages are in ₹ and are calculated for 19 major States of India.

Source: Perspective on Poverty in India: Stylized Facts from Survey data, World Bank, 2011 *http://www-wds.worldbank.org*

Fig. 8.8: The increasing Premium of Casual Non-farm Wages compared to Agricultural Wages

casual work in the non-farm sector. Still agriculture holds the key in determining poverty in rural India. We will have to wait for many years to witness non-farm rural employment overtaking and sidelining the farm work in India. India's non-farm growth is slower as compared to her giant neighbour China. Many of our South-East Asian neighbours are ahead of us on this count.

Growth of non-farm sector is the symptom of economic transformation taking place in rural India. The pace may be slower but the indication is encouraging. Development is always transformation process. It is an upward movement whereby people gradually move away from agricultural occupation and shift to manufacturing. The greater is the movement, the faster is the process. During the initiation of the process, agriculture remains the dominant occupation for the people. All the advanced nations in the present world had undergone the same process of shifting from agriculture to non-agricultural occupation over time. In today's developed countries of the western world, a very small segment of people, sometimes less than 5 per cent are engaged in agricultural occupations. This tiny group of farmers is not only catering to the food demand of the country but also producing surplus for export. Remarkable advancement of science and technology hundred years ago made it possible. Machine has displaced man in the western agriculture. This process is quite sluggish in the South Asian region where majority of population still tied to agriculture for living. Non-farm activities comprise of manufacturing, processing and servicing. Growth of non-farm sector depends on the demand generated in the rural area as a result of enhanced income in agriculture over a period of time.

Studies in India have revealed the pattern and co-relates of the growth of non-farm sector in recent years. One casual factor has been the attainment of education. Non-farm growth is rapid and robust in those locations of the country where level of educational attainments is relatively higher. One possible explanation for this connection might be pulling effect of skill. Education and skill among the rural workers might have paved the way for the growth of non-farm sector. Urban growth has been contributing to the expansion of the non-farm sector in the rural area. The role of urban growth in reducing poverty in India has already been highlighted. But this contribution is being made through stimulating non-farm economic activities. Urban economic growth has a wider reach. But it affects the adjoining villages and areas situated within commutable distance from the urban centre. Proximity to urban centre is also beneficial for the rural area. Occupational diversifications take place rapidly in consequence of closeness to urban centres. Some of the manufactured products including processed ones might be demanded by urban population when urban economy grows. The demand for rural-made product by the urban people boosts up non-farm sectors in the rural areas. Thus the benefits of urban growth on rural non-farm employment draw on such factors.

8.5 Health and Education: The Human Capital

India's recent poverty decline as confirmed by the official statistics provides a strong reason to rejoice. The pace of poverty reduction has been much faster now than it was in seventies and eighties. But her record in poverty reduction is at variance with her performances in other two human development parameters: health and education. Our euphoria for triumph over poverty in recent years would calm down when we compare with our eastern neighbour. Bangladesh, as a free nation was born in 1971, therefore, younger to us by 24 years. Our younger neighbour has suffered many times by political upheavals, military coup and derailment of democracy. Bangladesh is poorer than us. India's per capita GNP is $ 1,170 compared to $ 590 of Bangladesh in comparable units of purchasing power. Our per capita income is almost double of theirs. Our lead over them is limited in the realm of income. Let us look at our trails on other count of human wellbeings. India's remarkable economic growth that began after the reform measures almost stumbled in 2008 triggered by the worldwide economic recession. Until then, economic growth in India as measured by per capita real GNP surged ahead much faster than her eastern neighbour. India is placed ahead of Bangladesh in the Human Development Index ranking only on the back of her per capita income. If income is taken out from the index, just for fun, India is behind Bangladesh in Human Development score.

An average Bangladeshi can live up to 70 years in comparison to average life span of 64.4 years for an Indian. The population of underweight children in Bangladesh is 41.3 per cent. The same is higher in India at 43.5 per cent. Bangladesh's image to the world as backward Muslim nation burdened with overpopulation has faded. An image makeover is on the go. Fertility rate has noticeably come down and much lower than that of India. India's fertility rate of 2.7 is higher than 2.3 of Bangladesh. Mean years of schooling is 4.8 years in Bangladesh which is higher than India's 4.4 years. The literacy rate among female between fifteen and twenty four years of age is higher in Bangladesh. One of spectacular developments indicating a social progress in Bangladesh is her accomplishment in the literacy of young females. They are ahead of their male counterparts in the attainment of literacy. This, however, has not happened in India. The mortality rate of children under five is sixty six per thousand in India compared with fifty two in Bangladesh. We are behind them in infant mortality rate also. Our rate is fifty per thousand whereas the same is forty one for them. Child immunization with DPT is 94 per cent in Bangladesh; the same is 66 per cent in India. Professor Amartya Sen praises the achievements of Bangladesh in advancing the wellbeing of people despite her low income.

Comparison between India and Bangladesh in the sphere of human development performance does not seem to be worthwhile exercise. Comparison should be undertaken between two equals. China is rather comparable to India and let us explore how these two great nations fare in human development performances. Life expectancy at birth in China is 73.5 years compared to 64.4 years in India. The infant mortality rate is fifty per thousand in India compared to a lower figure of seventeen in China. Maternal mortality rate 230 per lakh in India which is just 38 in China. The mean year of schooling in China is 7.5 years and for India the same is 4.4 years. China's adult literacy rate is 94 per cent and the same for India is 74 per cent as per 2011 Census. As a result of India's effort to improve the schooling of girls, its literacy rate for women between the ages of fifteen and twenty four has risen; but that rate is still not much above 80 per cent, whereas in China it is 99 per cent (Amartya Sen). Child malnutrition was quite higher in India. Only 66 per cent of Indian children are immunized with triple vaccine (DPT) as compared to 97 per cent in China. Our giant neighbours are ahead of us in health and educational outcome. India's performance in adult literacy is comparable only to sub-Saharan African region.

One exercise on comparative performance over the last three decades would be pertinent in the present analysis (Fig. 8.9).

Illiterate population in their exercise of comparison includes unlettered population plus the proportion of population that has not completed full course of primary education. During 1984, 64 per cent of Indians were illiterate whereas in 1975 almost a decade earlier, China's illiterate population was 40 per cent. Way back in 1975, 32 per cent of adult population in China had secondary education. In contrast after almost 60 years, during 2004, only 16 per cent of India's population had completed secondary education. We could only achieve only half of what China had achieved 60 years ago. This issue has been invoked number of times in the scholarly works of Amartya Sen while delving on the subject of shared development in the post-reform India. Fruits of economic growth in the contemporary India are being cornered by the upper

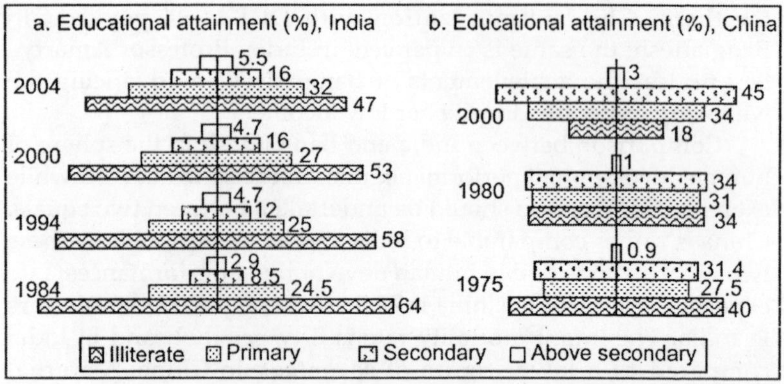

Note: Educational attainment among the share of the population aged 15 and older. Illiterate includes both the illiterate and below-primary-educated populations.

Source: Perspective on Poverty in India: Stylized Facts from Survey data, World Bank, 2011http://www-wds.worldbank.org

Fig. 8.9: India's Educational Attainment was below China 30 Years Ago

echelons leaving out nothing for the underdogs of the society. This development as he points out is largely caused by the lack of education and appropriate skill among the larger section of Indian society. The independent India did not prioritize universal basic education which China did during the same time.

The emphasis of the Chinese state on secondary education during the early years after her emergence as a Communist nation was farsighted. China had demonstrated by her own example that poverty and underdevelopment did not stand on the way of her challenging drive to universalize basic education and health care. The example of China and her public policies in the realm of human development are great lessons for India to learn. Both of us began our journey as independent nations with the baggage on our shoulders, filled with endemic poverty, teaming population, widespread illiteracy and pervasive ill health. We took recourse to democratic means to eliminate the human sufferings. Makers of modern India had cherished to institute democratic polity in which voices of opposition would be heard, respected and considered for the best interest of the Indians. Our Constitution adopted after the birth of the free nation provides for freedom of press, universal adult franchise, regular election and decentralization of power. The elected government is accountable to the people. This obligation of the state makes it cautious of any possible adverse consequences of state action. Adverse impact on the people creates the possibility of total rout in the next election. Fear of fall always haunts the people at the helm of affair. China now did not go that way under the leadership of Mao Tse-tung.

The monolithic power structure in the post revolution China leaves no room for people's participation in governance of the state. India's multi-party democracy stands sharply in contrast to one party rule in Chinese state. Decision taken at the top level of party hierarchy is thrust upon the grass root people leaving no room for questioning. Very rigid party hierarchy in top down mode, well oiled by communist ideology and teaching, has been delivering the governance. The totalitarian regime in the absence of popular dissension, freedom of press and public debate, run the risk of taking unguided course. The whole step decided by a few in the four walled dark room, may bring about disaster on massive scale. It can kill millions of people within a short time. This had happened unfortunately in China during the period from 1959 to 1962. The demonic famine unprecedented in Chinese history had swallowed 30 million Chinese. Famine was triggered by the faulty agricultural policy by the Chinese state in the fifties. Absence of the freedom of press on the one hand and the lack of public discussion on the other helped in the onset of famine. The men in power at the top of the pyramid did not invite nor they receive any opinion or early warning of the looming scourges. Contrastingly democratic India since her birth as a free nation has not witnessed famine. Democratic political structure can prevent such menace to get in.

While agricultural policy was disastrous, but universal health care and compulsory basic education for all children in China were marvellous. The benefits are being reaped in the post-reform China. Contemporary China is refered as manufacturing hub of the world. Chinese people could make use of the opportunities created by liberalization of trade and investment in the wake of economic reform adopted in 1979. Economic reform measure in the post-Mao China was a radical departure from socialist path for social transformation. But economic reforms in China did not follow nor precede political reform. State socialism has given way to market socialism. The former can be credited for remarkable human development outcome in China. Just before the initiation of economic reforms, the average life span in China was 14 years more than that of India. Economic reforms of 1979 greatly improved the working and efficiency of Chinese agriculture. Industries in China were given to private investors. The Chinese state virtually withdrew itself from industries. The reform paved the way for foreign investment and technology to turn Chinese industries competitive, efficient and outward looking. Economic gain brought about by reform in China has been enormous.

Economic reforms entailed withdrawal of entitlement to universal public health care. People were asked to buy health insurance from the market. The resultant effect of this action hit miserably the people at large. Chinese lead over India in longevity drastically came down at the turn of the new millennium and after two decades of economic reform. Chinese authority realized the loss for the society and altered its stand. In 2004, it introduced right to medical care. China, as of now has greater health care coverage than India. The gap in longevity between the two nations has gone up. The Chinese lead is now 9 years, a rise of 2 years by this time. China's remarkable human development outcome has a root in its past public policy of prioritizing basic education and health. The expansion of secondary education in China way back in 1975 was an extraordinary task accomplished by the totalitarian state. The year 2000 can be taken up for comparison (Figure 8.10) as we have the data for both the nation pertaining to that year. Illiterate Indians constituted 53 per cent of all compared to only 18 per cent in China in the year 2000. In the same year proportion of persons with secondary education was 45 per cent in China as against only 16 per cent in India.

Health outcome as an important aspect of human development process is not satisfactory, if not quite dismal in India. The National Family Health Survey in its Third Report for the year 2005-2006 reveals poor attainment in health. The report lays bare that 43 per cent of children below five years of age were under weight. The same further reveals that 48 per cent were stunted and 20 per cent were wasted. More than half of adult women are anaemic. One-third of all adults in India has lower body mass index (BMI). South Asians, the majority of which are Indians are shortest people in the world. The adult shortness is also the result of childhood neglect of nutrition and care (Fig. 8.10).

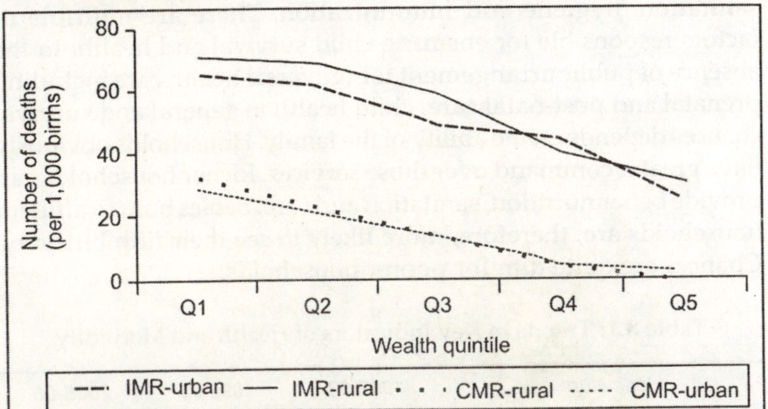

Note: CMR = Child mortality rate; IMR = Infant mortality rate; Q1 – Q5 = Asset index-based quintiles of population.

Source: Perspective on Poverty in India: Stylized Facts from Survey data, World Bank, 2011http://www-wds.worldbank.org

Fig. 8.10: Health Outcomes are substantially Worse among the Poor

The infant mortality rate among poor children is double than among rich children in both rural and urban areas. In 1999, only about two-thirds of fully immunized compared to nearly all children belonging to the richest quantity. The southern states in India with Kerala in the lead have been exhibiting human development achievement consistently for last two decades. Their accomplishments are comparable with those of western country. In contrast, performance of the BIMARU States comprising of Bihar, Madhya Pradesh, Orissa, Uttar Pradesh and Rajasthan.

The third report of Family Health Survey reveals that child health outcomes are dependent on household's economic standing. Poor households are more likely to witness the death of their children or infants than their richer counterparts. Infant mortality rate and child mortality rate are the highest in the poorer households. The positive connection between better child health outcome and households' relative prosperity indicates widespread inequality in nutrition and health care. The survival of the baby and her life journey up to the threshold of 5 years depends on many factors. Among them most important is mothers' health particularly her prenatal nutrition and care. It depends on post-natal care, breast feeding practice, mothers' nutrition, sanitation, hygiene and immunization. There are multiple of factors responsible for ensuring child survival and health. In the absence of public arrangement for universal health care including prenatal and post-natal care, child health in general and survival chances depends on the ability of the family. Households obviously have greater command over those services. Richer households can provide better nutrition, sanitation and care. Babies born to affluent households are, therefore, more likely to see their fifth birthday. Chances are quite dim for pcorer households.

Table 8.1: Trends in Key Indicators of Health and Morbidity

Indicators	*1992-93*		*1998-99*		*2005-06*	
	Rural	*Urban*	*Rural*	*Urban*	*Rural*	*Urban*
Life expectancy at birth (years)	59.0	65.9	61.0	67.6	61.8	68.5
Infant mortality rate (%)	85.0	56.1	73.3	47.0	62.2	41.5
Child mortality rate (%)	119.4	74.6	103.7	63.1	92.0	51.7
Total fertility rate (%)	3.7	2.7	3.1	2.3	3.0	2.1
% Children fully immunized	30.9	50.7	36.6	60.5	38.6	57.6

***Note*:** Total fertility rate for the 1- to 36-month period preceding the survey.

Source: Perspective on Poverty in India: Stylized Facts from Survey data, World Bank, 2011 *http://www-wds.worldbank.org*

The key indicators of health and morbidity brought to light by Table 8.1 leaves room not for complacency but for something to worry about. The percentage of children fully immunized at a certain point of time is an important indicator of children's health status. It speaks much of the governments concern and action for health of her budding citizens. The progress in this regard on the whole is dismal in India. The pace of coverage is not only slow over the years; it has rather tapered for the urban area during the period from 1998 to 2006. The coverage was 60.5 per cent for urban children in 1998; it came down to 57.6 per cent in 2006. Take the case of total fertility rate over the years in India. The impact of family planning measures initiated in India since independence could be assessed by the total fertility rate. Speedy decline of the rate over a period of time speaks of the spectacular success of the programme. The faster pace augurs well for the country like ours yawning for breath pressed by the pressure of growing population. Sustainable development, the realization of which requires lessening of population size, has been the cherished objective of India's development initiatives. The pace of decline of TFR over a period of 13 years is sluggish. Average longevity has gone up but the rise here is also slow. For example, rural India's average life span was 59 years in 1992; it has increased to 61.8 in 2006. This is a small increase over a period spanning 13 years.

Infant mortality rate was 56 per cent during 1992-93 for urban India, instead of going down, it has gone up to 62.2 per cent in 2005-2006. It has decreased by around 22 per cent for rural India during the same period. Rate of decline in child motality is, however, quite satisfactory. The result on key health indicators in India during the period of study is, however, mixed. Success in some areas seems to be shadowed by failures on the others. Concerted drive is necessary to have satisfactory outcomes in all aspects of health and wellbeing. The rate of decline in the proportion of underweight children, set against the average cross country data, is dismal. The cross country data suggest that the rate of decline tends to be half the rate of growth of GDP per capita. By this trend, the rate of decline should be 38 per cent for the period between 1980 and 2005. But actually the rate is 29 per cent. The rate of growth of average adult height has been much slower than that of the case in several European countries in the past and in China in recent decades (Deaton and Dreze, 2009) (Table 8.2).

In the desert of despair, there is also an oasis of hope. Praise worthy progress is visible in the elementary school attendance. Children are attending schools in large number now. Early childhood school attendance has increased quite substantially during the period under study. Using National Sample Survey data for the period from 1993 to 2004; clubbing all age groups for learners attending educational institution (5-29 years), the attendance ratio for rural children has jumped from 37.9 per cent to 53 per cent for boys and girls together. Elementary school attendance has been quite impressive. Almost 80 per cent of rural girls are attending school in 2006, up from less then 60 per cent during early 90s. An ideal scenario in school education is judged by age appropriate grade enrolment. Presence of over-aged in each

Table 8.2: Attendance increased substantially in the Past Decade, particularly in Elementary Schools

Age group	*1993/94*				*2004/05*			
	Rural		*Urban*		*Rural*		*Urban*	
	Male	*Female*	*Male*	*Female*	*Male*	*Female*	*Male*	*Female*
Age 5-29 years	45.4	30.5	47.7	34.9	53.2	43.6	54.1	51.9
Age 3-5 years	17.2	15.0	35.5	32.3	30.6	29.0	49.0	47.9
Age.6-14 years	74.5	58.2	87.0	82.4	86.9	79.5	91.0	89.5
Age 6-10 years	74.0	60.4	87.5	83.8	87.6	83.2	88.7	85.0
Age 11-14 years	75.3	54.5	86.4	80.6	85.8	74.1	88.4	86.9
Age 15-18 years	43.0	22.3	59.1	52.0	49.4	36.0	61.0	59.3
Age 19-29 years	8.0	2.4	16.8	9.9	8.6	3.9	17.4	12.3

Source: Authors' estimates based on NSS data.

Note: Table reports percentage of age group currently attending school.

Source: Perspective on Poverty in India: Stylized Facts from Survey data, World Bank, 2011 *http://www-wds.worldbank.org*

grade of schooling is an unhealthy symptom. But the situation has greatly improved by this time. The magnitude of overage students is on the wane. The gender gap in school attendance has also come down. The surge in attendance has occurred in poor households in educationally backward States. The gender gap and urban rural divide in primary school attendance have been substantially bridged. But the gap in higher grade is bridging at a slower pace. Literacy percentages among Indians have been on the rise since 1951. This will further go up in the coming days as manifestation of increased school attendance in recent years. India's generational mobility in educational attainments across social groups and wealth categories has also increased. Educational attainments are higher now in the present generation than the earlier generations for the same family.

8.6 Learning Very Little in Schools

Quality of Learning

Does quantitative expansion in school attendance and enrolment across length and breadth of India commensurate with learning achievement? The issue is not only pertinent. This has a significant implication for country's development prospects. This is not a healthy picture that little children are crowding the school but coming out without learning anything or with a little learning at the end. Four to five years of primary schooling should equip the learners with three R's: reading, writing and arithmetic. These basic skills are imparted to the younger children during the primary level of learning. Unfortunately, learning attainment for children might be a cause of worry for our planners of education. The concern is aired that quality is running far behind quantity. Research studies by different organizations, both at Centre as well as in the State levels are being undertaken since mid 90s to assess the learning attainment of students. One such study was taken up by the National Council of Educational Research and Training (NCERT) in 2009. The study was named as National Midterm Achievement Survey. The target group was class five students. The study reported that average score was 48 per cent in mathematics and 60 per cent in language.

Annual Survey of Education Report, ASER in short, is being published by PRATHAM regularly. PRATHAM is an NGO of wider repute, engaged in assessing quality attainment of primary school-going children in the entire country. Academic competency is measured in relation to the syllabus designed for each grade of primary education. They measure the gap between what a child actually knows and what she needs to know as per her age in a given grade. Pratham's reports are widely accepted by academicians and scholars as authentic references in discourse on quality and quantity of primary education in India (Fig. 8.11).

The organization's report for 2010 can be taken up to make an idea about the state of quality in primary education. One shocking revelation is that 9 per cent of children in Grade 5 could not identify numbers up to 100. Grade 5 students are supposed to read a very short paragraph. The shocking revelation is that 44 per cent could not read a short paragraph of Grade 2. It was also found that 29 per cent were unable to divide and subtract. The assessment was undertaken on the children reaching almost the end of primary education of five years. Out of three R's, the two R's—Reading ability and Arithmetic competency—were taken up for testing among them. After 5 years of Primary schooling, 7 per cent of them can only recognize letters, no words and no sentences.

Among these children, 13 per cent could read the words and 25 per cent could read text meant for Grade I. Learning attainments

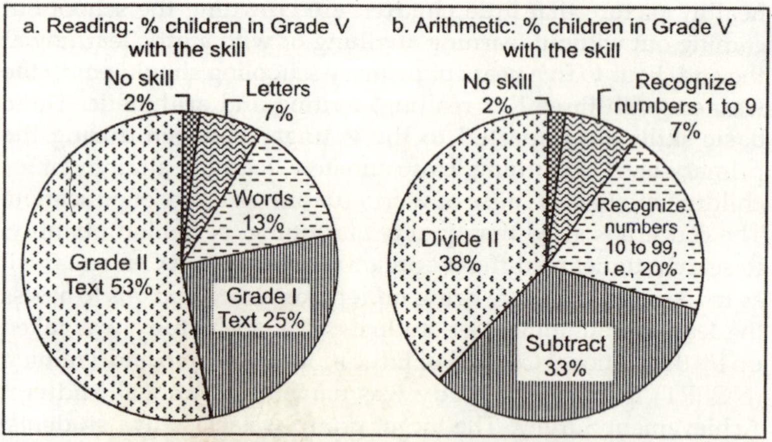

Note: The panels are to be interpreted as follows: 7 per cent of children in Grade V can only recognize letters, 13 per cent can recognize both letters and words, and so on.

Source: Perspective on Poverty in India: Stylized Facts from Survey data, World Bank, 2011 http://www-wds.worldbank.org

Fig. 8.11: Children Learn Little even after spending 5 Years in Schools

are not only below the ideal mark but also highly unequal among the young learners. Quality of learning varies across States in India. The other dimension of quality is intra-State variation (NCERT, 209; Pandey, Goyal and Sundaraman, 2008). Children in remote villages in any State in India having schooling facilities much below the mark are less likely to learn that meets the standard set of assessment of academic competency. School facilities incorporate adequate teachers, text books, attendance, teacher-pupil ratio, school buildings and class rooms, teaching aids, teachers' training as well as play ground for stimulating body and mind of little learners. Facilities for schooling are not distributed squarely across the State despite the introduction of Operation Black Board, DPEP in the 90s and Sarva Sikisha Abhiyan in recent years. Attempts are being made to bring about uniformity in schooling infrastructure. But the skewed structure in the distribution of facility built over more than six decades cannot be dismantled overnight. But the drive must go on. Variation in quality attainment across school can be attributed to differences in school facilities. Family background does matter in learning attainment of children. Education of parents, particularly of mothers, can greatly influence learning attainments of their offsprings at school. Unlettered parents are always at the receiving ends because of their inability to teach and guide at home.

Social stratification can also influences education outcome. For example, children belonging to tribal communities are always at disadvantageous position *vis-à-vis* the general caste or other categories. The weak standing of tribal children is generated by their lack of grip over the State language in which teaching learning is transacted in class rooms at school. Obviously, these children are uncomfortable with the State's dominant language which they do not speak at homes. Learning outcomes are also influenced by economic power of the families to which the children belong. Deficiency of learning at schools can be compensated by supplementary coaching at homes. Ability to provide coaching by the parents, therefore, is also an influencing factor. Pratichi study report prepared by Pratichi Trust instituted by Noble Laureate Amartya Sen has brought to light the widespread deficiencies in learning achievement at the primary schools in the selected villages in West Bengal. The study found the prevalence of private coaching among the underprivileged families in the study villages. The astonishing and painful revelation is that families living from hand to mouth have been keeping aside a part of meagre income for private tuition. Poor parents are coughing up their hard earned incomes for the sake of their children's education. Poor parents are spending on such items for which the State is obligated to provide free of cost as per the Constitution. The nation is looking forward to Right to Education Act that came into effect in our country on and from 1st April, 2010.

Human Development for the poor is posing serious challenges to the growing India. The contemporary growth performance of the Indian economy has earned appreciation worldwide. India's conventional image as a caste-ridden over-populated poor nation in the South Asia is fast fading. Her new image in the new millennium as a growing economic power is being built up. Her new image is made by her thriving service sector. We are now world leader in information technology services particularly in developing software for the developed countries. But the economic growth should not be the final end of any nation. This is just means to achieve wellbeing of people. It just provides the opportunity for the state to make use of the increased income for enhancing capability of people. Income as such has no value unless it is translated into good life. But sustainability of the growth depends on human capital formation process which should be the priority of the government action. Child malnutrition is such an issue at the moment in India which must receive priority attention. The child with stunted growth is almost sure to become unproductive adult in her turn. Undernourished and sickly children of today are on their way to become incompetent adults in future. The country needs skilled, healthy and intelligent youths in the coming days to sustain the growth momentum. Economic opportunities being created by the ongoing growth are being pocketed by privileged class in Indian society.

Fruits of growth in the contemporary India are not being shared by all sections of Indian society. The underdogs are manifestly bypassed. These deprived lots include unlettered, unskilled, perennially ill, terminally sick, socially marginalized, tribal communities, indigenous and ethnic people and so on. The unskilled adults are those who missed quality schooling in their childhood. These ranks of idle youth cannot contribute to nation building through their participation in economically productive activities. Rather, the state has to take care of them through various material provisioning. They could be an asset for the country had they would attend schools to acquire skill. The state invests now for education for her children. The return would accrue during their productive youth. This universal quality schooling for all children in India is not only a legal obligation of the state but all economically beneficial action of the state. Child health is as important as child education. We need healthy youth for India's future growth. Full course child immunization for all children can not be compromised. Physical incapacity in today's youths has a root in her neglected infancy. Crippled childhood beleaguered by ailments and deformities have a root in prenatal neglect of mothers. Thus reproductive child health must be set in priority task.

8.7 Rising Inequality

Poverty and inequality have been intimate bed fellows for long time. They are together since the beginning of our journey on the planet as human race. Inequality can occur on various features. Height of adults of a country can be one aspect about which inequality can be present and one may be interested as a subject of interest to know the extent of inequality in the distribution of heights. There are many such aspects of human existence in which inequality can be quite pervasive. Some discipline of study can be interested in that particular aspect. Economists are interested in the pattern of distribution of economic resources among families and individuals. Ownership of economic resources and the ability to protect and expand them decide the economic power. The latter are just purchasing power in the market measured in income. Thus productive resources are means and incomes are outcomes. Land, livestokes, manufactured capital, human capital are examples of productive resources commanded by the individuals or by families. These productive resources help in producing commodities and services valued in the market. One has to buy the product in the market and the resultant income is accrued to the owner. Inequality persists in the distribution of resources as well as in the distribution of income. But the extent of economic inequality varies across nations. This is extremely high in some countries and quite low in some other places. Differences in social conditions, polity and legacy largely explain the variation in the extent of economic inequality across the nation.

Before the birth of human society and when human civilization was yet to usher in, our ancestors lived in the lap of nature. Anarchy rather than rule of law marked the world of nature where powerful always took away the bigger pie of the fruits of nature. Physical prowess decided the share of the cake each individual would get for survival. The powerless obviously suffer and perished. Rule of society did not come forward for protection of frails, ailing and elderly people during these pre-civilization existence of the primitive nature. Thus inequality in the distribution and access to resources in the state of nature was the defining mark. Human society came into being after this long spell of anarchy. Human minds began to think over the issue of inequality among members of society. Inequality was diagnosed as a social wrong at much later stage of human civilization. State, as an ultimate protector of individuals, would device means to eradicate inequality of economic opportunities. The democratic state, particularly, would strive for creating opportunities for development for all of its citizens. Equality of opportunity is the hallmark of democratic society. There is a view opposite to the usual outcry against inequality, in favour of inequality of economic status among people. Those who are in favour argue that equality of income or resources and equal provision of opportunities among the citizens would hold back the nations' growth and prosperity. Man would not think to work hard, take risk and innovate if the material return does not accrue to him.

Material gain has always been the driving factor for a person taking a different course in life. There must be enough incentives for someone in undertaking hard work for pursuit of profit. People would be demoralized if the state forcefully takes away the gain and distribute them to all on equal measure. Entrepreneurship, innovation and talent would not flourish in such a dispiriting system. The nation would remain perpetually entrapped by poverty and backwardness. Development economists have been debating on the issue of the connection between economic growth and economic inequality. The dominant view is that economic prosperity over time gradually reduces inequality. Developed countries are less unequal than the less developed ones. Simon Kuznets with whom the name of the famous Kuznet's hypothesis is associated had studied on the connections. He found a relation that resembles the inverted U-shape on the basis of empirical study on the relationship between per capita income growth and a measure of income equality named after him as Kuznets's ratio. The curve tells that inequality would be rising when the country would be developing. The curve reaches its maximum height at a point when per capita income growth reaches a midway, being at half of the scale between lowest income and highest income. Sub-Saharan African nations resemble the lowest income countries in the lower segment of the scale where economic equality is on the rise. Inequality reaches its peak in the middle income category. The highest rate of income inequality persists among middle income countries located mainly in South and Middle America. As the country grows richer, inequality comes down. The world's most egalitarian nations belongs the league of most affluent countries in the northern Europe.

Scandinavian nations notably Denmark, Finland and Norway are pioneering nations in accomplishing remarkable reduction in economic inequality. India's spectacular growth performance in the wake of economic reform measures unfortunately is accompanied by increasing income inequality. However, two different units of measurement provide different extent of inequality in contemporary India. Economic inequality measured by using consumption data is low in India by international standard (Fig. 8.12).

Interestingly we are in the same league along with Brazil and South Africa, infamous for harbouring extreme inequality in the world when income data is used in place of consumption data. The poverty mapping exercise undertaken earlier to study the regional concentration of poverty in India surprisingly revealed that consumption inequality is high in the rural area, no less than that of urban India. Even in Andhra Pradesh economic inequality in rural area is higher than the same in urban area. This unequal economic status in rural area is pregnant with other worse possibilities. One is the deepening and perpetuation of social injustice against the social underdogs.

Too high economic inequality in rural area paves the way for concentration of power and influence among powerful few. This tiny group wields much political power in the rural society because of economic strength. These rural rich can corner much of the benefits of rural welfare programme of the State and Central government. This possibility should alert the government about misdirection of government social welfare schemes towards those ineligible wrong hands. Rural income inequality as measured by Gini Index went on decreasing over a longer period, beginning from the 50s down to 1980. The rural income inequality has been on the rise in the 80s. The same is on faster rise during the period from 1990 to 2000 (Fig. 8.13).

The same feature is also manifest in the urban income distribution. Urban inequality declined in India until 1980 and thereafter it started rising. The interesting revelation is that rural growth tended to be pro-poor during the period from 1983 to 1993-1994. Thereafter, the growth ceased to become rural biased. It turned out to be neutral during the period from 1993-94 to 2004-05. While rural economic growth remained neutral during this period, urban economic growth favoured the urban rich (Fig. 8.13).

Thus overall economic inequality came down during the period from 1983 to 1993-94. But it rose slightly after that (Fig. 8.14).

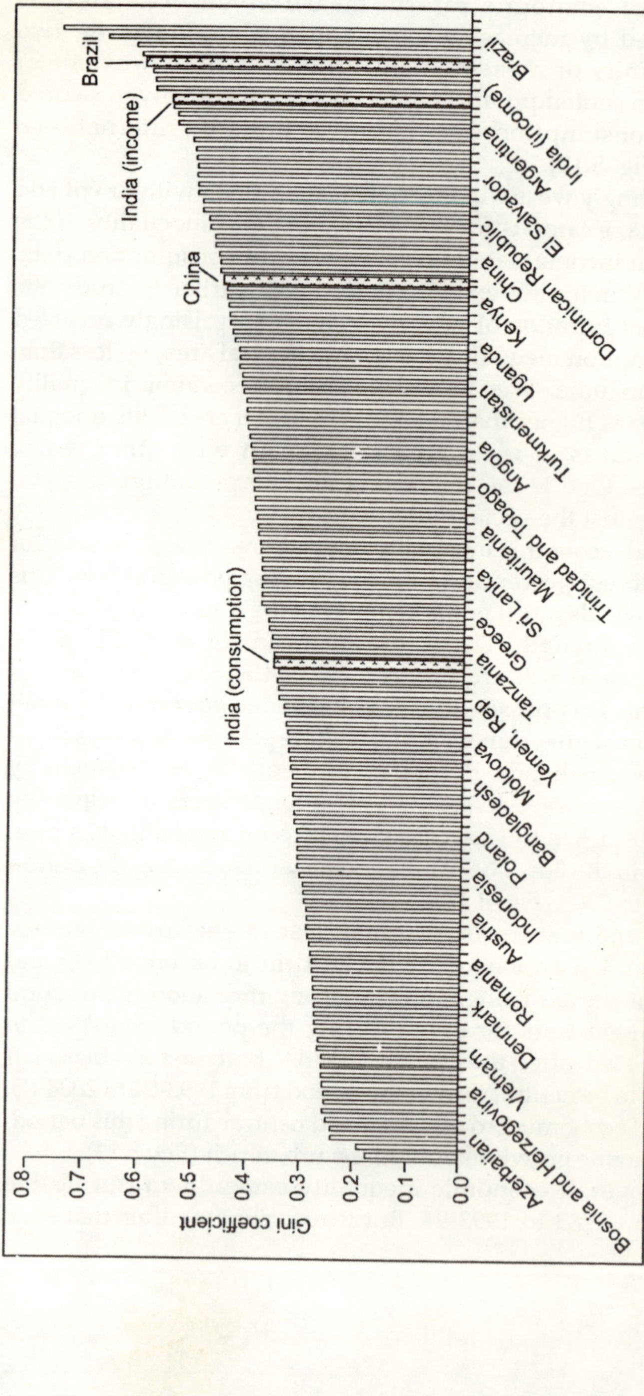

Source: Consumption Gini from NSS 61st round; income Gini from 2004-05 NCAER–University of Maryland India Human Development Survey (Dubey 2008). *http://www-wds.worldbank.org*

Note: Consumption Gini = 0.325; Income Gini = 0.535.

Fig. 8.12: India in International Comparisons of Inequality

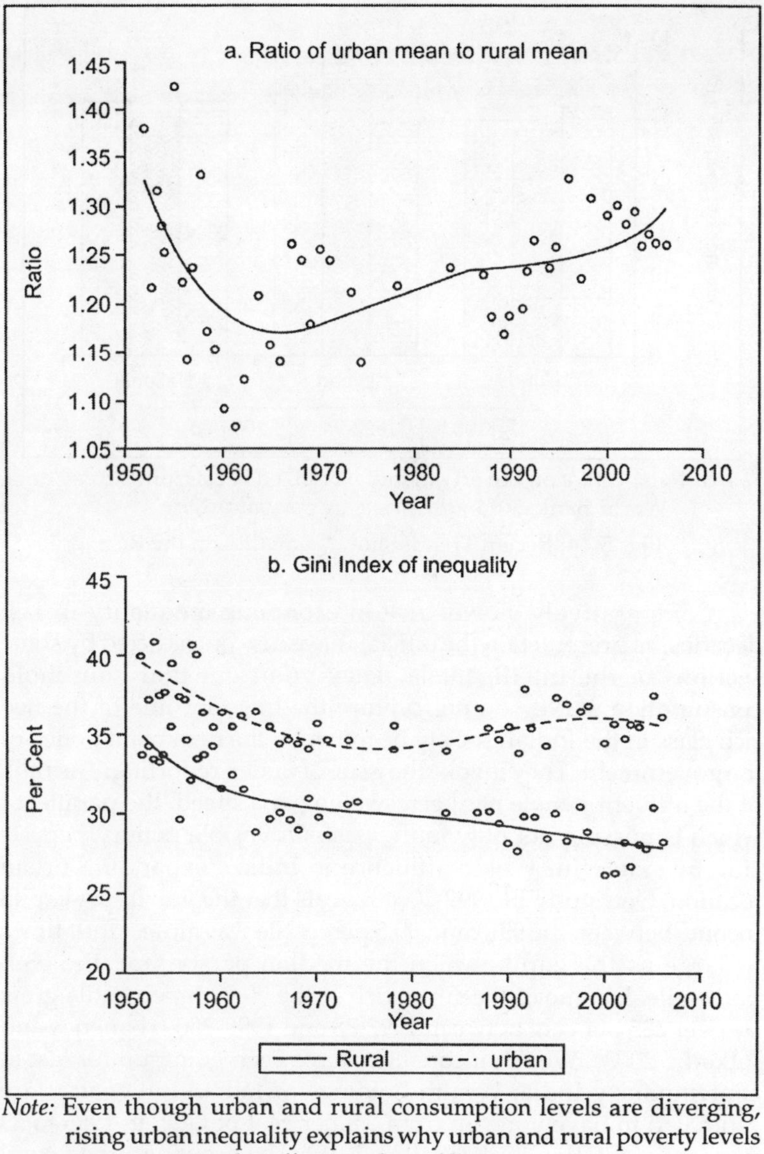

Note: Even though urban and rural consumption levels are diverging, rising urban inequality explains why urban and rural poverty levels are converging *http://www-wds.worldbank.org*

Fig. 8.13: Rising urban inequality in India

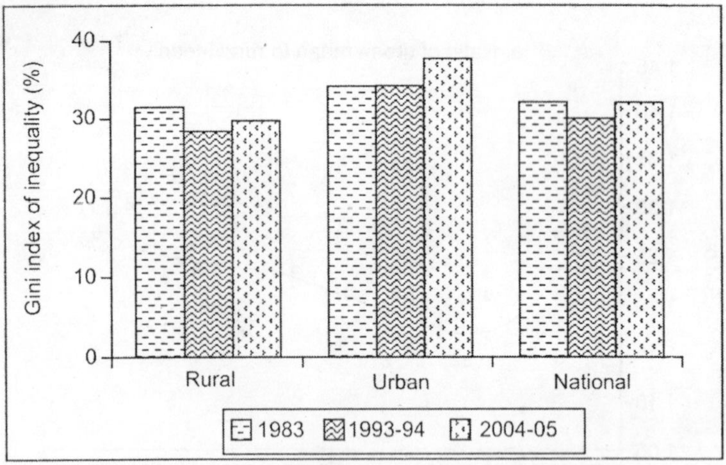

Source: Perspective on Poverty in India: Stylized Facts from Survey data, World Bank, 2011 *http://www-wds.worldbank.org*

Fig. 8.14: Recent Trends show Inequality on the Rise

Comparatively slower rise in economic inequality in last decades, as presented in the official release is contradicted by some sections of the intelligentsia. They point out that household consumption survey do not capture the huge income of the neo rich class in the Indian society begotten by the neoliberal policy of the government. They invoke the issue of under-reporting. The rank of the affluent people has been swelling at a speed, the parallel of which is missing not only in the past. Ostensible penury persists side by side with visible affluence in India's expanding urban location. One study in 1999-2000 reveals that the gap in per capita income between the 99th and 99.5 percentile was almost four times as large as the gap between the median person and the 95th percentile. Income of the super rich at the 99.99th percentile grew by over 285 per cent between 1997-88 and 1999-2000 (Banerjee and Pitketty, 2003). Wealth inequalities have been going up for fast in contemporary India. Wealth holdings of Indian billionaires are estimated to have gone up from 0.8 per cent of GDP in 1996 to 23 per cent of GDP in 2008 (Walton 2010). The growing urban-rural gap in mean income is identified by some as main trigger in causing overall income inequality in India. Inter- State difference in mean income is also held responsible for generating income inequality.

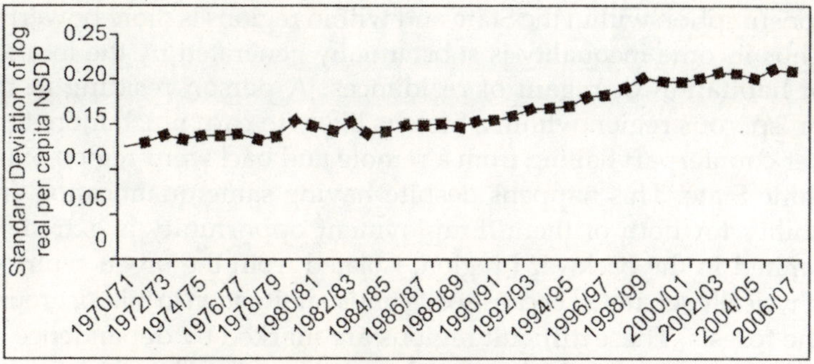

Source: Perspective on Poverty in India: Stylized Facts from Survey Data, World Bank, 2011.

Fig. 8.15: Spatial Differences have grown

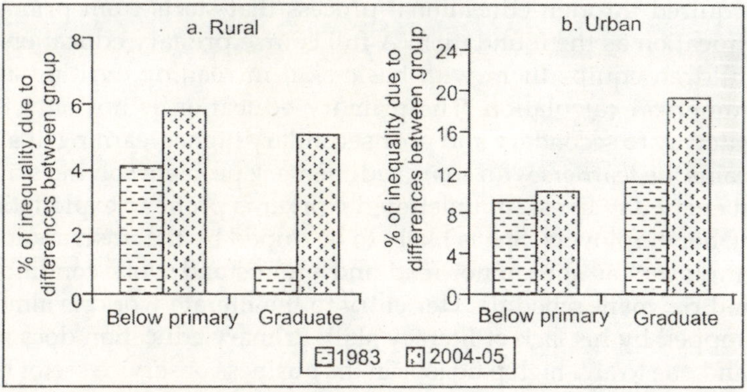

Note: Percentage of inequality due to difference between given education category compared with the rest of the population.

Source: Perspective on Poverty in India: Stylized Facts from Survey data, World Bank, 2011 *http://www-wds.worldbank.org*

Fig. 8.16: Increased Returns to Education are Driving Rising Inequality

The national account figure as presented in Figure 8.15 points out the growing inter-State inequalities in mean income. During the 70s well before the onset of neoliberal economic regime rich states used to have average income twice those of poor States, now the ratio is almost four times. However, a decomposition analysis using survey data reveals that only a small share of overall consumption inequality can be attributed to inter State or between State difference in mean income. It came to light that inequality of consumption within the State and within regions is more powerful. Thus income inequality is substantially generated by the location of habitation or regain of residences. A person residing in the prosperous region within a State is likely to earn much more than her counterpart hailing from a remote and backward region of the same State. This happens despite having same qualification and ability for both of them. Employment opportunity is extremely limited in the backward region, isolated from the urban centre or physically separated because of its unusual situation in hills or around the forests. These difficult regions are marked by dependence on mono cropping agriculture as the source of livelihood.

The other factor that contributes to economic inequality is the differential return to education of the earners. Wage differential is quite high between skilled and unskilled workers. Skill is acquired through educational process that starts from primary education as the foundation. A full course primary education of children equips them with basic skill in reading, writing and numerical calculation. The primary education is not only the gateway to secondary and post-secondary higher learning, it also trains the learners with some rudimentary problem solving skills, in every day lives. An unlettered worker is prone to exploitation by her employers. She is likely to be duped by the unscrupulous employers as she cannot read and understand work conditions and payment schedule. Her entry to the literate world is almost stopped by his lack of literacy skill. Primary education does not land one to any high paid jobs in the business or service sector but it still make a difference in lower end job. The literate small peasant fail to read the instruction printed in the box containing pesticides or inorganic fertilizers. Those written lines give the instructions for proper dose for single use or for blending to achieve best result in the field. Peasants having a full course of primary education stand ahead of those who do not have. Income earning capacity is correlated with educational attainments.

Decomposition analysis conducted to locate the factors giving birth to inequality points out that the influence of primary education on urban income inequality is present but very insignificant. But graduate education makes a large difference. The share of income inequality explained by graduate education was only 11 per cent in 1983 (Fig. 8.16). The share almost doubled to 20 per cent in 2004-05. The increasing return to education for workers in India is the testimony of the assertion that non-farm economic activities are overtaking agriculture in India. Non-farm activities require skill in diversified fields whereas farm sector can manage with very little rudimentary skill. Education would be needed as the countrysides of India shift from agriculture to non-agriculture activities. Even primary education completers can escape low paying agriculture. It seems to be strange and hard to understand why so much of differences in income is caused by the differences in educational attainments. Access to education, particularly to elementary education has expanded spectacularly. The expansion began from second half of the 90s under the auspices of the DPEP. Sarva Shiksha Mission followed by Right to Education came in the new millennium. Access to primary education is near universal for the children. But what is far from universal is quality learning.

Unfortunately inequalities in learning achievement are high in India. Rewards to skill are becoming more unequal (Dutta, 2006; Kijima, 2006). India's rising income inequality is caused by enormous difference in learning outcomes after completion of education. While schools are accessible by all children with little effort, quality schooling is limited to the privileged few who can afford it. Higher educational institutions are being built up by private companies to seize the opportunity of growing demand for quality professional education. Some of the higher educational institutions run by the government have been producing world class experts and professionals in the field of management, technology and medical sciences. But these institutions are few and far between. Admissions to these institutions are highly exclusive. The rest of the public institutions are of varied standard. Private higher educational institutions, mostly in the field of technical education, have been mushrooming in India since the period when the gate was made open for private investor. In the frantic effort to set up business through establishing and running private colleges many of them are imparting low quality education. The quality learning imparted to the learners in the higher education sector is skewed in favour of the reputed few. Income inequality in the emerging sector in the contemporary India can be explained by this.

The relationship between poverty and inequality as a subject has drawn attention of scholars of development studies from the days of the end of colonialism. However, the link is certainly not straightforward as one would expect. They do not move in the same direction with equal intensity. Some poor countries are less unequal than the others. But no one can contradict that a rise in inequality would dampen the poverty reducing impact of an increase in per capita income. Some would opine that growth acceleration might not be possible without an increase in inequality. This trend best exemplify contemporary India where return to education has a hand in India's growth performances. But the transitory inequality is less harmful than the structure inequality that characterize Indian society for thousands of years.

8.8 Social Exclusion

Transitory inequality in course of development of a country, as shown by Simon Kuznet by his famous inverted U-structure, is more or less universal. With economic prosperity this inequality slows down. Economic inequalities in the growing India are driven by the differential return to education. That works as endowment or advantages and opportunities for growth exists for people equipped with education and skill. This endowed class reaps the opportunities brought forward by neoliberal policies. The underdogs remain on the sideline. The gap in economic benefits widens fast. But the structural inequality, as an offshoot of India's hierarchical social order, is more harmful. Economic inequality is further reinforced by social exclusion. India's caste-ridden society is unique in the world. Caste and class division simultaneously persist here for hundreds of years. The twin handicaps of low caste and poverty for the large section of Indians are virtually holding them back. Birth to a low caste family spells doom for the new born baby who is expected to grow as adult in her turn. She would certainly grow as crippled adult, feeling isolated, bereft of self-esteem and missing the meaningful education throughout her life. The caste system is associated with Hindu society, the largest religious communities in India. It originated in later Vedic period and had reached its peak during medieval period in India. Social structure was built on rigid caste lines. People born to a particular caste would be identified on the basis of caste throughout their lives. One is tied to her caste lifelong. She could not scale up caste ladder by her good deeds and achievements. Occupations or livelihoods are identified with caste and occupational mobility was virtually impossible. Occupation and caste were tied. Power and privileges were usurped by the upper caste people. The powerful upper caste dominated the lower caste in all aspects of life. The social exclusion that still exists implicitly in the modern and democratic India has its roots in our historical legacy.

Decomposition analysis conducted for whole of India showed some influence of social group division on consumption inequality in India. That equally applies to her constituent States. The said analysis outlined that 4 per cent of India's consumption inequality could be explained by social grouping of the respondents households in Scheduled Tribes (ST), Scheduled Castes (SC), Muslim and others. In Bihar, the Scheduled Caste households fall behind the rests of the population. Social groups are also heterogeneous. For example, not all Scheduled Caste households are equal in economic standing. Within group inequalities are more significant than the inter-group inequality. The income gap between the richer classes within a socially disadvantaged class is wider than that between the social groups. ST and SC population are at the lowest rung in the social ladder, while the former is at the bottom followed behind by the latter.

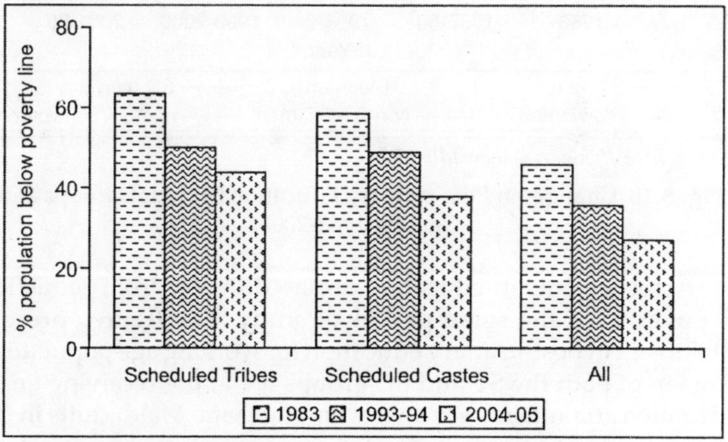

Source: Perspective on Poverty in India: Stylized Facts from Survey data, World Bank, 2011http://www-wds.worldbank.org

Fig. 8.17: In terms of Poverty, Scheduled Tribes are 20 years Behind the General Population, and Scheduled Castes are 10 Years Behind

The bottom social groups, predominated by STs and SCs have come a long way. They are certainly better now than what they were during independence. Many indicators of development, particularly relating to education and health for them have been improving over the years but they are still far behind the general caste population. Let us look at the pace of poverty reduction across social categories in India for two decades, from 1983-84 to 2004-2005. During these long years, poverty rate came down by 20 per cent for all India. But poverty rate among the ST social groups in 2004-05 was the same as in the case of general population 20 years ago in 1983. This same rate was present among SC community 10 years ago (Fig. 8.18).

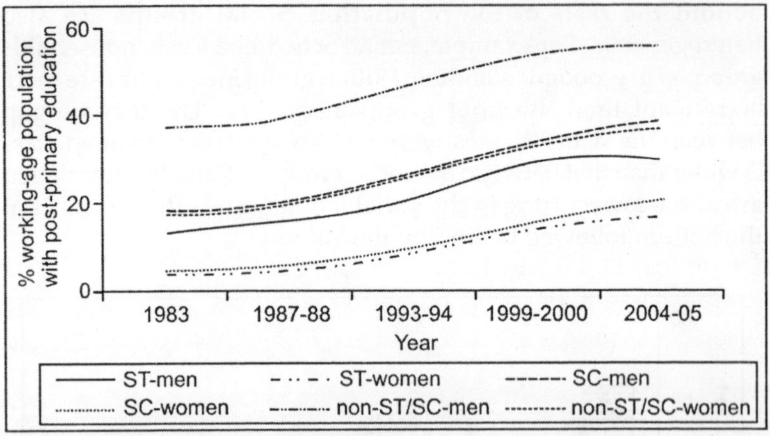

Source: *http://www-wds.worldbank.org*

Fig. 8.18: Changes in Post-primary Education by Social Groups and Gender, 1983-2005

Achievements in education are no different from reduction in poverty for the same period of study. The figures present attainment in post-primary education for working age population. Women of both the ST and SC groups are at the receiving ends. Education attainments are lowest among them. Male adults in the general category are at the top in post-primary education attainment. Disparity between male and female in this crucial field is substantially large among the upper caste Indians. Our nation has come a long way since her independence. Our economic progress during last couple of decades is quite impressive as evident in our spectacular GDP growth. We are now in the league of high growth nations to which the world is looking forward for future leadership for the third world region. Education holds the key for nation's economic progress. The gender inequality, so high among the general caste, does not augur well for India.

Infant mortality rate and child mortality along with maternal mortality are indicators of human wellbeing. Reduction in these indicators reflects improved state of affairs among population. The Scheduled Tribe community in India's caste divided society stands at the bottom of human development indicators. Child mortality is highest among them in tune with their worst performances in education. The quality of employment for the lower caste Indians reflects the other manifestations of disadvantage and discrimination. For example, nearly 30 per cent of ***dalits*** are engaged in low skill jobs, compared to 8 per cent in the general category people. The ***dalits*** are less likely to start and run their own business, more so in urban areas. They are employed in low paying and low end jobs. Low paying menial jobs are in store for them only because they lack appropriate education and skill. Many scholars, however, contradicts this observation. They tend to argue that education is not the casual factor; the social standing is an influencing factor. The wage gap is caused by the ability of access to decent occupations. ***dalits*** are thus sidelined to be perennially tied to their caste based occupations in villages. They do not switch over to other self employment activities, abandoning their traditional jobs. This immobility as a result of caste-rootedness seriously restricts the earning ability.

Even in the urban private formal sectors, recent research establishes, they are less likely to secure a job despite being as qualified as applicants of other castes (Deshpande and Newman, 2007). The *dalits* in India comprising of Scheduled Castes as designated by the Government of India are socially oppressed community. They do not live in complete isolation from the social mainstream. They live in locality populated similarly by other castes and communities. Despite historical oppression and neglect of them, social mainstreaming is possible and taking pace slowly. But tribal population in India is far off the mainstream society because of their habitation isolation. Tribal areas in India are least connected by communication network. Surface as well as telecommunication, not to speak of the up-to-date information technology, are yet to cover many remote tribal areas. The communication difficulty comes in the way of getting government services that consist mainly of education and health care. Over last two decades they have been alienated from the traditional sources of their livelihoods: land and forest (Planning Commission, 2008). Economic marginalization has led to political marginalization. They have very little role in political decision making process.

Paradoxically, India's indigenous and tribal communities are being displaced by development project. Instead of tasting the fruits of development, they are bearing the burden of development. They are forced to leave their 'home lands' to allow the mining projects to come in. They are paying the price of infrastructure development projects coming up during recent times. The tribal habitations where they have been living for thousand of years are not only rich in forest resources over ground. The underground is endowed with mineral resources. Multinational mining companies are extracting minerals on getting permission from the Government. No other communities in India have suffered as much as they have. They constitute 8 per cent of India's population but 40 per cent of the 21 million people displaced between 1951 and 1990 were tribal (Burra 2008). Consumption inequality may be less worrying, but what is worrying is educational deprivation for them (Fig. 8.18).

Female disadvantages are deep and widespread in India despite her quite impressive economic growth registered during last six decades. But the process is slow enough to be cause of worry. A baby girl born to a disadvantaged family is less likely to see her first birth day. Infant mortality rate is higher among females compared to males. Disadvantages goes up two fold for a girl child born to a poor and lower caste family. Disadvantages of poverty are reinforced by the added disadvantages of parental low caste. Girl children are valued less than the boys in the family. Girls are considered as bad investment for a poor working family. They are destined for other family. So investment on education for girls is always unrewarding for the families. From survival chances to development opportunities females are at the receiving ends. The other features of women's disadvantage in economically disadvantaged class is the prolonged cycle of child bearing and

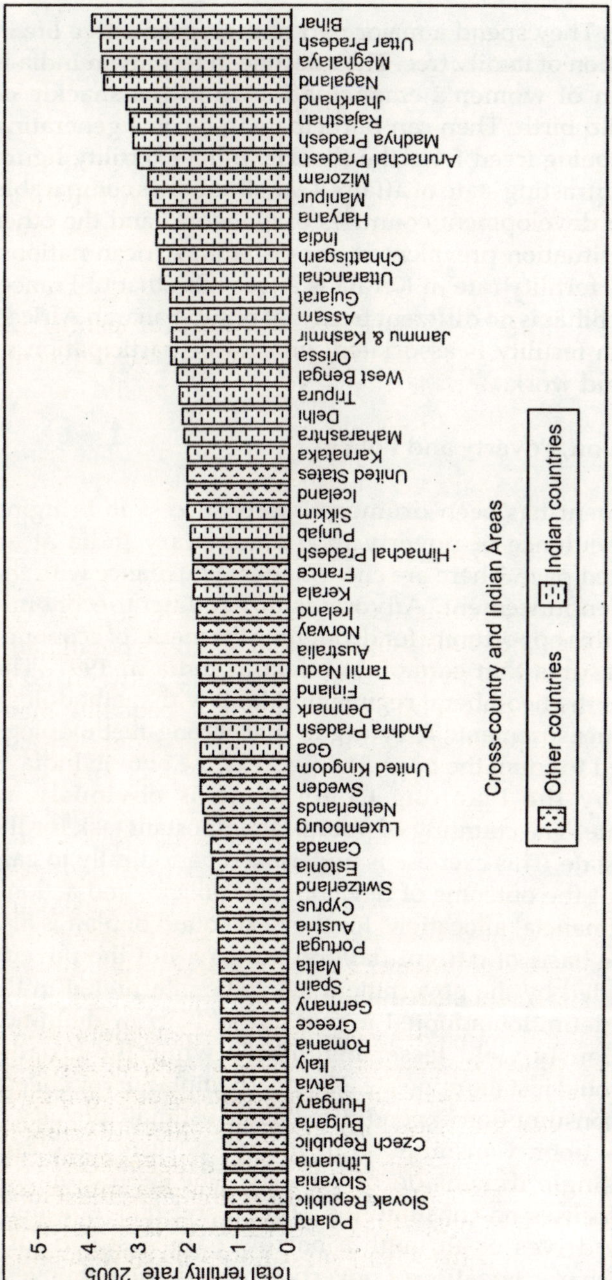

http://www-wds.worldbank.org

Note: Data from 2005, NFHS & EUROSTAT 2008, STATEAN AUSTATS

Fig. 8.19: Fertility is declining, and many Indian States resemble more developed countries Births per woman

child rearing. They spend a major part of their productive life in the continuation of family tree. Thus decline in fertility in India is the reflection of women's emancipation from the shackle of recurrent child birth. Then can participate in income generating activities on being freed from the shackle. India's fertility figure presents a contrasting state of affairs. One situation is comparable to that of the development countries of the world and the other resembles a situation prevalent in sub-Saharan African nations. For example, fertility rate in Kerala is lower than that of France. The same for Bihar is no different from that of sub-Saharan African nations. High fertility is associated with lower participation of women in paid work.

8.9 Deprivation, Poverty and Policy

The government has been drumbeating its success in bringing down the incidence of poverty in contemporary India at an unprecedented pace. There are cheer leaders who dance with the euphoric pronouncement. Advocates of neo-liberal economic policies take this opportunity for drumming the merits of economic reforms measures that came into effect in India in 1991. The opponents of the neo-liberal regime find fault with methodology of poverty measurement. They argue that wrong methodology has been used to count the poor. The figure of the poor in India as presented by the Planning Commission is obviously an underestimate. The counting of poor is an important task for the democratic state. This exercise is undertaken periodically to gain an idea about the outcome of development policies and actions. Target and financial allocations for the next round of plan is also made on the basis of current data on poverty. But the poverty figure provided by the government has to be interpreted in the light of the definition adopted to measure it. Narrow definition would obviously yield lesser magnitude while the broader definition would just the opposite. National Sample Survey collects household consumption expenditure data to estimate poverty or to count the poor. Consumption or income poverty manifestly speaks of single dimension of poverty. The definition that singularly focuses on consumption of food and non-food items perceptibly drives us through a narrow path destined for a constricted characterization of poverty. The definition of poverty must go beyond the narrow confines of consumption basket. The government must accept the foundational spirit and principle that the human poverty is not characterized by consumption or income deficits. This is wellbeing deficits that stem from multifaceted deficits. The deficits stand in the way of leading a life with dignity and freedom. Poverty must be interpreted as absence of freedom. It encompasses not only freedom from hunger and malnutrition as premise in the official construction of poverty in India. It must entail freedom from illiteracy, from ill health, from neglect and torture, from persecution, from social oppression, from discrimination on the basis of caste, gender and places of birth, from unlawful detention, from denial of political participation, from social and community engagement and from many other obstacles to decent and dignified living by all citizens. Poverty eradication projects must aim at achieving the freedom. Economic growth provides the opportunity for the state to mobilize more resources for pro-poor development initiatives. The state must come forward to take the fruits of growth to the vulnerable people. Economic growth is always welcome for the sake of the poor. Trickle down of growth without active state intervention would be elusive. Targeted anti-poverty programme must be undertaken vigorously with a firm political will. Direct cash transfer of subsidies to the poor must be undertaken provided that appropriate rural infrastructure has been created to pay cash subsidy to the deserving poor. The existing system of provisioning of subsidized food and other essentials through sale points across length and breadth of India is caught up in corruption. Subsidies allocated for poor are reaching non-poor middle men. Direct wage employment programme currently underway in India is right based. This scheme has been crafted on the basis of many lessons learnt from the failure of similar programmes in the past. Despite it manifest merits; NREGS has been crippled by many diseases. One of them is obsession of the State government with payment and disbursal without focussing on the quality of productive assets planned to be created by the wage work programme. Politics of populism is spoiling this wonderful anti-poverty programme. Strict monitoring of the work to ensure the creation of permanent productive assets in the villages must receive top most priority of governance. Self employment programme and wage employment schemes must continue as twin instruments to fight poverty. But the state must move forward to build human capital through provisioning of universal quality health care and basic education. The opportunities created by economic growth could be reaped by the underprivileged if appropriate skill is imparted to them through public action.

CHAPTER 9

Summing Up

Poverty alarmingly persists in 'fast growing' India. Spectacular opulence among the privileged class in contemporary India stands as stark contrast to the persistent poverty among the underdogs of Indian society. Prosperity of the privileged few coexists with pervasive destitution for millions of Indians. India is emerging as economic power but millions of her citizens are economically powerless. Growth sustainability is at stake in the continuation of economic destitution of a huge section of Indians. The disparity and destitution in contemporary India are at variance with her global position as the largest democracy in the world. India is a part of the world generally but part of the developing world particularly. India's massive poverty is not only swelling the rank of world's poor. Her imposing presence in the South Asian region turns this region into a 'poverty den' placed just after sub-Saharan African region. Poverty as a form of human distress is not confined to a particular geographical boundary; it keeps going in wide-ranging depth across the globe. It has a local past as well as global past. The latter goes back to our earliest ancestry well before the birth of society as human organization. Human living under the reign of nature was brutish, short and nasty. People had desired to get rid of anarchy and had embraced social living organized under set of informal rules of conduct for all members of human society. Poverty or material scarcity of food, clothing and shelter did not appear as adversity so long as nature was bountiful and were available to all human beings in plenty.

Scarcity befell on our early ancestors when nature around them had failed to sustain them any more. The migration of our early ancestors to unknown lands was evidently driven by the urge to meet the basic human need for food. Why did they migrate? Poverty certainly had pushed them out of their usual places of settlement in some corner of the present day Africa. The number of feeding mouths swelled over the years. Nature took too much time to reproduce after replenishment. Survival needs were compelling poverty as we understand as a living adversity thus pervaded our ancestors millions of years ago. Poverty in India has to be understood in the global context, particularly in relation to the dark zones of poverty in the contemporary global map. The World Bank has recently presented a horrible picture on Sub-Saharan African region comprising of 48 African states. The Bank reveals that almost half of the people of this region live on $ 1 per day which is the global mark for severe destitution. The chronic Poverty Research Centre, an arm of the UN has identified 16 countries of this region as ***'desperately deprived'***. The local context certainly matters. The tropical ecology gives rise to risk and vulnerability in agricultural operation. When agriculture is damaged by ecological disaster, it hurts the majority of the people. Poverty is being reinforced by internal strife, race riots, ethnic cleansing, terrorism as well as AIDS epidemic. The ill effects of this horrible state of affairs are reflected in the lowest standing in the ranking of Human Development Index. Two million people of this region died of AIDS in 2006.

Low capability of the people in this region is caused by the combination of the absence of quality health care and quality education for all as public goods. These states are expected to provide two important public goods. Exclusion from political, social and economic institution is part of the vicious cycle that give rise to extreme economic disparity. The nature of politics prevailing in this region is fundamentally non-developmental. Development and elimination of poverty can be accomplished by giving shape to institutions to be founded on the premise of nationhood, citizenship, fairness and democratic state. India has to teach and to learn from them. South Asian region, much smaller than the African region, comes next in sheltering the poor people in huge proportion. This region's far eastern neighbours gave shape to what is known to the world as 'East Asian Miracle'. These two Asian regions despite being close to each other geographically offer contrasting scenario. The remarkable economic prosperity in the East Asian region was primarily driven by human capital formation. Japan showed the way, the others followed the lead. The wave did not reach the shore of India. Free India inherited the huge baggage of underdevelopment from her colonial master. Eradication of poverty was the biggest challenge for the leaders of India. The World Bank has presented the state of head count poverty in this region for a period spanning 15 years.

Poverty has come down in Bangladesh, in Nepal as well as in India. Surprisingly, it has gone up in Pakistan and almost unchanged in Sri Lanka. Contrastingly GDP growth rate for Pakistan as well as Sri Lanka during the same reference period are higher than that of India. Economic growth in these two nations has failed not only to reduce poverty, growth has rather deepened it. For the region as a whole, the incidence of head count poverty is on the wane but the poor South Asian living on less than $1.25 per day has gone up from 549 million in 1981 to 595 million in 2005. Pro-poor fiscal transfer must be an immediate task. Productive base has to be enhanced by public investment in appropriate technology, promotion of markets and provisioning of quality education and health care. Endemic poverty persisting in the 'suffering zone' of the contemporary world is gravest challenge to the world community. But the genesis of poverty has to be linked with the beginning of human civilization millions of years ago. Society and state were born out of men's collective desire. Men had abandoned the state of nature for the sake of orderly life to be ruled by social order. Enlightenment thinking had sprouted during seventeenth and eighteenth century. Human distress in general and poverty in particular were diagnosed as wrong state of affairs. The thinking on poverty was shaped, in its embryonic stage by the enlightenment philosophers. Age of reason set in slackening of grip of the orthodox churches on men and control over human minds.Hegemony of rulers on the subjects began to be loosened.

The Enlightenment philosophy propagated that people's wellbeing is not decided by any unseen force or external agency beyond the control of human beings. Human minds could explain and interpret the natural surroundings around men. The physical world moves on fixed laws or rules, the understanding of which became the pursuits of scientists led by Galileo through the discovery of solar system. Copernicus, Kepler, Francis Bacon, Rene Descartes, Sir Isaac Newton formed the galaxy of stars to shed light on the mystery of the universe. The hold of church in explaining the human existence was unsettled by the series of discoveries. Material living of mankind was explained by social thinkers, enriched and equipped with new knowledge in philosophy of life. The social order in which human distress and material scarcity generates and persists can be altered by collective human action. The enlightenment philosophy taught us that social world could be understood and explained by human minds. The causes of poverty could be identified and understood by the rational minds. Man was placed in the core of social thinking and actions. The enlightenment philosophy gave birth to humanitarianism. Persistence of poverty goes against the spirit of humanitarianism. Logical understanding of the state of affairs and the light of humanism could only alter the situation. Poverty exists because of material adversity, deprivation and discriminations. It could be altered through appropriate public actions. The age of reason set in motion this understanding.

Historical documents on the incidences of poverty, as we define it now, are few and far between. Economic historians face the inadequacy of historical evidences on the nature of human distress in the ancient period. The sites of the river valley civilizations discovered during last century by archaeologists shed some light on the pattern of living of our ancestors around five thousand years ago. The artefacts and utensils found in the sites tell very little about material distress of a few or of all of them. The religious texts and epics provide some ideas about the period and the people of the time when their great literatures were scripted. But those descriptions cannot be taken as historical documents to construct history of that period. Post Vedic literature in India narrates about the celebration of ***yagna*** (sacrifice) as royal duty towards the subjects. This royal act had religious implications too. But many subjects were benefited by the royal benevolence. This royal act of charity in the garb of religious rituals points out to the persistence of destitution among a sizable section of the subjects. But this inference is also constrained by the absence of hard data of any form. One reason that appears to have caused the missing of the evidences on poverty during such long period in history is lack of value judgment. The social outlook on poverty as an unacceptable human living condition was developed in enlightenment era that gave birth to humanitarianism. Humanism demands that each human being should live happily without going through any harrowing experience of acute scarcity of material endowments.

State was born as an outcome of social contract as an institution or entity holding the power to rule. Social living under informal rule and convention for many years gave way to formation of state as a political entity. State emerged as super-guardian for people living within a certain sovereign territorial boundary. The state wields power to make rules, enact formal laws, enforces them and run the administration for the sake of peace, stability and development. State is mandated by the people to govern on behalf of people. Democracy, as a system of governance came into being to fit that pattern, where people decide and act in the governance indirectly. The world so far has witnessed varieties of state. States can be either police or ***'welfare focused'***. A police state only looks after law and order, nothing else. The welfare state, on the other hand, strives to provide as much welfare as possible for the citizens. Reduction in poverty in the aftermath of the evolution of state system is attributed to two processes; economic growth process and political process. The former create opportunities for better living overcoming poverty and the latter develops and perpetrates institutional arrangements that tend to work for safety nets and redistributive provision. Welfare states must engage themselves with these functions. State formation has two obverses: economics and politics. One is growth focused and the other is welfare focused.

Totalitarian states are least bothered about the destitution of their citizens. Dictators and autocratic rulers are preoccupied with their clinging to power. They fill their coffers by imposing exorbitant taxes on the people only to strengthen their military might. They do not bother the displeasure of the people. So long their armouries are plentiful the dictators are immune from external attack or internal rebellion. Democratic states on the other hand are for the people. The party in power has to face the next round of election. People observe and evaluate its performances during its term of office. Good work returns them to power for the next term. Failure can cause drubbing. Democratic functioning in overpopulated poor states is inhibited by different impediments. Poverty can be great handicap in the way of people's participation in governance. Spirit of democracy stands the chance to be subverted. But poverty eradication can be a priority agenda of the state if poverty can become an electoral issue in all elections. The credit score of the ruling government goes high up if a good number of poor could be lifted out of poverty by government's affirmative action. But democratic states may not be always development states. The efficacy of the democratic states in reducing poverty depends on the institutions whose functioning, in turn depends on the internal dynamics and politics. All modern states that come up in course on Great transformation from agricultural to industrial society confronted challenges of building and strengthening of national economy and provision social welfare benefits. Poverty elimination was set as a longer terms goal.

Like nature of state, culture of the land or of the community can influence the perpetuation of poverty. Cultural theorists support this contributing role of culture. They invoke the issue of mental state of inertia or apathy towards taking up challenges. Some cultures teach the people to remain happy with the present state of affairs. Samuel Huntington is the leading figure in the contemporary cultural theories. He cites the examples of Ghana and Korea to prove the practical relevance of culture in shaping economic destiny of a nation. Amartya Sen, however, contradicts this explanation. He invokes other important factors that include public policy on education and health, geopolitical location of Korea and not culture exactly as contributing factors in taking Korea far ahead of Ghana in economic advancement. But poverty in India has to be understood in the light of her history, economic opportunities and culture. The state of India that emerged after a long spell of colonial subjugation took up the task of eliminating poverty in shortest possible time. This could be accomplished through planned development as our founding fathers had hoped. The government constituted the Planning Commission to lay out Plan for India's balanced economic development. Poverty and the poor in India were to be defined, counted and to be identified.

This task has to be completed before implementing targeted antipoverty programme. Poverty line was defined and adopted by the government to count the number of poor. This is a money metric measure of ability to buy and consume the poverty line basket of goods and services. The basket contains food as well non-food items for consumption.

Nutritionists in India prescribed a 2400 kcal and 2100 kcal for rural and urban areas respectively for an able bodied and male working adult. They also identified the amount of foodgrains including cereals and lentils that would contain the prescribed calories to keep a healthy body capable of working. The National Sample Survey Organization provided the distribution of Indian population according to Monthly Per Capita Consumption Expenditure (MPCE) size class. The MPCE class satisfying the prescribed caloric norm food expenditure was taken up as poverty line yardstick. The Non-food expenditure corresponding to the food expenditure was accepted as a basic minimum. Poverty line class is thus identified in India since its introduction. But World Health Organization had insisted, way back in 1985, on 2780 Kcal for working adults. Professor Partha Dasgupta argues for heightening the cut-off to 3550 Kcal. Workloads have gone up for urban informal workers in the wake of neo-liberal policies. They would need now more calories to keep body and soul together. The minimum calorie requirement as determined during the early 70s has lost its substance in the context of contemporary India where lives for both urban and rural working poor have become harder, struggling and strenuous. Clinging to outdated norm has given rise to yawing mismatch between the numbers of poor and number of malnourished in India. While head count poverty is on the wane, number of malnourished Indians did not go down correspondingly. There is a need now to re-examine the calorimetric poverty line. The food component in the poverty line basket is need-based but the corresponding non-food basic need is imprecise. Escalating private cost on health care and quality education are not being incorporated in the official poverty line.

Thus poverty line approach is evidently reductionist and embedded in what Professor Amartya Sen has described as ***'commodity space'***. It ignores and discounts a wide variety of development deficits that cripple the underdogs in our society in various ways. Income or money metric poverty line does not consider the issues of intra-household disparity in asset ownership, the extent of household indebtedness, demographic differentiations, household morbidity and many such features. Gross calorie intake is not always equal to net caloric absorption; the body metabolic system comes in the way. The link between gross caloric intake and health outcome is not obvious at all. A large number of poor are moving away from coarse cereals. Pro-reform and anti-reform scholars have been at loggerheads for quite some time on the issue of the link between reform and poverty. Pro-reform economists tend to lay all credits to the reform measures for unprecedented reduction in head-count poverty during the period form 1993-94 to 1999-2000. Poverty fell by around 11 per cent in rural areas and close to 9 per cent in urban areas. The anti-reform groups point out that divergence between expenditure poverty and caloric poverty is widening very fast. Economic inequality in India is on the rise Professor Arjun Sengupta had found that 78 per cent of India's population has been surviving on ₹ 20 per day. In the face of so many outcries against government's claim, Tendulkar Committee was constituted to reveal the incidences of poverty in India. The Committee adopted new methodology in the light of the growing demand from all corners to broaden the definition of poverty. The Committee kept the urban poverty unchanged at 25.7 per cent but came out with an enhanced figure of 41.8 per cent for rural poverty in India. Calorie anchored poverty line fails to explain the mismatch between reductions of poverty and increase or stagnation in malnutrition prevalence among women and children. Tendulkar Committee's recommendations was accepted by the Government and was appreciated by a number of scholars. But the limitations were also pinpointed by some observers of poverty in India. The sceptics argue that the Committee did not verify empirically the claim that caloric requirement has come down in rural India.

The poor families are to be identified for the sake of targeting as recipients of social welfare programmes. Below Poverty Line (BPL) families are to be provided with subsidized foodgrains through PDS. The government has to identify them. During 80s, the beneficiaries' list was made on the basis of annual family income. The limitation of money income as an indicator of destitution came to the fore. Income as a sole criterion was discarded in the next survey. The BPL survey conducted in 1997 to record ownerships of productive and non-productive durable assets of rural households. Households owning at least one of the ***'enlisted'*** assets were surveyed and the BPL list was made on the basis of monthly consumption expenditure. Five years later, in 2002, a complete new survey tool was used. Altogether 13 socio-economic parameters were taken up for assessing relative prosperity or destitution of households. A cut-off score was fixed below which families were identified as targeted beneficiaries. Again is 2009, Saxena Committee was constituted for devising better tool for indentifying the poor in the highly charged backdrop of agitations against wrongful BPL listing. The Committee recommended some features to be taken into account for inclusion as well as exclusion from the list.

Single focus on GNP per capita as a measure of economic wellbeing is out of fashion. The first departure from one-dimensional focus was visible worldwide when the World Bank and the United Nations adopted Human Development Index as a measure of quality of life for the people in the member-states. The world community accepted that income or per capita G.N.P. as weak measuring yardstick. Health and education are important drivers of human wellbeing. The World Bank is now constructing Multi-dimensional Poverty Index (MPI). It came to light that 51 per cent of South Asians are Multi-dimensionally poor.

Persistence of endemic poverty poses a serious threat to political stability. The contemporary Maoist insurgency in the tribal dominated poverty ridden Hindi-heart land of India is the manifestation of such outburst. Can poverty and democracy co-habit? There are poor democracies in the world. But the spirit of democracy is undermined in the presence of massive poverty. Political participation of people, as a feature of democracy, would be severely undermined by the persistence of poverty. Poverty persists in totalitarian African states also. Singapore, Korea, Taiwan or even China are examples of totalitarian states whose record in eliminating poverty within this respective areas are remarkable. Thus reduction of poverty does not always depend on the form of government. It depends on the outlook, vision, political culture and appropriate public policy of the rulers. Democratic state is committed to the people. The state has to strive for alleviation of poverty. Economic growth process in the democratic state is expected to eliminate poverty in course of time. But the ***'trickle down'*** could be missing or would be very little. Democratic states undertake anti-poverty programmes. India's Integrated Rural Development Programme (IRDP), Swarana Jayanti Swarojgar Yojna (SGSY) and National Rural Employment Programme (NREP) are examples of some of the prominent antipoverty programme.

Broadly, these programmes are of two types: self-employment and wage employment. The latest addition in the band of the wage employment programmes is the right based National Rural Employment Guarantee Programmes (NREGS). These programmes could have contributed immensely in fighting poverty in India but they could not succeed fully not only because of shortcomings in planning but also because of official neglect and lack of monitoring during implementations. Reaching the target numbers, releasing the funds, payment and spending within stipulated time are overwhelming tasks of the implementing officials. Government seems to be less concerned about the real outcome of the massive public spending. Household poverty is the disadvantage for the unit as a whole but some of the members are hit more than the others. Children, women and aged in the poor families are always at the receiving ends. Child poverty relates to child disadvantaged in the poor families. Disadvantage begins from the womb itself and continues for the entire span of childhood. Children in a poor family are most likely to be born to a malnourished mother. She did not receive prenatal care, nutritious diets, rests and leisure as primary necessities to give birth to a healthy baby. Infant mortality and child mortality rates are high in poor families because of pre-natal and post-natal neglect. Child poverty could be eliminated not only through economic empowerment of the families but also through child-centred development initiatives focusing on child care, nutrition, sanitation and education. The women members like children in the family bear the brunt of economic adversities.

Feminization of poverty is a contemporary coinage by the opponents of the neo-liberal policies. They argue that females in the poor families are more hit compared to males by the onslaught of reforms-driven poverty. The unequal intra-household resources distribution is further widened by the reform measures. Adult male members migrate to cities and towns to seek likelihoods there. Women and aged are left behind to fend for themselves. Anti-globalizers argue that the inroad of market economy in place of state control and allocation of resources has been displaying danger signal for the underdogs. The compulsion of reform measures is turning the states into passive onlookers to the plight of the underprivileged. Social welfare measures of the poor and vulnerable are disappearing fast. Mother-headed families are coming up in large numbers in which single mothers are burdened with the double duties of household chores and income earning work outside homes.

Advocates of globalization press the point that economic interconnection reduces poverty by creating opportunities for employment in the new areas of productive undertaking. Investment, technology and new ideas are helping not harming the developing world. The opponents paint the neoliberal regime as demon on its way to swallow the poor of the third world countries. State protection for the poor is being withdrawn. Multinationals are having free run. Those who are in between the two divergent poles of arguments on the effects of globalization try to reconcile the two contrasting arguments. They argue that public policies of the globalizing states determine the outcome of globalization. But poverty, as it persists in many locations of the world, is anathema to freedom, the enjoyment of which is worldwide accepted as human rights. Freedom from hunger is the worst casualty of poverty. Poverty curbs the freedom to live a life full of dignity. The poverty is thus unfreedom.

Viewed from the angle of capability, poverty is the state of capability deprivation. Capability is the opportunity or ability a person to do what she has reason to do. One should have the opportunity to become certain person. Income is not the signifier of human wellbeing. Incomes have to be translated into good life. A person may be capability poor but may not be income poor. The state must provide enough opportunities to convert income into highest possible human wellbeing. Poverty impedes human agency to flourish and develop. The Universal Human Rights adopted at the United Nations, calls for promotion of human freedom for all human beings on this planet. Perpetuation of poverty at any location of the world goes against the spirit of universal human rights.

Growing and shining India is home to 300 million poor as per government estimate released in 2005. But incidence of head count poverty has remarkably come down if one goes by government data. Two well known agencies of the government, National Sample Survey (NSS) and National Accounts Statistics (NAS) are tasked with making estimate of poverty differ on the progress of poverty reduction. Divergence should give way to convergence for the sake of better planning. Pattern of growth significantly determines the impact of it on the pace of poverty reduction. Agriculture, thus still sustains majority of Indians, grew very slowly in the post-reform years. Thus pace of poverty reduction is halted by stagnant or ***'snail like moving'*** agriculture. Consumption poverty has declined during the decades after economic reforms measures in 1999. Surprisingly, caloric poverty has not declined and as many as 80 per cent of rural Indians were caloric-poor in 2004-2005. Why does it happen? Economists of the neo-liberal camp argue that people at large are moving away from coarse cereals to expensive foods as a result of enhanced purchasing power. They justify this argument by invoking the findings of two research surveys. One is self-reported hunger study that reveals drastic fall in hunger perception during the period from 1983 to 2005. The other is the world Gallup Poll survey conducted in 2006 which reports that half of the respondents in India were getting better now materially. But inter-State and intra State variation in the level of poverty in India is certainly worrisome. One feature of India's contemporary growth scenario is that urban prosperity has been contributing to reduction in poverty in the rural areas encircling the urban centres. Expansion of urban economy has been helping the rural non-farm economy to grow where agriculture is languishing, rural workers are moving toward non-farm jobs. But the quality of non-farm employment is on the wane. Steady reduction of consumption poverty in India does not match with her deplorable score card in human development indicators. While the score for the nation as a whole is upsetting, some States have already touched the level of the developed countries in this regard. Scores of some other States resemble those of poor African nations. India as a nation should emulate her own'best achieving' constituting state. Indicators of child wellbeing, as estimated by the government agencies, are causes of concern for all. School enrolment has remarkably gone up in recent times. But children are learning very little in the overcrowded schools. Poverty comes in the way of gaining quality learning. While decline in consumption, poverty is a cause for rejoicing, the increase in income inequality in the 'growing' India is enough cause for worry. We are now on the way to join the league of high unequal countries of the world along with Brazil and South Africa.

The widening inequality in India is driven by differential return to education of the participants in economically productive activities. The caste division, still powerful in modernizing India, have a say in the distribution of the fruits of development. Poverty and low caste are familiar bed fellows. Social exclusion and economic exclusion have been reinforcing each other. The lesson we learn from India's growth trajectory since her birth as a free nation is rich to learn and disseminate. Economic growth, on its own does not take care of disempowered people. Appropriate public policies can only drive the growth juggernaut in such way that it lifts the underdogs, incapable of getting in to it independently. Those powerless Indians have to be empowered through public action, the major part of which must be meaningful education and quality health care for all.

Bibliography

Ahluwalia, M S. (1978), 'Rural Poverty and Agricultural Performance in India', *Journal of Development Studies*, 14(2): 298-323.

Banerjee, A. and E. Duflo (2007), "The Economic Lives of the Poor", *Journal of Economic Perspectives*, 21(1):141-167.

Banerjee, A., and T. Piketty (2003), "Top Indian Incomes: 1956-2000", *World Bank Economic Review*, 19(1): 1-20

Bardhan, P.K. (1970), 'On the Minimum Level of Living and the Rural Poor', *Indian Economic Review*, 5(1): 129-36

———(1971), 'On the Minimum Level of Living and the Rural Poor: A Further Note', *Indian Economic Review*, 6(1): 78-8.

———(1973), 'On the Incidence of Poverty in Rural India of the Sixties', *Economic and Political Weekly*, 8(4/6): 245-54.

Basu, K. (2001), 'On the Goals of Development', in G.M. Meier and J.E. Stiglitz (eds). *Frontiers of Development Economics: The Future in Perspective*. New York: Oxford University Press, pp. 61-86.

———(2006), 'Globalization, Poverty, and Inequality: What is the Relationship? What Can Be Done', *World Development*. 34(8): 1361-73.

Bhatty. I.Z. (1974), 'Inequality and Poverty in Rural India', in TN. Srinivasan and P.K. Bardhan (eds). *Poverty and Income Distribution in India*. Calcutta: Statistical Publishing Society, pp. 291-336.

Borooah, V. and S. Iyer (2004), 'Vidyi, Veda and Varna: The Influence of Religion and Caste on Education in Rural India', *Journal of Development Studies*, forthcoming.

Caglar, O. and M. Sewadeh (2010), "How important is migration?", in E. Ghani (ed.), *The Poor Half Billion in South Asia*, Oxford University Press.

Cali, M., and C. Menon, (2009), "Does Urbanization Affect Rural Poverty? Evidence from Indian Districts." Spatial Economics Research Center Discussion Paper 14, London School of Economics, London, U.K.

Calvo, C. and S. Dercon (2003), 'Adjusted Indian Poverty Estimates for 1999-2000'. *Economic and Political Weekly*, January 25, pp. 322-26.

_______, (2005), 'Measuring Individual Vulnerability', UNU-WIDER Jubilee Conference, Helsinki. Finland.

Chakraborty Sudip (1999), *Rural Poverty and IRDP*, Ncrthern Book Centre, New Delhi.

Chakraborty Sudip (2011), *Food Security and Child Labour*, Deep & Deep Publications, New Delhi.

Chattopadhyay, A., and T. K. Roy (2005). "Are Urban Poor doing Better than their Rural Counterpart in India? A Study of Fertility, Family Planning and Health." *Demography India*, 34 (2): 299–312

Chen, S. and M. Ravallion (2000), How Did the World? Poorest Fare in the 1990s?' Working Paper. August. World Bank. Washington, D.C. Available at *http://'ideas. repec.org/p/wbk/wbrwps/2409.html.*

_______ (2008), 'The Developing World is Poorer Than We Thought; But No Less Successful in the Fight against Poverty'. Policy Research Working Paper 4703, August. World Bank Development Research Group, World Bank. Washington. D.C.

Chiappero Martinetti, E. (1994), A New Approach to Evaluation of Well-being and Poverty by Fuzzy Set Theory', *Giornale Degli Economisti e Annali di Economia.'* 53(7-9): 367-88.

Cornia, G.A. and F. Stewart (1995), Two Errors of Targeting'. *Journal of International Development*. 5(5): 459-96.

Craig, D. and D. Porter (2003), 'Poverty' Reduction Strategy Papers: A New Convergence', *World Development*, 31 (1): 53-70 [also cited in Devereux (2002)].

Dandekar, V.M. and N. Rath (1971), *Poverty in India*, Pune: Indian School of Political Economy.

Dandekar, V. M. and N. Rath (1971), 'Poverty in India–I', *Economic and Political Weekly*, Vol 6, No 1.

Dasgupta, P. (1993), *An Inquiry into Well-Being and Destitution*. Oxford: Clarendon Press.

Datt, G., and M. Ravallion, (1996), "India's Chequered History in the Fight Against Poverty: Are There Lessons for the Future?" *Economic and Political Weekly*, 31: 2479-86.

Datt, G., and M. Ravallion, (2009), "Has Poverty in India Become Less Responsive to Economic Growth?" Background Paper prepared for "India Poverty Assessment Report", World Bank, Washington, DC.

Datta, K.L. and S. Sharma (2002), *Facets of Indian Poverty*. Concept Publishing Company, New Delhi.

Deaton, Angus (1997), *The Analysis of Household Surveys: A Microeconometric Approach to Development Policy*, The John Hopkins University Press.

_______, (2001), 'Adjusted Indian Poverty Estimates for 1999-2000', Research Programme in Development Studies, Princeton University.

Deaton, Angus, and Alessandro Tarozzi (2000), Prices and Poverty in India', Research Programme in Development Studies, Working Paper No 196, Princeton University.

Deaton, Angus and Jean Dreze (2002), 'Poverty and Inequality in India, Re-examination', *Economic and Political Weekly*, September 7. pp. 3729-48.

Deaton, A. and V. Kozel (2004), 'Data and Dogma: The Great Indian Poverty Debate', *http://www.wws.princeton.edu/~deaton/papers.html*.

Deichmann, U., M. Fay, K. Jun, and S.V. Lall, (2004), "Economic Structure, Productivity, and Infrastructure Quality in Southern Mexico." *Annals of Regional Science*, 38: 361–85.

Deshpande, A. (2000), 'Does Caste Still Define Disparity? A Look at Inequality in Kerala, India', *American Economic Review*, 90, pp. 322-25.

Dev, Mahendra S. (2005): 'Calorie Norm and Poverty', mimeo. Centre for Economic and Social Studies, Hyderabad.

Devarajan, Shanta, (2006), "Can South Asia Eliminate Poverty in a Generation?" World Bank, Washington DC, World Bank.

Devereux, S. (2003), 'Conceptualizing Destitution', Institute of Development Studies Working Paper 216, Brighton, Sussex.

Di Nardo, John, Nicole M. Fortin and Thomas Lemieux (1996), 'Labour Market Institutions and the Distribution of Wages, 1973-1992, A Semi-parametric Approach', *Econometrica*, Vol. 64, No 5, pp. 1001-44.

DiNardo, John and Justin L. Tobias (2001), Nonparametric Density and Regression Estimation', *Journal of Economic Perspective*, Vol. 14, No. 4, pp. 11-28.

Dreze, J. and P.V. Srinivasan (1997), 'Widowhood and Poverty in Rural India: Some Inferences from Household Survey Data', *Journal of Development Economics*, 54, pp. 217-34.

Dubey, A.; S. Gangopadhyay; and W. Wadhwa, (2001), "Occupational Structure and Incidence of Poverty in Indian Towns of Different Sizes." *Review of Development Economics* 5: 49-59.

Duclos, J.Y. and A. Araar (2005), *Poverty and Equity: Measurement, Policy and Estimation with DAD.* New York: Springer. Available at *http://web.idrc.ca/en/ev-97152- 201-l-DO_TOPIC.html.*

Economic and Political Weekly (EPW) (2008), 'How Many Poor in the World?', *Economic and Political Weekly*, 25 October, 43(43): 5-6.

Fafchamps, M., and F. Shilpi, (2003), "The Spatial Division of Labour in Nepal." *Journal of Development Studies*, 39 (6): 23–66.

Ferré, C.; F.H.G. Ferreira; and P. Lanjouw. (2009), "Is There a Metropolitan Bias? Urban Poverty and Access to Services by City Size in Six Developing Countries." Draft, World Bank, Washington, DC.

Fisher, G.M. (1992), 'The Development and History of the Poverty Thresholds', *Social Security Bulletin*, 55(4): 3-14.

Gardner, K., and F. Osella (eds.) (2003), "Migration, Modernity and Social Transformation in South Asia: An Overview and Contributions to Indian Sociology": *Contributions to Indian Sociology* 37, (1–2): 109–39.

Ghani, Ejaz (2010), The *Poor Half Billion in South Asia—What is holding back lagging regions?*, Oxford University Press

Glaeser, Edward (2010), *Making Sense of Bangalore*, Legatum Institute, London

Gopalan, C.; B.V. Rama Sastri; and S.C. Balasubramanian (1999): *Nutritive Value of Indian Foods*, National Institute of Nutrition. ICMR, Hyderabad.

Government of India (1979), *Report of the Task Force on Projection of Minimum Needs and Effective Demand*, Perspective Planning Division, Planning Commission, New Delhi.

________ (1993), *Report of the Expert Group on Estimation of Proportion and Number of Poor*, Perspective Planning Division, Planning Commission, New Delhi.

________ (1995), *Nutritional Intake in India 1993-94*, National Sample Survey Organisation, Ministry of Statistics and Programme Implementation, New Delhi.

________ (2001), *Nutritional Intake in India 1999-2000*, National Sample Survey Organisation, Ministry of Statistics and Programme Implementation, New Delhi.

________ (2009), *Report on Conditions of Work and Promotion of Livelihoods in the Unorganized Sector.* New Delhi: National Commission for Enterprises in the Unorganized Sector.

Government of India (2001), *Census Town Directory*, New Delhi: Office of the Registrar General.

_______, (2009), *Report of the Expert Group to Review the Methodology for Estimation of Poverty*, New Delhi: Government of India, Planning Commission.

Greer, J. and E. Thorbecke (1986), 'A Methodology for Measuring Food Poverty Applied to Kenya', *Journal of Development Economics*, 24(1): 59-74.

Groedhart, T.; V. Halberstadt; A. Kapteyn; and B. van Praag (1977), 'The Poverty Line: Concept and Measurement', *Journal of Human Resources*, 12(4): 503-20.

Hagenaars, A. and B. van Praag (1985), 'A Synthesis of Poverty Line Definitions', *Review of Income and Wealth*, 31(2): 139-54.

Hardle, W.; M. Muller; S. Sperlich; and A. Wcrwatz (2004), *Non-parametric and Semi-parametric Models*, Springer.

Harvey, A. (1976), 'Estimating Regression Models with Multiplicative Heterosccdasticity', *Econometrica*, Vol. 44, pp. 461-65.

Henderson, J.V.; Z. Shalizi; and A. J. Venables (2001), "Geography and Development." *Journal of Economic Geography*, 1: 81-105.

Himanshu, (2008), "Agriculture and Non-Farm Employment: Exploring the Inter-linkages in Rural India", Draft, Jawaharlal Nehru University, New Delhi.

Horowitz, J. (1992), 'A Smoothed Maximum Score Estimation for the Binary Response Model', *Econometrica*, 60, pp. 505-31.

Ichimura, H. (1993), 'Semi-parametric Least Squares (SLS) and Weighted SLS Estimation of Single-Index Models', *Journal of Econometrics*, Vol. 58, pp. 71-120.

Jayaraj, D. and S. Subramanian (2009), 'A Chakravarty-D'Ambrosio View of Multidimensional Deprivation: Some Estimates for India', *Economic and Political Weekly*, 45(6): 53-65.

Kapadia-Kundu, N., and T. Kanitkar, (2002), "Primary Healthcare in Urban Slums", *Economic and Political Weekly*, 37: 5086-89.

Kapteyn, A.; P. Kooreman; and R. Willemse (1988), 'Some Methodological Issues in the Implementation of Subjective Poverty Definitions', *Journal of Human Resources*, 23: 222-42.

Kapur, D., and J. Witsoe, (2008), "The Role of Spatial Mobility in India's 'Silent Revolution': A Case Study of Migration from Rural Bihar", Background Paper prepared for *Indian Poverty Assessment Report*, Center for the Advanced Study of India, University of Pennsylvania, Philadelphia.

Kijima, Y. (2006), "Why did wage inequality increase? Evidence from urban India 1983-99, *Journal of Development Economics*, 81(1): 97-117

Klasen, S. (2008), 'Economic Growth and Poverty Reduction: Measurement Issues using Income and Non-Income Indicators', *World Development*, 36(3): 420-45.

Klein, R. Ind R. Spady (1993): 'An Efficient Semi-parametric Estimator for Binary Response Models', *Econometrica*, Vol. 61, pp. 387-421.

Krishnaji, N. (1984): 'Family-size. levels of Living and Differential Mortality in Rural India Some Paradoxes', *Economic and Political Weekly*, 19, pp. 2- 8-58.

Krugman, Paul (1999), "The Role of Geography in Development", *International Regional Science Review*, 22(2): 142-161.

Kundu, A. (2009), "Elite Capture and Marginalization of the Poor in Participatory Urban Governance. A Case of Resident Welfare Association in Metro Cities", in *India Urban Poverty Report 2009*. New Delhi: Oxford University Press.

Kundu, A., and N. Sarangi. (2005), "Employment Guarantee in India: The Issue of Urban Exclusion", *Economic and Political Weekly*, 40: 3642–46.

Lall, S.V.; U. Deichmann; M.K.A. Lundberg; and N. Chaudhury, (2004). "Tenure, Diversity, and Commitment: Community Participation for Urban Services Provision", *Journal of Development Studies*, 40: 1-26.

Lall, S.V.; E. Schroeder; and E. Schmidt (2008), "Geographically Prioritizing Infrastructure Improvements to Accelerate Growth in Uganda", Background paper for 2009, *World Development Report: Reshaping Economic Geography*, World Bank, Washington, DC.

Lanjouw, P., and R. Murgai. (2009), "Poverty Decline, Agricultural Wages, and Non-farm Employment in Rural India: 1983-2004", *Agricultural Economics*, 40 (2): 243–64.

Lanjouw, P., and E. Rascon (2010), "Child Malnutrition and City Size in Urban Mexico", Draft, Development Economics Research Group, World Bank, Washington, DC.

Leftwich, Adrian, *Indian Journal of Human Development*, Indian Institute of Human Development, New Delhi. Vol. 5, No. 2, 2011.

Ligon, E. and L. Schechter (2003), 'Measuring Vulnerability', *Economic Journal*, 113(486): C95-C102.

Lipton, M. (1977), *Why Poor People Stay Poor: Urban Bias and World Development*. London: Temple Smith.

Meenakshi, J.V. and B. Vishwanathan (2003), 'Calorie Deprivation in Rural India, 1983-1999/2000', *Economic and Political Weekly*, 38(4): 369-75.

Meenakshi, J.V. and R. Ray (2002), 'Impact of Household Size and Family Composition on Poverty in Rural India', *Journal of Policy Modelling*, 24, pp. 539-59.

Meenakshi, J.V. and B. Vishwanathan (2003), 'Calorie Deprivation in Rural India', *Economic and Political Weekly*. Vol. 38, No. 4.

Meenakshi, J.V. and B. Vishwanathan (2003), 'Calorie Deprivation in Rural India, *Economic and Political Weekly*, 38(4), pp. 369-75.

Mehta, J. and S. Venkataraman (2000): 'Poverty Statistics. Bermicide's Feast', *Economic and Political Weekly*, Vol. 35, No. 27.

Mehta, J. and S. Venkatraman (2000), 'Poverty Statistics: Barmicide's Feast', *Economic and Political Weekly*, 35(27): 2377-82.

Minhas, B.S. (1970), 'Rural Poverty, Land Redistribution and Development Strategy', *Indian Economic Review*, 5(1): 97-128.

_______, (1971a), 'Rural Poverty and the Minimal Level of Living: A Reply', *Indian Economic Review*, 6(1): 69-77.

_______, (1971b),'More on Rural Poverty, or a Glimmer of Progress', *Indian Economic Review*, 6(1): 88-94.

Minhas, B.S. (1971c),'Rural Poverty, Numbers Games and Polemics', *Indian Economic Review*, 6(1): 97-102.

Minhas, B.S. (1991), 'On Estimating the Inadequacy of Energy Intakes: Revealed Food Consumption Behaviour *versus* Nutritional Norms', *Journal of Development Studies*, Vol. 28, No. 1.

Mishra, P. (2006) *Butter Chicken in Ludhiana. Travels in Small Town of India*. London: Picador.

Nayyar, R. (1991), *Rural Poverty in India: An Analysis of Inter-State Differences*. New Delhi: Oxford University Press.

Orshansky, M. (1965),'Counting the Poor: Another Look at the Poverty Profile', *Social Security Bulletin*, 28(1): 3-29.

Osmani, S.R. (1992), 'On Some Controversies in the Measurement of Undernutrition', in S.R. Osmani (ed.), *Nutrition and Poverty*. Oxford: Clarendon Press, pp. 121-61.

Palmer-Jones, R., and A. Dubey. (2007), "Poverty Measurement, Poverty Lines and Consumer Price Indexes in India: A Critique." Presentation at the "International Seminar on Revisiting the Poverty Issue: Measurement, Identification and Eradication", A.N. Sinha Institute, Patna, July 20-22.

Pagan, Adrian and Aman Ullah (1999), *Non-Parametric Econometrics*, Cambridge University Press.

Panda, M. and R.K. Rath (1999), 'Price Changes and Some Underlying Aspects of Measurement of Poverty', Indira Gandhi Institute of Development Research Discussion Paper No. 152, IGIDR, Mumbai.

Pandey, P.; S. Goyal; and V. Sundaraman, (2008), "Public Participation, Teacher Accountability and School Outcome. Policy Research Working Paper 4777, World Bank, Washington DC.

Patnaik. I. (2004): *The Republic of Hunger*, Public Lecture on the occasion of the 50th Birthday of Safdar Hashmi, organised by SAHAM AT (Safdar Hashmi Memorial Trust) on April 10, New Delhi.

Patnaik, U. (2004),'The Republic of Hunger', *Social Scientist*, 32(9-10): 9-35. (Text of a Public Lecture on the occasion of the 50th Birthday of Safdar Hashmi on 10 April 2004, New Delhi.)

Patnaik, U. (2004): 'Alternative Ways of Estimating Poverty and Implications for Policy: A Critical Appraisal of the Indian Experience", www.networkideas.org.

Patnaik, U. (2007), 'Neoliberalism and Rural Poverty in India', *Economic and Political Weekly*, 48(32): 3132-50.

Planning Commission (1962), 'Perspective of Development: 1961-1976, Implications of Planning for a Minimum Level of Living', Government of India, New Delhi [Reprinted in Srinivasan and Bardhan (1974)], *Poverty and Income Distribution.*

Planning Commission (1979), *Report of the Task Force on Projections of Minimum Needs and Effective Consumption Demand.* New Delhi: Government of India.

Planning Commission (1984), *Report of the Study Group on the Concepts and Estimation of Poverty Line.* New Delhi: Government of India.

_______, (1985), *Seventh Five Year Plan* (Vol. I). New Delhi: Government of India.

_______,(1993), *Report of the Expert Group on Estimation of Proportion and Number of Poor.* New Delhi: Government of India.

_______,(2009), *Report of the Expert Group to Review the Methodology for Estimation of Poverty.* New Delhi: Government of India.

Pogge, T.W. (2008), 'Where the Line is Drawn: A Rejoinder to Ravallion', One-Pager Number 69, October. International Poverty Centre, United Nations Development Programme (UNDP), Brasilia.

Pogge, T.W. and S.G. Reddy (2006), 'Unknown: The Extent, Distribution and Trend of Global Income Poverty'. Available at http://www.columbia.edu/~sr793/povpop. pdf.

Powell, J.L.; J. H. Stock; and T. M. Stoke (1989): 'Semi-parametric Estimation of Index Coefficients', *Econometrica*, Vol. 57, pp. 1403-30.

Pratham (2009), "Annual Survey of Education Report", Pratham Resource Centre, New Delhi.

Qizilbash, M. (2003), 'Vague Language and Precise Measurement: The Case of Poverty', *Journal of Economic Methodology*, 10(1): 41-58.

Ravallion, M. (1998),'Poverty Lines in Theory and Practice', Living Standards Measurement Study, Working Paper 133, World Bank, Washington, D.C.

_______, (2004), 'Monitoring Progress against Global Poverty', *In Focus: Dollar A Day How Much Does it Say?*, September, 6-8, International Poverty Centre, UNDP, Brasilia.

_______, (2008), "'How Many Poor in the World?: A Reply", *Economic and Political Weekly*, 43(45): 78-9.

_______, (2010),'How Not to Count the Poor? A Reply to Reddy and Pogge', in J. Stiglitz, S. Anand, and P. Segal (eds), *Debates in the Measurement of Poverty*. Oxford: Oxford University Press.

Ravallion, Martin, S Chen, and P Sangraula (2009), "Dollar a Day Revisited", Policy Research Working Paper No. 4620, World Bank, Washington DC.

Ravallion, M.; S. Chen; and P. Sangraula. 2007. "New Evidence on the Urbanization of Global Poverty." *Population and Development Review* 33 (4): 667-702.

Ravallion, M.; G. Datt; and D. van de Walle (1991), 'Quantifying Absolute Poverty in the Developing World', *Review of Income and Wealth*, 37(4): 345-61.

Ray Ranjan, Geoffrey Lancaster (2005), 'On Setting the Poverty Line Based on Estimated Nutrient Prices: Condition of Socially Disadvantaged Groups during the Reform Period', *Economic and Political Weekly*, Vol. XL, No I, January 1.

Ray, R. and G. Lancaster (2005), 'On Setting the Poverty Line Based on Estimated Nutrient Prices: Condition of Socially Disadvantaged Groups during the Reform Period', *Economic and Political Weekly*, Xl(l): 46-56.

Reddy, S.G. (2004), 'A Capability-based Approach to Estimating Global Poverty', *In Focus: Dollar A Day How Much Does it Say?*, September, 6-8, International Poverty Centre, UNDP, Brasilia.

_______, (2007), 'The Great Indian Poverty Debate', *Development*, 50(2): 166-71.

_______ (2008), 'Differently Distorted: The World Bank's "Updated" Poverty Estimates', *Economic and Political Weekly*, 43(43): 44-7.

Reddy, S.G. and T.W. Pogge (2010), 'How *Not* to Count the Poor', in Stiglitz, Anand, and Segal (eds), *Debates in the Measurement of Poverty*. A longer version is available at www.socialanalysis.org.

Rudra, A. (1974), 'Minimum Level of Living—A Statistical Examination', in Srinivasan and Bardhan (eds), *Poverty and Income Distribution*.

Sachs, Jeffery D; Ashutosh Varshney; and Nirupam Bajpai (1999): *India in the Era of Economic Reform.'*, Oxford University Press, Oxford.

Saith, Ashwani (2005), Poverty Lines *versus* Poor, *Economic and Political Weekly*, October 2005.

Sen, A.K. (1983), 'Poor, Relatively Speaking', *Oxford Economic Papers*, 35(2): 153-69.

_______, (1985a), *Commodities and Capabilities*. Amsterdam: North-Holland Press.

_______, (1985b), 'A Sociological Approach to the Measurement of Poverty: A Reply to Professor Townsend', *Oxford Economic Papers*, 37(4): 669-76.

_______, (1992), *Inequality Reexamined*. New York: Russell Sage Foundation and Oxford: Clarendon Press.

Sen, Abhijit (2000): 'Estimates of Consumer Expenditure and its Distribution: Statistical Priorities after the NSS 55th Round', *Economic and Political Weekly*, December 16, pp 4499-518.

Sen, Abhijit and Himanshu (2004): Poverty and Inequality in India, *Economic and Political Weekly*, September 18, pp 4247-63.

Shorrocks, A.F. (2004), 'Inequality and Welfare Evaluation of Heterogeneous Income Distributions, *Journal of Economic Inequality*, 2(3): 193-218.

_______, (2005), 'Inequality Values and Unequal Shares', UNU-WIDER, Helsinki, Finland. Available at *http://www.wider.unu.edu/conference/conference-2005-5/ conference-2005.5.htm.*

Shorrocks, A.F. and S. Subramanian (1994),'Fuzzy Poverty Indices', Mimeo, University of Essex.

_______, (2006), 'Poverty: An Overview', Mimeo, UNU-WIDER, Helsinki, Finland.

Srinivasan, T.N. and P.K. Bardhan (eds.) (1974), *Poverty and Income Distribution in India*. Calcutta: Statistical Publishing Society.

Subramanian, S. (1987), 'Poverty Statistics: Real Phenomena or Arithmetical Illusions? A Note', in Malcolm S. Adiseshiah (ed.), *Mid-Year Review of the Economy 1986-87*. New Delhi: Lancer International, pp. 135-41.

_______, (1990), 'Poverty', in Malcolm S. Adiseshiah (ed.), *Eighth Plan Perspectives*. New Delhi: Lancer International, pp. 221-54.

Subramanian, S. (1997), 'Introduction: The Measurement of Inequality and Poverty', in S. Subramanian (ed.), *Measurement of Inequality and Poverty* (Readers in Economics Series). New Delhi: Oxford University Press, pp. 1-53 (Reprinted as Oxford India Paperbacks: 2000, 2002).

_______, (2005), 'Unravelling a Conceptual Muddle: India's Poverty Statistics in the Light of Basic Demand Theory', *Economic and Political Weekly*, XL(1): 57-66.

_______, (2009a), "How Many Poor in the World?": A Critique of Ravallion's Reply', *Economic and Political Weekly*, 44(5): 67-71.

_______, (2009b), 'A Practical Proposal for Simplifying the Measurement of Income Poverty', in K. Basu and R. Kanbur (eds), *Arguments for a Better World: Essays in Honour of Amartya Sen, Volume 1: Ethics, Welfare, and Measurement*. Clarendon: Oxford University Press, pp. 435-52.

Subramanian, S. (2005): 'Unravelling a Conceptual Muddle: India's Poverty Slatistics in the Light of Basic Demand Theory'. *Economic and Political Weekly*, January I, pp. 57-66.

_______, (2010), 'Identifying the Income-Poor: Some Controversies in India and Elsewhere', Discussion Paper 46, Poverty, Equity and Growth Discussion Papers Series, Courant Research Centre, Goettingen, Germany.

_______, (2011a), "'Inclusive Development" and the Quintile Income Statistic', *Economic and Political Weekly*, XLVI(4): 69-72.

_______, (2011b), 'Money-metric Poverty Identification: A Cautionary Note', *Journal of Economic Analysis*, 2(1): 35-56.

_______, (2011c), 'The Poverty Line: Getting it Wrong Again', *Economic and Political Weekly*, XLVI(49): 37-42.

Sukhatme, P. V. (1978): 'Assessment of Adequacy of Diets at Different Income Levels', *Economic and Political Weekly*, Special Number.

_______, (1993), 'Note' in *Report of the Expert Group on Estimation of Proportion and Number of Poor*. Perspective Planning Division, Planning Commission, New Delhi.

Sundram, K. and S. D. Tendulkar (2003a), 'Poverty has declined in the 1990s: A Resolution of Comparability Problems in NSS Consumer Expenditure Data', *Economic and Political Weekly*, January 25, pp. 327-37.

_______, (2003b): 'Poverty in India in the 1990s: Revised Results for All-India and the 15 Major States for 1993-1994', *Economic and Political Weekly*, November 15, pp. 4865-72.

_______(2003c), 'Poverty among Social and Economic Groups in India in 1990s', *Economic and Political Weekly*, December 13, pp. 5263-76.

Suryanarayana, M.H. (1996), 'Food Security and Calorie Adequacy Across States: Implications for Reforms', *Journal of Indian School of Political Economy*, 8(2): 203-65.

_______, (2000), 'How Real is the Secular Decline in Rural Poverty?', *Economic and Political Weekly*, 35(25): 2129-40.

Tarozzi, Alessandro (2002), 'Estimating Comparable Poverty Counts from Incomparable Surveys: Measuring Poverty in India', Princeton University, processed.

_______, (2004): 'Calculating Comparable Statistics from Incomparable Surveys, Application to Poverty in India', Duke University, processed.

Townsend, P. (1979), 'The Development of Research on Poverty', *Social Security Research: The Definition and Measurement of Poverty*. London: Department of Health and Social Security, HMSO.

_______, (1985), 'A Sociological Approach to the Measurement of Poverty: A Rejoinder to Prof. Amartya Sen', *Oxford Economic Papers*, 37(4): 659-68.

_______, (2004a), 'Basic Needs', in A. Kuper (ed.), *Social Sciences Encyclopaedia*, New York: Routledge.

Townsend, P. (2004b), 'Poverty', in Kuper (ed.), *Social Sciences Encyclopaedia.*

_______, (2004c), 'Relative Deprivation', in Kuper (ed.), *Social Sciences Encyclopaedia.*

UN (United Nations). (2009), *India Urban Poverty Report, 2009*. New Delhi: Oxford University Press.

Van de Walle, D. and D. Gunewardena (2001): 'Sources of Ethnic Inequality in Vietnam', *Journal of Development Economics*, 65, pp. 177-207.

Visaria, Pravin (2000), 'Poverty in India during 1994-98: Alternative Estimates', Institute for Economic Growth. New Delhi, processed June 9.

Watts, H. (1968), 'An Economic Definition of Poverty', in D.P. Moynihan (ed.), *On Understanding Poverty*. New York: Basic Books.

World Bank (1990), *World Development Report 1990*. Washington, D.C.: World Bank Press.

_______, (2001), *World Development Report 2000/2001*. New York: Oxford University Press.

_______, (2009) *World Development Report 2009: Reshaping Economic Geography*. Washington, DC: World Bank.

Yatchew, Adonis and Zvi Grilichcs (1985), 'Specification Errors in Probit Medels', *Review of Economics and Statistics*, Vol. 67, pp. 134-39.

Index